MONEYSTAMPS

THE SAFE-HAVEN
INVESTMENT
IN AN UNSAFE WORLD

Governments can create more Money

Companies can issue more Stock and Bonds

Miners can extract more Gold & Diamonds

But no one can create more Investment Grade Stamps

Table of Contents

Introduction

This book provides convincing facts and arguments as to why stamps truly are the ultimate safe-haven asset and then gives you actionable information on individual stamps to get started. The term moneystamps is used to differentiate the ten percent of stamps, issued before 1950, that have true investment potential, from the ninety percent which are of interest only to postage stamp collectors. Stamps' ability to serve a diversity of needs combined with their fixed supply quantities gives them a broad appeal, stability and ever rising value. In securities' evaluation, financial metrics have been developed to help make rational choices. And guess what, the same metrics approach works even better for stamps as I prove herein. Chapter 2 shows how well my past recommendations have performed.

The selection of which stamps have the best potential for preserving and growing in value, i.e. moneystamps, has been my specialty for the last 25 years. My non-stamp experience is in the financial arena. Having spent the last 20 years writing about income investing for Forbes magazine and managing client portfolios helped me to develop a keen appreciation for the uncertainty investors are suffering in the current securities markets. Income yields are disappearing from the market, and investors are facing ever increasing risks of capital losses in their search for income. Since selling my advisory business, my focus is on investing in assets whose principal attribute was asset preservation. Such assets are termed safe-haven assets. These assets are not well understood but offer a genuine shelter from today's uncertainties.

The investment world has changed significantly in the last decade. As of the latest reading, some $17 trillion dollars of worldwide capital is now invested in financial instruments with negative rates of return. Another symptom of change is that, according to the Wall Street Journal, $100 denomination US currency notes to the tune of $900 billion has left the United States and disappeared. These are clear signals to national governments of an opportunity to take control over what is essentially idle capital. For instance, the German government recently sold a 30 year bond issue with a zero interest rate and the US Government is looking into a similar 50 year issue. What this is telling us is that the world is awash with so much capital that borrowers with impeccable credit can borrow for free. Just promise to give them their money back. In investment lingo this is described as investors putting the return **of** capital ahead of the return **on** capital. We will cover this in our discussion of the various type of investors in Chapter 1 and how stamps fill a variety of needs beyond this primary one. What is clear from this fundamental change in capitalism is that governments see an opportunity to take control over what they perceive as idle capital in the name of the public good.

Whether you come away from reading this book and deciding to build your own stamp investment portfolio, or decide to use a professional stamp advisor, you'll find that investment grade stamps can be an effective part of your long-term asset diversification needs.

Expanded and continuous guidance can be found on our website www.StampFinder.com.

Richard Lehmann
Boca Raton, Florida
Stampfinder.com

Chapter 1 – What Makes Moneystamps the Ultimate Safe-Haven Asset

Safe-haven investment covers a broad category of assets into which an investor may wish to diversify to reduce portfolio risk both in terms of specific asset category, or to obtain un-correlated price and market performance to more traditional investments such as stocks and bonds. Such assets are physical in nature, such as gold, silver, diamonds and rare coins. They are long-term investments that do not pay a current return.

Finding the ultimate safe-haven asset requires a review of their attributes and drawbacks an asset may possess. To meet the stature of 'ultimate' an investment needs to have more positive characteristics than all other investments of the same category or class. The most important attributes of a safe-haven asset are:

- **Value Appreciation**
- **Inflation & Currency Protection**
- **Anonymity**
- **Price Stability**
- **Stable Supply**
- **Diverse Appeal**
- **Worldwide Availability & Demand**
- **Durability & Portability**
- **Other uses**
- **Future demand**
- **Legal Considerations**

Value Appreciation – Gold has a rate of appreciation over the last 25 years of 230% or an average of 9.2% a year. Silver has appreciated 204% or 8.2% over this same time period. Diamonds have not done as well and may have declined over the last 25 years. Rare coins appear to have been doing quite well over at least the last 25 years. The performance here appears to be greatly influenced by the price of gold and silver which may be a good proxy, albeit coins tend to outperform their metal content.

An index of over 25,000 investment grade stamps is maintained by StampFinder and shows 25 year appreciation of 238% or 9.5% a year for mint and 183% or 7.3% a year for used stamps.

Inflation & Currency Protection – Inflation and currency protection are always at the forefront in the mind of investors who have accumulated an extensive amount of capital precisely because they are historically the most potent destroyer of wealth.   Gold and silver have always been the first asset people think of when inflation is a concern and for good reason. Their prices tend to over-react in the short term to both real and perceived inflation risk. No other safe-haven asset has this ability to react to short term inflation risks, however, coins and stamps can react to short term currency movements since they trade on a global scale.

Anonymity – While gold and silver are a favorite haven of all serious investors, they are universally recognized and therefor require protective custody. Diamonds have a similar need. Rare coins are less easily recognized except when they are made of gold and silver, but then their rarity, which usually gives them the greater part of their value, is still hard to detect. Stamps take the prize for this attribute because their value is unknown to 95% of the populace. Even then, stamps are subject to a variety of variables since each specimen is unique.

Price Stability – Gold and silver have the longest track record of being prized for the constancy of their value. This constancy comes from the fact that until about 100 years ago, they were the currency or its backing in most of the world. Today gold has been vulnerable to large price swings because its trading in an international market has been so greatly simplified that the number of market participants is unlimited. It suffered price declines in 9 of the last 25 years. Gold still serves as a reserve asset for central banks, who are its largest holders. It is subject to price manipulation by such banks to help them manipulate their currencies. Diamonds are also vulnerable to price swings due in part to being part of a cartel which produces well in excess of market needs. Hence it needs to prop-up prices. Rare coins have long been a safe-haven asset and appear only to be vulnerable to breaks in the prices of gold and silver or adverse economic conditions.

By Comparison, investment grade stamps have an amazing price stability and consistent upward mobility. One benefit of stamps over gold in that you are diversifying over hundreds or thousands of different items which appreciate at different rates while gold is one asset diversification, one price. Hence, they are not as vulnerable to price swings or manipulations.

Stable Supply – Gold and silver are resources in limited supply, but new sources are constantly being found. Still, the supply of newly mined gold and silver is insufficient to keep up with demand so prices will continue to rise. Diamonds are also in great supply, but to such an excess that a cartel is needed to manage a stable supply, i.e. hold back supplies. Rare coins have no new supplies except when coins are discovered in an ancient shipwreck or a buried cache.

With investment grade stamps you are dealing with a static, ever shrinking supply of items which, in economic terms means it has inelastic supply. Countries stopped printing investment grade stamps from between 70 to 178 years ago. Time and misuse has diminished the supply to where we can be fairly sure that a stamp that sold for pennies when issued and today commands a price of $25 or more is in short supply. With stamps, supply is driven by demographic factors, i.e. only when collectors die do additional stamps become available for sale, economic hardship and dealer inventories notwithstanding.

Diverse Appeal – The more diverse the audience of a safe-haven asset, the more stability and value it will retain. Gold and silver have shifted from being in demand as a currency to their use as a reserve asset by central banks and an asset diversification by investors. They have attracted new users with the growth of the electronics industry while continuing to grow in their traditional use in jewelry.

Stamps and coins are the oldest hobbies activities in the world, stamps more so since their use was for worldwide communication while only precious metal coins and ancient coins were collected beyond country borders. *While 90% of stamps will never have real investment appeal, they do give rise to the market-place machinery where investment grade stamps also trade. This provides the liquidity essential to a mature market and price stability.*

Worldwide Availability & Demand – All of the safe-haven assets I have discussed here have a worldwide appeal. What is important is how easily specific assets can be bought and sold in any given country. Stamp and coin collecting are by far the largest hobby activities in the world in terms of monetary value. Stamps more so, as domestic coin collecting is a country specific hobby for the most part. *The Internet has served to enhance the availability and liquidity of stamps and made a cottage industry into a world market. It has opened stamps up to new uses such as an alternative currency. In this respect they provide an alternative to Bitcoins which lack tangible worth and price stability.*

Durability & Portability – While durability is not a serious issue with most safe-haven assets other than stamps, portability has limitations for all the rest. *In many parts of the world, the ability to move an asset across a national border is an essential part of its worth.* We in the West are relatively free to carry an asset across a border, whether declared or not. This freedom is far from universal. Citizens in many countries of the world are searched leaving and entering their home country and items of value are subject to expropriation and fines, or worse.

The area where stamps are most vulnerable is their fragility, especially for classic material dating back centuries. They also need a climate-controlled environment in order to preserve their condition. The upside to this is that over time, the supply of investment grade stamps will continue to shrink through deterioration and accident so that careful maintenance more than pays for itself. It is, however, stamps' fragility which provides it with one of its strongest and most sought-after attributes, its portability. People have been using stamps for decades to escape from countries like Russia, China, Cuba, and Iran to name some of the more obvious. The ability to hide a stamp among other papers makes it a clear favorite for use as flight capital. An added attraction is that such use is not even illegal in any country we know of. That is not to say they would not be confiscated if found and recognized given that the rule of law is not a universal principal.

Other Uses – The world if filled with countries where democracy is unknown, corruption is how business is done, economic instability reigns and the rule of the jungle is the law. There are people in these countries who need an asset they can hide, can carry across any border without fear of detection and use for transactions without the use of currency or banks. This is in addition to their main use by stamp collectors or philatelists who have the money to invest in their hobby. Investor participation provides additional demand for investment grade stamps with the more expensive the better. *As was famously noted, "for their size and weight, investment grade stamps are the most valuable hard asset in the world." It is the multiple purposes for which stamps are used which adds to the demand and thereby the price. That isn't something any investor will complain about.*

Future Demand – We live in a golden time for the purchase of investment grade stamps. Most stamps reside in the industrial countries of the world and are in the hands of collectors who are rapidly approaching their demise. And those taking up the hobby will be buying the cheapest material first. Some may think that such demographics are leading to an overall decline for the industry, but this is not what is occurring. The market for investment grade stamps shows a steady rate of appreciation because such stamps are attractive to investors as well as collectors.

Collectors are buyers who buy only one copy of a stamp to fill an album for a specific country. Investors are buyers who see specific stamps as a good buy and will buy as many of them as they can get. This means investors have the opportunity to acquire investment grade stamps in what is basically a buyer's market. A second factor in the stamp market is that the growth in collectors will come mainly from the developing world where you have a rapidly growing middle class. Unfortunately, most of the developing countries have improved their economies far more rapidly than their political condition. Hence, corruption and uncertainty is ever present and anyone with capital needs to be highly interested in anonymity and mobility. Investment buying will be popular in such countries.

The above factors mean the next decade will be a time of high availability of all types of stamps which will be transiting from the industrial world to the third world. These factors mean the availability of investment grade stamps in quantity and at reasonable prices will be better than it has been in a long time.

Legal Considerations – Stamps have been under the radar, so to speak, because they are perceived as a collectible. The variety of uses outline above have arisen mainly due to the Internet which made them much more multi-purpose and easier to trade. In democratic and socialist countries, they are not the subject of any specific restrictions. In more oppressive countries, they would fall under enforcements pertaining to objects of wealth. The main restrictions would be regarding the use of stamps as a currency. In any case, reporting and use restrictions have not caught up with government rules for the time being and, considering the strides being made by digital currencies, it appears that stamps will continue to be unregulated for the foreseeable future.

Conclusion

The above analysis forms the basis for my conclusion that investment grade stamps are the 'ultimate' safe-haven investment. This is not just due to their stellar financial performance, but also, the attribute strengths which give them a broader demand. But all stamps are not investment grade. In fact, 90% are not even candidates. In Chapter 2 you will learn about how we have developed a system of metrics for analyzing individual stamps in order to select out those stamps which are good investments from those which are just expensive. This ability to analyze stamps much like stocks and bonds gives a buyer greater confidence about this investment choice. That coupled with the fact that investment grade stamps, as a whole, are greatly undervalued today making their 'ultimate' safe-haven designation well deserved. In Chapter 3 you will see why they meet a variety of needs even beyond just being a good asset diversification.

CASE STUDY #1

In a meeting with Michael Bloomberg about featuring investment grade stamps on the Bloomberg financial system, he related the following as told to him by a friend of his. The friend, a general in the Iranian army, knew his career was over and life was in jeopardy when the Ayatollah Khomeini returned to Iran as the supreme ruler. When he left the country with his wife and children it was obvious he was not coming back, so his baggage was ripped apart for anything of value which could be considered contraband and expropriated. Previously his entire wealth had been in real estate, jewelry and some gold and diamonds. Yet when he left the country, his entire net worth was now in a paperback novel he carried onto the aircraft. A novel within which were secreted a few rare Persian postage stamps. The book never even got a look.

Chapter 2 – The StampFinder Rating System and Its Performance

Beginning in 1992 we began publishing the StampFinder Stamp Selection Guides for various countries culminating in a 1994 summary guide titled "Best Buys In Postage Stamps." We had by then developed a five star rating system which ranked stamps based on evaluating their 5, 10, 20 and 30 year appreciation rates. Star ratings were assigned based on actual appreciation for those periods as well as such factors as the quantities printed, price disparities between major catalogs, stamp types and price direction. Forbes magazine took note of this new investment opportunity in a December 21, 1992 article titled "The stamp arbs" (you can read it at www.stampfinder.com/stampnews/details/29). Readers who acted on the advice given there and bought the 7 recommended stamps would today have had a 301% gain (11.1% per year) on a $1920 investment.

Performance of Mint (Unused) Stamps

Given the passage of now some 25 years, it was time to go back and determine just how well past predictions turned out and how good an investment such stamps had performed. It was also important to see what assumptions could be made about future performance through a more detailed analysis and through adding new assumptions based on stamps which had achieved extraordinary results. *What we found was that stamp appreciation performance could be predicted much more reliably than can be found in most other investments.*

We analyzed some 16,209 items ($19,512,244) with the following performance results:

1. We had recommended 6,144 items ($2,860,000) which returned 195.5% or 7.8% a year.

2. Of the items with negative returns 914 (5.4%) we had recommended only 171 (1.0%).

3. Of the 2,378 items with an average return of over 20% a year for 25 years we had recommended 774 (32.5%).

4. Some 8,053 items were not recommended and these returned an

average of 6.2% a year. This demonstrates just how strong the stamp market has been over the last 25 years. Also, given that the recommended items appreciated 7.8% or 25.8% better than the average of all items, it demonstrated that appreciation potential can be forecast in a finite manner.

5. The stamp universe we reviewed (16,209) broke down to annual average return percentages as follows:

0% to 2%	20.0%
2% to 5%	26.9%
5% to 10%	23.2%
10% to 20%	12.3%
20%+	17.1%
Negative %	0.5%

6. The 5 highest appreciation unused stamps in the last 25 years were the following:
    a. Tuscany #16 went from $180 to $ 16,000 (28,788%)
    b. East Africa & Uganda #59 went from $167 to $40,000 (23,852%)
    c. New Britain # 29F went from $140 to $32,500 (23,114%)
    d. Switzerland #18 went from $52.50 to $11,600 (21,995%)
    e. Russia #195d went from $40 to $8500 (21,150%)

7. Although our buy recommendations did not include any of the above, the analysis did flag the following which occupied the indicated ranking:

a. Jammu & Kashmir #4b went from $425 to $45,000 (10,582%) (20th place)

b. Sardinia #7b went from $40 to $3,600 (8,900%) (22nd place)

c. Sarawak #77a went from $300 to $25,000 (8,233%) (24th place)

d. China #42a went from $100 to $7500 (7,400%) (27th place)

e. Roman States #4b went from $40 to $2500 (6,150%) (29th place)

Performance of Used Stamps

While the performance of unused stamps has been very rewarding for past investors, stamp collecting was, until the 1930s, mainly an activity of collecting postally used stamps. This was because such material was cheaper and more readily available in addition to posing lesser mounting and storage problems. Because of this, the supplies of mint stamps were comparatively small except where postal authorities sold-off unused supplies of stamps after they were demonetized. This preference for used stamps was still strong over the last 25 years and the appreciation statistics demonstrate this.

The analysis covered some 11,552 used items ($29,026,877) with the following performance results:

1. The 4,164 recommended items, now valued at $13,807,210, returned 255% or 10.2% per year.

2. Of the 5,242 (45.4%) items with an average return of 5% or higher each year for 25 years, the recommended items totaled 1797 (43.2% of our recommendations). Contrast this with the 575 (5.0%) items with a negative rate of return of which we recommended only 179 (4.3% of our recommendations)

3. Some 7,388 items were not recommended. They returned an average of 8.8% per year. As with mint stamps, the higher average return versus that for non-recommended stamps (15.9% higher) is clear testimony that using financial analysis metrics on stamps does produce more positive results.

4. The used stamp universe we reviewed (11,552) broke down to annual average return percentages as follows:

0%	3.3%
>0% to 2%	20.9%
2% to 5%	25.4%
5% to 10%	24.0%
10% to 20%	13.6%
20%+	7.8%
Negative %	0.5%

5. The 5 highest appreciation used stamps in the last 25 years were the following:

   a. Two Sicilies #3e went from $12 to $9,000 (74,900%)
   b. Wurttemberg #O146a went from $20 to $13,400 (66,900%)
   c. New Britain #29F went from $90 to $30,000 (33,233%)
   d. Russia #31a went from $375 to $62,500 (16,566%)
   e. Two Sicilies #5d went from $100 to $15,000 (14,900%)

6. While used stamps outperformed mint by a significant amount, they also showed more sizeable declines by certain countries. Below are the countries with the highest percentages of stamps showing declines, which may be an indication of the overall strength of that country (note the USA showed only 3.1% of issues declining):

   a. Greece – 13.2%
   b. Monaco – 27.2%
   c. Japan – 23.3%
   d. Belgium – 13.2%
   e. Germany including states & colonies – 11.4%

   The overall performance of used stamps exceeded that of mint stamps (up 10.2% versus 7.8%) as did the aggregate value of stamps in the over $25 category ($29,026,877 for used versus $19,512,244 for mint). This reflect the fact that collecting used stamps has a much longer history than for mint ones. However, it stands to reason that mint stamps from these early years must generally be much rarer and have many more quality issues, making mint never hinged or mint with decent gum a much more difficult find. Hence, *over time, mint stamps should significantly outperform used ones.*

Conclusion

Note that this early survey and results covers the time period 1994 to 2019. The 1994 recommendations were based on an analysis of the 30 years performance of these same stamps prior to 1994. Hence, we have 55 years of cumulative history which demonstrates that investment grade stamps have been a spectacular asset holding for a very long time. <u>I publish a newsletter on my StampFinder.com website titled "Monestamps Advisor" which focuses on specific countries and topics as well as upcoming auction offerings which would be of interest to stamp investors</u>. It goes into greater depth on individual countries and value trends. Our long price history allows us, through regression analysis, to identify the attributes which make specific stamps rise in value. Information which we translate into Best Buys recommendations.

Stamp dealers and many collectors are constantly voicing a fear that stamp collecting is a dying hobby. They will cite the negative demographics of the hobby, i.e. four collectors dying for each new one. While this may be true for the 90% of non-in-vestment grade stamps, it is not the case for moneystamps, as 55 years of data clearly shows<u>. The reality is that the investor stamp market is driven by money rather than bodies. By this I mean that collectors will buy just one investment grade stamp to fill a specific space in their collection. Investors will buy a dozen or more of a stamp they consider a good buy. Hence, supply rather than demand will always be the constraint here. This is why prices for moneystamps have defied demographics and will continue to rise.</u>

CASE STUDY #2

An extremely wealthy individual is diversified into gold and diamonds in order to have assets which are uncorrelated to his securities holdings. His major concern is that these two commodities trade at prices which are subject to market manipulation by central banks or a cartel. He sees his portfolio of investment grade stamps as an additional diversification, a safe-haven investment where the market price of each stamp is independently determined with limited exposure to manipulation.

Chapter 3 – Who Should Consider Stamps for Investing

The current universe of stamp investors is composed mainly of stamp dealers and wealthy stamp buyers of trophy stamps with six and seven digit prices. A third larger group of stamp investors also exists. These are life-long collectors who built their holdings over decades and mostly at prices that never caused them to think of their collection as something they should value as part of their estate. In fact, such collectors could not even tell you what their collection is worth. Pity their heirs who are thus left clueless.

What has come into play over the last few decades is that governments around the world have become more aggressive in meddling in the affairs of successful individuals and finding new ways of sharing their wealth via regulation, taxation, expropriation, inflation, litigation, and shaming. Those who recognize this as a growing trend have seen the need to diversify their investments into safe-haven assets which offer various degrees of protection against the uncertainties the future has to offer. We are all aware of things like gold, diamonds, and coins as such assets; but few have realized that stamps offer protection against the largest variety of adverse events. Here is a list of some of the benefits you want or adversities you fear where stamps can be as good or even the best asset you can hold:

- You want the comfort of a portable resource whose value is known only to you

- You want to diversify your capital over a variety of uncorrelated assets

- You like the capital gains history and potential of stamps

- You want more inflation protection

- You like the risk diversity within a stamp investment

- You want to settle some estate matters other than through a written will

- You need to accumulate flight capital due to an unstable economic or political environment

- You need an alternative currency for use in certain countries

- You face a legal threat which may result in a seizure of any and all of your tangible assets.

- You face claims which will be based on an estimate of your net worth such as in a divorce

- You have assets abroad which cannot be safely settled through the banking system

- You have liabilities abroad which cannot be safely settled through the banking system

- You have donations or gifts you want to make anonymously

- You have obligations you want to settle anonymously

- You fear arbitrary government seizure or freezing of your assets

To those who live in countries where the rule of law is observed, some of the above would read as devious. But such people have not lived long enough or in one of the many corners of the globe where uncertainty is the rule and government is arbitrary and corrupt. The outrages against civility and order by government, which we hear about in the USA and usually see remedied, are daily events in most of the world and go unreported. Those who succeed in such places become a target because of their success and have legitimate reasons for hiding their success.

CASE STUDY #3

Case study #1 is not the end of the Iran story. Many Iranians have fled that country in the last 40 years and many have successful lives in the US and elsewhere. They often have left behind relatives who are suffering under the adverse economic conditions there. They can send them money through the banking system but such funds are taxed and, more importantly, leave a name and address of a family member abroad which can be used by a country that is a state sponsor of terrorism. Imagine receiving a letter from your relative informing you that a 'distant cousin' will be coming to their city in two weeks to do some business and they should provide housing and transportation during his stay. It is made apparent that this request is being made at the behest of the government. In short, your relative is now being held for ransom and you may be vulnerable to aiding in a possible terrorist attack.

It is so much safer to mail a relative an investment grade stamp with a known value. The people who deal in foreign currencies would gladly redeem the stamps for local currency since there are many people still in Iran who want to get money out. This situation explains why Iranian stamps show one of the best appreciation records over the past 25 years. Tables 6 and 7 show that in the last 25 years Iranian mint stamps have appreciated 518.9% and 539.4% for used stamps. I expect this to continue.

Chapter 4 – Where to Buy Stamps

The question of where to buy stamps depends on your physical location, and the price/value of the stamps. American or European collector have numerous payment options, no foreign remittance restrictions and stable currencies. This is not true, however, for most countries. There, residents may well be limited to local dealers or money changers (for stamps useful as an alternative currency). For those without such restrictions, the options are significantly better.

Buying at Auction

The principal source of investment grade stamps for an investor is a stamp auction. Several hundred auctions take place worldwide every year and every day on eBay. There is always an opportunity to buy and sell, albeit the winter months in the USA and Europe are the busiest. If you want to invest a significant amount in investment grade stamps you will need to go to stamp auctions to buy items costing $5,000 and above and for these, you would be wise to use an auction agent. In fact, stamp auctions are the best place to buy any items over $250. The advantages here are that the item's value is determined at a site where numerous buyers can bid and the seller wants the item to be bought that day. The price you pay is only constrained by the minimum the owner may have put on it and the mix of dealers, collectors or investors bidding against you. If there is only dealer interest, you do well; if collectors or investors, the item may set a new high. Of course, you could get lucky such as we are told happened once when a snowstorm hit in the city where the auction took place and the few bidders who showed up had a feast. Such events become legend, but with today's Internet and phone bidding, it's unlikely to reoccur. Still, every auction has items no one had in their sights so don't be afraid of making low-ball bids.

At an auction there will be four types of buyers; dealers, collectors, agents and investors. There will also be telephone call-ins, Internet bidders and phantom buyers, but let's keep this simple. You have the choice of attending the auction personally to bid. This can be quite entertaining, especially at a prominent auction where five and six figure items come up for sale. Such high-priced items will have a lot of focus and sophisticated buyers. Unless you are one, I recommend using an agent to do your bidding. An agent can size up a bidding situation and better sense when to continue or drop out. Remember that for most items, there will be another day.

If you go to an auction to bid in person sit in the back so you can try to size up the competition. If you identify the person bidding against you as a dealer, you are in good shape. Dealers will be bidding on numerous items. Auction agents will also be present and they represent collectors and investors. They will be more difficult to outbid. They can be identified by the fact that they give various buyer numbers when they win bids for different clients. Dealers are buying for resale and therefore cannot afford to pay anywhere near the retail value of an item. Hence, they will drop out soon after the bidding reaches the estimated value put on the lot by the auction house. Dealers are also the bidders who start giving you stares once they sense you are either a collector or investor (they know the other dealers in the room already and may have even conversed with them before the auction began, all above-board no doubt). If you are having success in bidding, expect to be approached whenever there is a break in the bidding. I have been asked flat out what else I am going to bid on and I have flat out told them. Hopefully it will be a short list in which case they will leave you in peace.

You can also mail in your highest price offer and the auction house will bid for you up to your limit in the published increments. This is not recommended unless there is no other choice such as an overseas auction where no agents are known to the agent you deal with otherwise. It's not that the auction houses are not honest, it's just that I find that my winning bids are not as close to my maximum bids as when I used an agent. You can also use our affiliated firm StampAuctionNetwork.com to do your bidding electronically for you. They will protect your maximum bid information as an agent would do. Their fee is also a modest 1% of the winning bid amount.

While buying investment grade stamps is stamp specific, it does not preclude bidding on collections. The trick is finding enough investment grade stamps in the collection to make it worth buying. While auction houses tend to take out items over $250 to sell individually, this still leaves a lot of items valued at between $25 and $250 to make up a significant part of the total value. If you are knowledgeable in stamps, this is also where you can go treasure hunting since auction houses often miss a lot in evaluating a collection when they are pressed for time. In fact, dealers value a collection by looking for the material worth from say $25 and up and limit their upper bid amount to say 40% of the value of those items and ignore the rest. Your problem is that they can make this value determination quickly because of their years of experience. You don't have the time you would need to do the same unless the collection can be viewed in detail on the Internet. What you can do, however, is determine which bidders on the floor are dealers and let them lead the bidding, only stepping in if the collection if going below its auction house estimate. It's not foolproof but can yield some amazing results. It's using the dealer's knowledge advantage to your advantage. Note however that this strategy does not always work. For example, when you have Chinese, Iranian or Indian dealers buying for resale in their home markets where a stamp is more often valued for its use as an alternative currency. If you intend to invest a serious amount of money into stamps you may well need to consider buying entire collections. In that case, you should use an advisor to help you select the items and determine how much to bid.

Note that if you buy a collection you want to selectively remove the investment grade items and put the remainder back into the next auction. Collections that come in pre-printed albums are often attractive and lead to the temptation to fill the blank spaces and complete the collection. Next thing you know you will be buying stamps with no investment potential, thereby turning you into a **stamp collector!** In selecting the stamps to remove note that the investment grade stamps which are part of a complete set should be taken as a set since this gives them added value provided the set is complete and uniform. This is especially true for mint never hinged sets which are often worth a multiple of a mint hinged set. Mint never hinged singles which are part of a set will not have the mint never hinged value premium they have in a complete set. Something to keep in mind when buying singles. You can enhance the value of what you buy as singles just by building them into complete sets, especially where a large mint never hinged price premium exists.

Buying on the Internet - Internet sellers

Sales sites for stamps number in the thousands, so a roadmap is in order. Most established dealers have their own websites and would prefer selling to you from there to avoid the sales commissions they have to pay on a multi-dealer site. The problem with these is that, if the dealer is located in another country, your recourse to any dispute would be costly to not non-existent. Even if US based, you just don't want to get into this kind of situation. Dealers join the American Stamp Dealers Association (ASDA), the National Stamp Dealers Association (NSDA), or the Philatelic Traders Society (PTS) to provide customers with comfort that you could complain to their trade association for a remedy. Aside from this, who has time to search dozens of sites to find what you want. Only collectors enjoy this since using lots of idle time is part of the hobby, especially since it can be done while viewing their favorite sport on TV.

Multi-dealer websites offer you one stop shopping with competitive pricing and guaranteed quality and right of return. They also often feature timed auctions for specific items allowing for an opportune buy. Such sites, however, allow anyone to become a seller. I always assume the seller is a collector selling off their collection in their retirement. Such a seller will often misrepresent the quality of a stamp, or its exact variety or even its catalog value. They will quote a price from their catalog which may be ten years old or non-existent. I rarely find such prices as lower than today. While errors can mean they are not very knowledgeable it can also mean they have only one collection to sell and then they are history. One feature of multi-dealer sites is that individual dealers can have stores on the site where all their listings appear together. This may be an alternative since you are less likely to suffer grief with such a seller. You may also choose to deal with him via his own website or via a want list once you have confidence in his integrity.

Below are the websites which do the most Internet stamp trading:

eBay.com – multiple sites in the US, Australia, Argentina, Belgium, Brazil, Austria, Canada

Delcampe.net - Europe based

Hipstamp.com – US based, formerly bidstart.com when owned by Stanley Gibbons

The American Philatelic Society at www.stamps.org

Sellers on eBay or similar multi-dealer sites have no urgency to sell unless they start soliciting for bids or have it on an auction clock. They also may be dealers who have purchase the item at auction and have little price flexibility. The question of a stamp's quality is also a much bigger issue since it has a huge impact on what is a fair price. Auction houses go to great length to describe a stamp accurately. They don't want it returned and have to make good on a stamp subsequently found to be incorrectly described and the seller having already been paid. eBay sellers are also held to an accuracy standard if they want to continue to sell on that platform. However, they are often inexperienced or amateurs and not even aware of their errors. Hence, you have to be especially vigilant with regards to forgeries, misidentified, re-gummed, re-perfed and repaired stamps. All are reasons to have a stamp certified. More on this in Chapter 14.

Stamps on the Internet are also sold by individual dealers on their own proprietary sites. Here you face issues such as does he operate from a foreign location where there is little legal recourse for foreigners? Or is he known, but not to you, for unfair dealing? Here is where his credentials such as affiliation with the ASDA and NSDA are helpful but check with those organizations to see if his membership really exists. Trade periodicals are also a source for stamps, but this is not recommended. I personally experienced buying a lot which was inaccurately described. When I complained to the periodical, after getting no satisfaction from the dealer, I found that he was a large advertiser and I was swiss cheese.

CASE STUDY #4

A businessman is visiting a country in Asia, which shall remain unnamed, in order to negotiate a presence in that country. His local agent advises him that, in order to obtain the necessary government permits and licenses, certain "customs" need to be observed. This country is known for rampant corruption which is periodically prosecuted along with the corrupter. Using the banking system is not safe for either party since it is totally transparent to the government. Using a cutout such as a local agent is not practical since they are unreliable and local "customs" must be repeatedly observed. Since postage stamps are popular in this country, their use as a gift has become a preferred means of doing business. A moneystamp is better than cash because it appreciates in value over time and provides a safe passage means to enter and leave almost any country especially if one is fleeing.

Chapter 5 – Stamp Pricing Sources

In philately, the pricing of stamps is a complex subject. As a collector becomes familiar with various catalogs, the valuation of the individual stamps become a puzzle due to the fact that some of the catalogs are controlled by companies that also deal in stamps. Collectors who rely on certain catalogs learn the valuation quirks and adjust their pricing expectations accordingly. However, with the prominent role now being played by the Internet there is a need for more clarity. Let's look at the valuation criteria for a sampling of prominent catalogs.

- In the USA there is the Scott Catalogue. New and used issues will start at a minimum price of 25 cents or twice the face value in dollar equivalents for Mint/Never Hinged items. For pre 1950 issues the pricing is for stamps graded as Very Fine.

- The UK has Stanley Gibbons Catalogues. A minimum price for the British Pound equivalent of about 9 cents US is specified for new issues in Mint or Used condition. Modern mint prices seem to be selectively priced. For pre 1950 issues the pricing is for stamps graded as Fine.

- Germany has Michel Catalogs. New issues start at a minimum price of the Euro equivalent of 75 cents US or twice face value for Mint or Used stamps. For pre 1950 issues the pricing is described as for stamps in flawless condition (equivalent to very fine grade).

- France has the Yver&Tellier Catalogues which prices stamps a minimum of the Euro equivalent of 25 cents US. Prices are based on stamps in flawless condition with various percentage uplift notations for classic stamps in Mint Never Hinged condition.

- In the Facit Catalogue, which specializes in the Scandinavian countries, new issues start at a minimum price of the Swedish Kronor equivalent of $1.20 cents US or about twice face value, although this is not as consistent as in the other catalogs. For pre 1950 issues the price is for stamps graded as very fine with used stamps with light, readable and dated cancellation.

- In the Zumstein catalog for Switzerland and Liechtenstein new and used stamps start at a minimum equivalent to $2 US for Mint Never Hinged or Used stamps. Higher face values are equivalent to 2.5 times face value, again for Mint or Used stamps. For pre 1950 issues the price is for stamps graded as very fine with Mint stamps priced as never hinged with a discount factor of 20% to 50% specified for Mint hinged items. The catalog seems to specify very fine quality for Mint stamps but is vague about the quality assumption for Used stamp prices. Pricing is in Swiss Francs.

- In the Unitrade Catalogue for Canada the minimum price starts at the equivalent of 30 cents US or twice the face value for Mint/Never Hinged items. For pre 1950 items prices are given in both fine and very fine grades with a multiplier for Mint Never Hinged.

Another valuation disparity is that catalogs are very slow to update their pricing, waiting as much as ten years to do a thorough pricing review for less popular countries. In addition, the source of their pricing information for other than the prices for non-auction sold items is never disclosed and therefor suspect. We assume the information comes from specialist dealers who have their hands on the pulse of the market, but this may be only half the story. Those dealers have their proprietary knowledge and inventory levels to consider. Both these factors may come into play which can be why some prices in Scott are shown in italics. Only Michel publishes the names of their pricing advisors by area which, in my opinion, should be done by them all. Even better would be disclosing when a comprehensive review for each country was last made and color coding all price changes. But that's, perhaps, expecting too much.

Why do these differences matter? For higher priced items and collections in an auction, the price disparities can influence the bidding if the auction house chooses to use a higher valuation from a specific catalog to increase its value estimate. As for buying from dealers or the Internet, the catalog prices are always the reference point used by sellers to make their prices look reasonable. This, of course, implies that the lower than catalog price being asked is reasonable. But as most collectors know, the quality elements of Good, Fine, Very Fine and Extra Fine are very subjective and make a world of difference for higher priced stamps. <u>The real estate mantra about what matters being location, location, location applies with postage stamps as well - except that it reads quality, quality, quality.</u>

If you are not an experienced collector, you will not be able to make the judgement of whether a stamp is correctly graded and how much it should be discounted for a lesser grade. Chances are, you don't even own a current catalog and therefor don't know whether the catalog value being shown in an offering is false or is ten years old.

Currency value changes also play an important role in stamp prices. The most dramatic recent example is Canadian stamps. Canada has a strong local market where values plunged as their currency dropped from above parity to about 75 cents US to their dollar. A situation like this is when dealers need to learn the difference between measuring their profit based on first-in first-out (FIFO) and last-in first-out (LIFO) inventory accounting; a concept businesses have long accepted as part of doing business. A Canadian dealer who understands business will know this is the time to sell to US and worldwide collectors at the lower dollar equivalent value, prices which no non-Canadian based dealer will meet. His recovery lies in using the increased business this price drop will generate to buy replacement inventories domestically at the now lower values.

<u>In the end, the Internet is the great price leveler. Catalog pricing disparities are becoming less relevant since fewer collectors are buying them. It will not be long before an on-line market price catalog service comes about and then, the Amazon effect will come to the philatelic industry as well.</u>

CASE STUDY # 5

A successful local businessman in an African country, which shall remain unnamed, operates an enterprise that is subject to national laws restricting his line of business to people of a specific color and ethnicity. He therefor faces a constant threat of being shut down or expropriated. He cannot remit large quantities of money through the banking system for fear of becoming a target for the seizure of his business or for shakedowns for graft. In the past he parked large amounts of cash with family members but found this became unwieldly and exposed them to criminals and shakedowns. He now converts his excess cash flow to moneystamps.

They don't print $1,000 bills, and 500 euro bank notes are hard to come by. But moneystamps each worth $1,000 or more come in 100s of different colors and flavors and go unrecognized by 98% of the world's population.

Chapter 6 – Stamp Prices

When you look at the stamps which have appreciated the most over the last 25 years, you see that the top performers were stamps which rose from hundreds of dollars to tens of thousands of dollars in that 25 year time period. What is surprising is that these are stamps that have been outstanding since the 1800s. How could it be that a stamp that has been outstanding for 150 years could suddenly appreciate from hundreds of dollars to tens of thousands of dollars?

There are various possible explanations for this. A principal reason is that many true rarities can remain hidden for a century simply because they are so rare. When something never comes up for sale, price discovery is not possible. Even when they come up for sale, it can be sold by private treaty or by an auction firm that does not know the item or is a firm that is not closely followed. It can also be that, for lack of knowledge, the item is included in a country lot by a collector who bought it cheaply and never bothered to have his collection appraised. The reality is that all high value stamps are currently owned by someone. Generally, someone who always thought of himself as a collector and never as an investor, probably because he acquired his high value stamp decades ago when it was nothing exceptional. So, what causes a stamp to suddenly explode in value? Here is one theory.

Every country's stamps has one or more dealers who specialize in that country. That dealer become the go-to dealer by advanced collectors who get down to the 10 or 20 stamps they are all still missing. Over the years, that dealer has learned which stamps all advanced collectors of his specialties are looking for. He also knows which customers have the stamp since those customers share their want lists with this dealer on the promise that he will look out for the item for them (and 20 or so other equally good customers, so it helps to be the oldest). When one of his good customers dies, he will likely be the first call from the heirs and he will know what awaits him in his specialty. Since he has waiting customers for many of the expensive items in the estate, he can make the best offer, or not, but knowing he can recover his cost in a matter of weeks. It takes a dealer decades to get into such a strategic situation, so you can bet he keeps his knowledge as close to his chest as possible. When the catalog companies call him to provide input as to price movements in his specialty he will play up the pricing on what he has in stock and downplay the things he would love to be able to buy. The information dam will only break if the item comes up at an auction and the dealer and a knowledgeable buyer fight over it. Price information can also get out because the dealer is ready to retire and now wants to cash in on the items he has been hoarding, his IRA if you will. What I am describing here is not illegal or unethical, it's how business is done. As the saying goes, "The source of all wealth is information."

Another reason for the sudden rise of a stamp is that it is a variety or error which was not previously known. This can happen because a stamp's rarity means it is never seen in sufficient quantities to allow comparison by a knowledgeable dealer or collector. When this occurs, varieties previously not known will become known and errors, likewise. For example, when I decided to create a catalog for the Mexican foreign mail stamps issued in 1879 to 1883, I acquired three collections and a retired dealer's stock. This extensive array of items allowed me to identify dozens of varieties and errors never recorded anywhere. Assigning a value to such items was a challenge because the quantities which may be out there was often an unknown. I assigned values based on a modest markup from the value for the standard issue of such items for which the printed quantities were known since I did not want to discredit the StampFinder catalog as being too high in order to enhance my personal holdings. Time and the market will determine a market values here, but at least we now have a starting point. In such a situation, items I catalog at $200 can easily sell for a multiple of that once more investors see the potential in these stamps. (Note – the StampFinder Mexico Foreign Mail Catalog 1879 To 1883 can be viewed free of charge at my StampFinder.com website.)

The above example also points out another reality of stamp prices. When collectors are the main buyers, they compete to buy one copy of a stamp for their collection and then drop out of the market for that stamp. When investors compete for an investment grade stamp, they will be in the market multiple times, either to buy a certain dollar amount of that issue or a certain quantity of that stamp. Hence, *investment grade stamps have a built-in price escalator due to supply, not demand being the driving force.*

It should be noted that my percentage appreciation analysis is based on changes in catalog values. Stamps which you purchase from dealers and auction houses will generally be lower. This disparity in values does not materially affect the analysis however, since the discounting by dealers and at auction do not change over time. Hence, the percentage changes will be the same. The analysis does not show the actual prices since such information is proprietary to the catalogue companies. Also, we would not like to lead the reader to think that they need pay such a price in most cases since quality grading is the overriding consideration in the price of all stamps.

Until recently quality was in the eye of the beholder, a matter of judgement and experience (and whether you are the buyer or the seller). Today we can be more objective and give a stamp a numeric grade per the eye of the computer. It's something to remember to avoid errors or a swindle, even a small swindle. There is software that can help you do this. For example, EzGrader is a stamp grading program that can give you precise determination of centering and measure the perforations of your stamp. It even generates a certificate of its findings; not a substitute for expertizing, but a measure of confidence for lower priced stamps not worth certifying. There is also stamp comparison software to help identify stamp errors and misprints. These software programs work even for auction catalog images when considering what to bid for an item.

The price you pay for a given stamp is a key component in whether it will return your investment 10 or more years down the road. Transaction costs are steep. For example you pay a 15% buyers premium to an auction house and can expect to pay 10% to 15% as well when you sell. If you buy from a dealer, the transaction costs are even higher. This is why we say stamps are not a short term investment. Stamp investors are vulnerable here because they will be buying from a seller with more experience and knowledge of the product. It is also why having a stamp expertized and dealing with a reputable dealer or agent an important safeguard.

CASE STUDY #6

A Venezuelan judge has safe-haven assets such as gold and diamonds stored in a bank safe-deposit box. The box is known as his by bank officials in a country with few banking secrecies laws and a corrupt political system. He fears these assets are compromised and may be frozen by corrupt bureaucrats. But he fears more bringing such assets into his house since home invasions are a big problem in Venezuela. He finds stamps are an ideal store of wealth because they are easily hidden and available anytime should he need to depart suddenly. Judges there have been the targets of assassinations when they insist on following the rule of law.

Chapter 7 – Failed Stamp Investment Programs

Promoting stamps as investment has been done by private treaty sales and buying syndicates in the case of trophy stamps. Most such arrangements had prominent dealers as sponsors and were promoted mainly to wealthy philatelists who liked the idea of an ownership stake in a rarity as much as the potential for capital gains. Such arrangements would be for specific periods of time and with no guarantees of eventual outcome. Given the price trends in such trophy stamps, I suspect they were very profitable. Changes in tax laws and investor sophistication led to arrangements that allowed individual account ownership much as stocks and bonds are owned today. But unlike the securities market the stamp market is unregulated, so the opportunities for abuse naturally followed. Two recent examples of this serve as a lesson as to why the institutional approach can expose the investors to risks and losses never disclosed or even anticipated by the sponsors.

In 2006, there were two Spanish stamp companies, Afinsa and Forum Filatelico that were shut down by the Spanish government under suspicion of fraud. Some 350,000 investors in Spain and Portugal had invested some 6.5 billion Euro with these firms in what were essentially modern stamp issues rather than investment grade ones. The attraction for investors was that the portfolios of stamps held for customers paid out an annual 8% rate of return with a promise that they would be repurchased after 5 years at the original cost. The basis for valuation of the stamps, was in part, a catalog for Spanish and Portuguese stamps published by Afinsa. In addition to buying older stamps, Afinsa negotiated bulk purchases of the annual issue of Europa stamps various countries at a price of 40% of face value and then put them into investor portfolios at 200% of face (the normal catalog valuation for new issues). The 8% cash interest was paid out of the money generated from new investors, so in this context, it was a modified Ponzi scheme. However, since stamps are not subject to securities regulations, such an arrangement was not criminal. Their very success led to their downfall because they could not have served 350,000 investors with a static supply of classic stamps where supply does not respond to demand. Yet it is this very fact that gives investment grade stamps such strong investment traits.

The shutting down of operations by the Spanish government was precipitated by a hedge fund that had been speculating in the stock of Afinsa and then convinced the government that Afinsa did not have the stamps it claimed. Erring on the side of caution, the government seized the company's premises and proceeded to audit the company's books. What they found was that, in fact, all the stamp holdings reported to investors were present and accounted for. However, the publicity from the seizing of the company dealt a mortal blow to Afinsa's business and froze the stamps of the investors for so long that all the investment contracts matured making a sell-off of the collections at any reasonable prices impossible. As of today, these inventories have only been partially liquidated and no criminal charges were ever filed against the principals. However, the investors involved have yet to see a recovery of their capital.

A similar type of investment program was being operated in the UK by Stanley Gibbons, a respected stamp dealer that also published a catalog of all the items they sell, namely the British Commonwealth. Their scheme involved some 3,000 investors purchasing 54 million pounds in stamps ($65 million) at the SG catalog price on which they promised to pay 5% or 7% rates of return for stamps held for 5 or 10 years respectively. At the end of the holding period SG would buy back the stamps at the then SG catalog price with 80% of the value increase going to the investor. Their approach correctly focused on investment quality stamps. The flaw in their approach was that SG constantly increased the catalog prices of their stamps well above any other world catalog since they could then sell to their new investors at such prices. This worked until stamp collector demographics dictated falling prices causing new investment to dry up and old investors to cash out. Rather than making good on its promises to the investors and being saddled with hugely overvalues stamp returns, the company declared bankruptcy.

The take-aways from these bad experiences by investors are:

1) Take delivery of all stamps

2) Have all stamps purchased by yourself or your personal agent in an arms-length transaction

3) Buy only investment grade stamps and in the best quality available

4) Have the stamps certified by an independent appraiser.

Both the above companies attracted investors by turning stamps into a bond like investment paying a high rate of return and, in the case of Stanley Gibbons, a capital gain as well. Stamps are not that kind of instrument and trying to make them so was at the root of the collapses that followed.

The failure by the above two entities is no reflection on stamps as investments, but rather, a failure to understand what type of investment they are, even by their sponsors. Their most attractive investment characteristics are their tremendous price stability over a long time horizon and their short term price movements not being vulnerable to the same macroeconomic shocks such as occurred in 2008.

One of the most astute stamp investors, Bill Gross, made millions of dollars in buying rare stamps. He donated the proceeds from his stamp sales to charity since he was already a billionaire. Given that he made his fortune investing in fixed income securities, committing millions of dollars into investment grade stamps is a strong endorsement to their value by someone who knows both markets.

CASE STUDY #7

A wealthy investor with careful estate planning in mind crafted a will which he feels will satisfy his numerous, contentious heirs. He does not want to be remembered for leaving behind a legal battle or bitterness against his memory or against one another. Still, there are certain people he wants to reward without raising questions and others who he feels are more deserving or in need. He has acquired a number of stamps in the $10,000 to $50,000 range as safe-haven investments. Assets he has left out of his will. Each of these stamps will be quietly given to the intended recipient with an explanation and with instructions as to how to dispose of them for their maximum value. Wills are an essential document for the wealthy. But left to the legal process, they are often the source of bitter outcomes. High value stamps offer the secrecy needed in this situation.

Chapter 8 - Stamps as an Alternative Currency

For decades, postage stamps have evolved beyond their use for mailing letters or to satisfy worldwide philatelists collecting them as a hobby. Their universal appeal and marketability has allowed them to become an alternative currency. For the stamp investor, considering where there's a use of stamps as an alternative currency is certainly a consideration in the selection of investment grade stamps, and they figure in our analysis of which stamps to buy as investments. They add a value component that make certain high-priced stamps a greater attraction than their peers. Those who fear stamps may come to be used for money laundering need not fear. The stamp market is just not large or liquid enough to meet the massive needs of that activity.

The question of where are stamps an alternative currency can be answered by reading the weekly headlines. At present China and Iran come most quickly to mind for a variety of reasons. Bribing public officials is standard practice worldwide and goes undetected in most cases. In the USA it has developed into an art form best described by the term quid pro quo. Yet in China, a recent wave of prosecutions has made cash payments difficult since the banking system there is subject to government scrutiny of all bank accounts. Paying a bribe with postage stamps is better than cash since they appreciate in value and are easy to hide. Price appreciation for Chinese stamps has been the highest of any country for the last two decades and will continue until the Chinese learn Latin.

Iran is an even clearer case of need. The first and third case studies cited herein are clear examples of how stamps can and are used as an alternative to currency. The individuals involved have no interest in stamps as an investment. Yet they find that high value stamps are a safe alternative in an unsafe situation.

Stamps have also become alternatives to currency where governance breaks down or where you see repressive governments, weak rules of law, economic uncertainty, extensive corruption or tight monetary controls. Gold or diamonds serve much of this need but quickly become unavailable. Stamps offer the benefit of portability and marketability outside visible channels. In fact, they are of such low visibility that the rules and laws of very few countries even recognize their value or potential use.

Historically, the first large use of stamps as an alternative to currency was in Germany in 1921 to 1923. When the economy and governance broke down the currency deteriorated so rapidly that in 1921 a 5pf stamp had to be overprinted with a new 1.60 Deutchmark value. By 1922 the currency had deteriorated to where mailing a letter cost 100 Deutchmark and by 1923 to 1 billion Deutchmark. People, in desperation, bought postage stamps in the hope that this would be a currency that retained some of the value that cash could not preserve. This proved to be of little success. Ironically, had they actually used the stamps or had them cancelled at the time of purchase, they would today been worth 10 to 100 times more. This is because the value of the currency and postal rates changed so rapidly that most of those printed were not used and German stamp collectors prefer used stamps.

Venezuela today is playing out in a similar fashion. In the face of runaway inflation, stamps appear to represent a repository of value in a rapidly deteriorating situation. But here also, stamps will not be of help. The problem is that such a strategy does not work when using postage stamps of current issue because they break the first rule of stamp value, i.e. stamps rise in value due to scarcity and high demand. Stamps bought to hedge against inflation have neither attribute.

CASE STUDY #8

The investments manager for a very wealthy family has been charged with diversifying the proceeds of the sale of a family business over numerous safe-harbor investments. His mandate is to diversify over assets which have, as their principal attribute, the ability to maintain their value over several generations. The income generated should be sufficient to cover the annual expenses of running the estate and capital gains should be sufficient to allow tax deductible donations be sufficient to minimize taxes to the level of the net cash flow from operations. Moneystamps have a natural fit in such program because they generate capital gains which can be used for donations to mitigate taxes. Through diversification, they historically provide an attractive accumulation of capital gains with very little downward fluctuation. Building such a portfolio into the millions of dollars will take years of acquisition activity but can be done very cost effectively when a long time horizon is planned. Hence, a dedicated philatelic expert can be retained, thereby mitigating the acquisition costs. No, I am not talking about Bill Gross, but it is his approach which has proven very successful.

Chapter 9 – The Supply Side of Stamps

While records exist on stamp printing quantities for even the earliest of issues, there is no way to accurately predict what is the actual available surviving supply. Extremely rare stamps that have been identified for decades are known, but simply because the supply is less than a hundred known copies. Even for modern issues printed in the tens of millions, surviving supplies either mint or used are not known because there are no records of philatelic versus postal sales. Likewise, there is no way to determine how many millions of stamps are torn off envelopes and thrown into a shoe box and eventually make their way into someone's collection. Many printing errors are only discovered decades later by such happenstance.

Despite this relative void in information, stamps are protected by the fact that one can be sure that no new supplies of an older item will suddenly appear. This is why stamps are a more predictable inflation hedge than gold or diamonds. Gold is subject to continuous addition from mining, new discoveries and manipulation by central banks, the biggest holders of gold. Diamonds have the same vulnerability with the added factor that the supply and pricing is managed by a cartel at a price level supply alone would not support.

Of course, there are occasions where a rare stamp is suddenly found in an unknown sheet quantity. A recent example of this however, dealing with an early Chinese stamp, led to no softening in the price of the stamp since investors bought the entire blocks intact. As noted elsewhere, there is a real shortage of six and seven figure rarities. It is these orders of magnitude investors prefer. Coins, in fact, are more vulnerable to such things because they had intrinsic value when they were hidden away and because they are less likely to deteriorate from poor storage. For example, once when I bought several "Widows Mites", a coin with Biblical provenance, at a relatively low price, I was told this was due to a recent find of several thousand coins in the Middle East and that such finds are not unusual.

Unused stamps from the 1800s must, by definition, be in short supply. There were comparatively few collectors then. Therefore, few mint stamps were saved, often limited to remnants sold off by post offices after the stamps were withdrawn and demonetized. Most people in those days only knew a circle of friends and relatives living within a short distance. Also, many did not know how to read and write. Stamps of high denomination, intended for international usage, are therefore rare Mint or Used and rarer still on a cover. While many of these stamps are expensive, their prices relative to later material, which is in much more abundant supply, are often quite cheap. Time will almost certainly rectify this situation. However, for the moment, investors may consider such material of primary interest.

A word of caution here. Quite often, Mint material from specific countries is in plentiful supply because large quantities were printed for sale to collectors, usually at a discount to their face value. Printers were frequently compensated by postal authorities for their work by being given the right to make philatelic sales to collectors outside the country. In other cases, printers kept the printing plates and made unauthorized copies or reprints. Low prices for mint items are often explained by such events, especially for South American countries.

There is one final observation about supply that can be easily overlooked but plays an all-important role. In its simplest form price is a function of supply and demand. Examined more closely, however, supply is determined by quantity times turnover. It is the element of extremely low turnover which lies at the heart of investment potential for postage stamps. The popularity of baseball cards as a collectible led some people to believe that in the USA, it will permanently displace stamp collecting as the largest hobby activity. The element which will prevent this from happening, however, is turnover. Baseball card collecting involves a significant amount of buying and selling by collectors according to what they feel is going to appreciate. Hence, this collecting activity has a large segment of participants who are in it to make a quick profit and who will sell items they feel have reached their potential. Also, they may go to a card show intent on buying a Yogi Berra card and come back with a Mickey Mantle simply because it was a better buy. This behavior by collectors means a given supply of Mickey Mantle cards may turn over several times a year as collectors cash in.

Stamp collectors purchase a given stamp to fill a pre-defined space in their collection. For them, there is no substitute for the specific stamp they need and price is only relative to their budget, i.e. collectors who know stamps don't put off buying a stamp because they think next year it will be cheaper. If a stamp they own should suddenly jump from $10 to $100, a collector will congratulate himself for having made a good buy. He is very unlikely to remove the item from his collection and sell it. This difference in collector behavior is what provides stability to stamp values and makes stamps a much more reliable long-term investment vehicle*.

Turnover in stamps is measured not in turns per year but turns per decade. Death is the primary reason a rare stamp comes back into the market. Hence, given a fifty year lifetime of collecting, the average stamp in that collection will turnover only every twenty five years. From this, one can see that when a stamp has only 10 or 20 known copies, the appearance of one at an auction is a major event. Bidding for such items will be fierce because potential buyers know another copy may not come to market for years. Price jumps of 50% or 500% are common in such a situation. The British Guiana, the most expensive stamp in the world, recently came to market after 19 years and sold for $9.5 million, almost ten times its previous sales price 19 years earlier.

In economic terms, stamps are a commodity with inelastic supply, low price sensitivity and limited interchangeability. A commodity with these three attributes would normally price itself out of sight except for one essential constraint, stamps are a nonessential commodity. These characteristics do make stamps a more volatile investment vehicle that is susceptible to price fluctuations when investors become involved. This is a factor which, fortunately, argues for the upside more often than the downside.

Chapter 10 – The Demand Side of Stamps

While the supply of stamps is important, the major determinant of stamps prices is demand. This is because stamps are a non-essential resource. Demand should be viewed both on a global (macro) level and a more regional (micro) level. Arbitraging the difference in values due to the dislocation of stamps between their source country and their ultimate designation was a major dealer source of profit. The Internet has now simplified this process and investors have even shifted the direction of trading demand. Lets examine this in detail.

Macro Economic Factors

At the macro level, demand is principally influenced by inflation and expectation of inflation. Inflation led to huge, across the board increases in stamp values during the late 1970's and early 1980's and set off a speculation frenzy that eventually led to a price collapse. Another macro demand factor can be political events. The fall of Communism changed the demand prospects for numerous countries not previously permitted to trade with the West. Initially, these countries were net sellers of their own stamps as people there wanted to obtain hard currencies. More recently, as world trade brought prosperity to these as well as to many developing nations, they have become net buyers of stamps.

Another macro factor featured prominently today is demographics. The ageing of the populations in the industrial countries, which is where most stamp collecting has taken place over the last 100 years, means four collectors are dying for every new one. This means a huge accumulation of stamp inventories is currently underway in these countries and prices are weakening in much of the stamp market. Dealers are taking advantage of this high availability of stamps to load up on their inventories, but there is a limit to what they can absorb (they too are getting older and may want to cash out before the market turns back upwards.) Since many of the third world nations have grown sizeable middle classes, the people that collect stamps, it is expected they will absorb much of this inventory buildup in the industrialized world. Yet, this will take time.

A final macro factor I would point out here and elsewhere in this book is the global accumulation of wealth since World War II. We have had a massive build-up of capital due to global prosperity from free trade. This has in turn driven down rates of return on investments to below zero on trillions of dollars of assets. The result is wealthy people are searching for new safe-haven investments that offer asset diversification and prospects for capital gains as well. If we are successful in convincing these individuals that stamps are the ultimate safe-haven investment, we can expect dramatic growth in the philatelic market. As pointed out in Chapter 2, *the investor stamp market is driven by money rather than bodies. By this I mean that collectors will buy just one investment grade stamp to fill a specific space in their collection. Investors will buy dozens of a stamp they consider a good investment just as they buy multiple shares of stock of the same company.*

Micro Economic Factors

The micro economic factors affecting demand are the economic, political and currency factors at work in specific countries. The growth and size of the middle class and their freedom to travel and invest abroad are also essential considerations in evaluating the potential of a specific country's stamps. However, when one is looking at the stamp market in the USA and other major markets, the micro economic factors are different.

In major markets such as in the USA the stamps of all nations come into play, not just that for US stamps. While the Internet has made the stamp market global, there is still a market diversity. Many US dealers still resist trading on multi-dealer sites like eBay and even those that do have only a small fraction of their inventory there. In fact, many dealers do more buying than selling on the Internet because they find that for many stamps, they know the market better than many of the part time dealers who sell there.

The Internet does give certain trading advantages to those who are highly automated and can take advantage of sellers who are not. Here is an example. Early on my StampFinder site was set up as a sales site, but with the capability of specifically identifying every stamp offering against our universal stamp database. After about 5 million listings it occurred to me to compare those listings and see which stamps priced below $100 had never appeared for sale on my site. Some 1200 items came up with zero or only 1 offering. When I surmised with a prominent dealer that I thought these items were so rare that they were mispriced by virtue of their infrequent availability, he made light of my theory. Six months later he related to me a story of how he had come across two stamps cataloging $80 which he could not recall having ever seen in 40 years of dealing. Remembering our discussion, he decided to put my theory to the test and offered up the stamps for $800. They both sold within a short period of time. What this demonstrates is that single country collectors all eventually reach a point where they are all missing the same stamps from their collection, namely the very high priced stamps and the few $50 and $80 stamps which, for some reason he can never get. The reason he cannot get them is that a dealer who specializes in a country knows exactly which items all these collectors are missing, knows they are rare and is constantly browsing the Internet for such stamp offerings. When he finds them, he buys them and marks them up as my dealer friend did and never, never shares this information with a catalog company. What is surprising is that eBay, the largest stamp dealer on the globe still has not enhanced its stamp listing protocol so that it can harvest such demand and supply information, something we have been able to do since 1996.

Another micro economic demand factor in stamps is how many collectors are likely to be interested in various stamps. Specifically, I mean stamps which were issued by a territory or country where more than one country collecting group would have an interest. For example, stamps issued during wartime occupations would be of interest to collectors of the occupier as well as of the country occupied. This is particularly important when the two nations involved had large collector bases such as German occupation of France or British occupation of Heligoland before it was handed over to Germany, or the various nations issuing occupation or offices stamps in China.

One of the best investment grade areas are stamps errors or varieties of otherwise widely produced stamps. Their demand is not as great because few are included in pre-printed stamp albums, the single biggest driver of stamp demand. The quantities of such stamps is generally miniscule making it a must-have item for country specialists. Its attraction for the investor is that its scarcity means it is constantly in demand. Note however that all errors and varieties should be considered because of their low quantities. Avoid varieties which are inconsequential, such as being printed sideways on watermarked paper, a difference you cannot see without a chemical bath or stamp tagging varieties which you cannot see without a black light. These are strictly for die-hard collectors.

Chapter 11 Selling Your Stamps

Buying and selling stamps is an expensive proposition which is why you should plan on a long-term holding period. If you sell at auction, you can expect to pay about 10% of the proceeds in a sellers fee . This can be negotiated down significantly depending on the size of your portfolio and how many important items it contains. Individual high value items, i.e. $50,000 and above, are attractive to auction houses because it will draw bidders for other items as well. Hence, you can negotiate a lower fee since they will be collecting a sizeable commission from the buyer. The only drawback to using an auction house is that there will be a delay of several months in having the item sold and then receiving your sales proceeds. Delays can come from a delay by the buyer in wanting an item certified or re-certified.

A delay may also come from no buyer being willing to meet your minimum offering price. You would most definitely want to set such a price to protect against a poor turnout at the auction or some price rigging by the participants. If a quick sale is of the essence, you can negotiate to sell the item to the auction house and have them sell it for their own account. This is quicker and more likely to yield you more than if you tried to sell it to a dealer who would offer you half what you might achieve at auction.

Another alternative to consider is offering it to a firm such as mine which specializes in acquiring investment grade items for its clients. This is better known as a private treaty sale. It is quicker and more confidential. It may also get you a better price than you could get at an auction. In any case, it would give you an idea of how high a minimum price you should put on the item.

Chapter 12 – Taxation of Stamp Transactions

The IRS in the USA is very clear about the taxation of any gains or losses on the ownership of stamps, namely, "Gold, silver, gems, stamps, coins, etc., are capital assets except when they are held for sale by a dealer. Any gain or loss from their sale or exchange generally is a capital gain or loss. If you are a dealer, the amount received from the sale is ordinary business income." (Page 25 of IRS publication 544 for 2018). Note this is a recent change. Previously such gains were always treated as short term gains no matter how long they were held.

It is clear that stamps, like most other tangible safe-haven assets, are treated the same as stocks and bonds and have the same holding period requirements to be short or long term. Their tax treatment as capital assets applies as well when stamps are donated to a worthy cause, i.e. their current retail value is deductible when given to a 501(3)c charitable organization such as the American Philatelic Society (APS), the collector membership organization which disseminates educational material and helps to grow the hobby. I recommend them only because donations of stamps over $5,000 in value need to have an appraisal to be tax deductible and most important, the receiving organization needs to hold the donation for a period of three years in order to allow the IRS the option of examining the material to validate the appraisal. Most charities would not want to get into having to store and safe-guard stamps for such a long period. They can also name an appraiser who lives in the area. Stamp donations can be the source of significant tax savings if you buy the right material and handle the donation properly. You should discuss this aspect with whoever advises you on your stamp purchases.

The tax treatment of stamps in various foreign countries are also important drivers of stamp appreciation. For example, Indian inheritance laws provide tax exemption for family heirlooms making them a popular way to avoid taxation. Indian law also bans the export of antiquities which is defined as objects over 100 years old. This includes stamps, hence, the supply of stamps issued prior to 1919 cannot leave the Indian market thereby drying up supplies worldwide. Note, numerous countries have such antiquities laws.

Chapter 13 – Postage Stamps and Technology

Technology and the Internet will continue to dramatically affect stamp values well beyond an already significant influential effect. When you mix together a stamps' price history, trading history, issuance quantity, country of issue, safe-haven attributes, currency considerations, economic and political considerations, recent trading developments, etc. you have a diversity of elements no human mind can wrap itself around. Specialist dealers do this over a lifetime of trading for a very limited number of items which limits their success. A computer has no time constraints. It can accept all the above variables for a universe of thousands of different stamps and through regression analysis determine which elements are important and to what extent. In this way, rarity and prices can be defined and updated in a continuous manner.

Since all rarities have a unique fingerprint, it allowing their sale and resale in an open or completely covert manner with their full, unique history and provenance on file. This in turn will help us nail down the real supply of such items and further price discovery.

Stamps may become like bitcoins, but with a tangible asset value. Considering bitcoin's success with no collateral backing, a stamp backed pseudo-currency could be a big winner, especially since it does not face the value volatility with bitcoins.

The goal in all this is not to make stamps into a commodity that trade on a daily basis or for short term gains. However, a community of dealers specializing in only investment grade material is sure to arise and they will serve as the market makers in this stand-alone market. It will be a market which trades on a Bloomberg financial system terminal. Actual physical delivery of the stamps will be optional much as gold bullion is preferably held by a repository.

Chapter 14 – Resources You Will Need

Once you have decided on why you want to make stamps a part of your investments and which stamps may fit that purpose, you will next decide on how you will proceed. If you choose to do your own stamp buying you should be aware of the following available resources that will make the process easier and safer.

StampFinder & Stamp Auction Network

For those who value their time, StampFinder.com has developed a website function that allows you to list those stamps you wish to buy on their Want List service. Here you can specify your wants and receive notification when it comes up for auction. The service is coordinated through StampAuctionNetwork.com, which has all the major auction houses as clients and provides complete access to the upcoming auctions and their detailed offerings through the auction catalogs. They also provide you with the ability to bid on-line during the live auction. They also have a service which has over one million auction results which you can peruse in order to see how much any given item has sold for recently. This is valuable information since such results are dependent on whether an item was bought by a dealer, collector or investor. You don't know who will be bidding at the next auction, so you will want to know what an aggressive buyer paid versus a dealer by the pattern of results. Also, you will see how frequently the item becomes available which is also a major consideration in investment selection.

Auction Catalogs

Auction houses spend a great deal in preparing and describing the lots for sale. You will find they tend to over describe any defects in a stamp since having them returned for omitting a defect would be a problem. You can request a catalog by mail, but this is generally not necessary since they are displayed digitally on the StampAuctionNetwork.com and are much easier to search online. The online versions have the added advantage that they can provide an indication of how strong an interest an item already shows by virtue of listing the latest opening bid amount. Be sure to read the conditions statements for each auction house since they differ in their trade practices, especially with regard to stamp condition and certification after purchase.

Stamp Catalogs

As an investment buyer you will want to have as much information as possible on what is the current market price for any given stamp. Below are what I consider the catalog resources which provide the information you need without the burden of having to buy catalogs covering the 90% of the stamps you have no interest in.

The "*Scott Classic Specialized Catalogue of Stamps & Covers 1840 – 1940*" is the premier information source used in the USA and much of the rest of the world. It is available in hard copy or online. This 1,100 page catalogue covers the universe of investment grade stamps and avoids the need to acquire the annual 12 volume edition which deals with the 90% of stamps of no interest as investments. Its major limitation is that it does not cover the WWII years which generated numerous stamps of foreign army occupations and short usage life. (Note- It seems that the losers in war were always the issuers of stamps, probably in the hope they were going to be staying a while.)

A second fine catalogue is the "*Stanley Gibbons Catalogue Commonwealth & British Empire Stamps 1840-1970.*" This publication is the main source used by dealers and collectors worldwide in and for Great Britain and its former colonies. Since Stanley Gibbons is mainly a seller of stamps their pricing is much more frequently updated and higher than others, but this only means their prices are more heavily discounted by others. Ignore their listings post 1950 which was when most of the colonies became independent. It also marks the point in time when postal authorities in much of the world changed from issuing stamps for postage to issuing them mainly for collectors. Pricing is in British Pounds, a currency presently under pressure due to their exit from the European Union.

Another worldwide publisher for stamps is the privately owned German catalog company Schwanberger Verlag GMBH which publishes the Michel catalogs. Their offerings are delivered in some 80 different volumes and formats with various volumes only updated periodically. Their Germany catalog is issued annually and is available online. I judge them to be more reliable since catalogs is their only business and they publish the names of those supplying them with their pricing information.

They also make a serious effort to supply printed stamp quantities. The limitation here is that they publish in German. Pricing is in Euros.

France also has a worldwide catalog company which publishes periodically in some 20 volumes. The catalog for France and Monaco is published annually. It has a single volume worldwide dealing with investment grade stamps titled "*Yver&Tellier Catalogue Mondial de Cotation Classiques du Monde 1840-1940*." It provides a single volume guide for French speaking collectors and was last issued in 2010. Pricing is in Euros.

Each of these catalogs offers unique information such as on stamp varieties, issuance , forgeries and unauthorized issues and overprints. If you decide you want to specialize in investment grade stamps from specific countries, there are specialized catalogs that may better fill your needs. There are hundreds of such catalogs and their value is not just for pricing information, but also to allow you to identify varieties not known to the other catalogs and to dealers or other Internet sellers. Again, as the saying goes "The source of all wealth is information."

The American Philatelic Society

The APS is the largest stamp collector membership organization in the USA. It provides educational and expertizing services and has one of the most extensive libraries on philately and reference collection in the world. It sells stamps for and to members via circuit books and on-line. It publishes a monthly magazine which comes with the $45 annual membership. It is a 501(c)(3) organization and donations of cash or in-kind are deductible to the fullest extent allowed under the law.. It is a resource which any serious investor in stamps should consider, if only to have it when they need an independent source for information. Their website is www.stamps.org.

Stamp Expertizing

I cannot over-emphasize the importance of having your high value purchases expertized. Stamp forgeries, alterations, repairs, re-gumming, etc. has been a part of the hobby almost from the beginning. Some of the forgers were so good they are celebrated and their work recognized and even collected. In a collection I bought of the first two stamps ever issued by Peru no less than 3 forgers had made copies of them, even in colors never actually used. But this was 1857 and Peru was a far-off exotic place with unique animals like llamas. In those early years much of the world was a mystery and photography was still in its infancy. This may account for the early popularity of stamps. Hence, many stamps from those early years were produced, some via the back doors of European printers who produced the actual stamps and took payment through producing extra stamps for sale to the philatelic market.

Printing was a much more primitive art in the 1800s, but many countries insisted on producing their own stamps. This too resulted in the theft of stamps due to poor control and the production of errors, intentional or otherwise, which could be sold at a premium. I personally visited a stamp collector in Paraguay who showed me his collection of dozens of errors produced at the government printing office by a relative of his. Whether the varieties were made to order or just printers waste was not clear from my conversation with him in my limited Spanish, but I remember his coffee was excellent.

One of the vulnerabilities for the catalog companies in the past has been their dependence on the integrity of the dealers providing them with price guidance for stamps that are not frequently traded. In addition, collectors are vulnerable to changes in the listing policies of the catalogues, which can lead to serious market mis-pricing. Two examples will illustrate this point. The #1 issue of St. Vincent in the 1993 Scott cataloged was priced at $8,000 mint and $500 used and continued at this level until 1998. Then in the 1999 catalog it suddenly showed no price, which continued to be the policy until 2005 when the prices suddenly appeared as $50 mint and $15 used, a whopping price decline of -93.7% and -97% respectively. The Stanley Gibbons Catalogue showed a similar change, however they reported the price drop as early as 1998. The reason for the change was that the stamp existed with 2 perforation varieties; an 1861 clean cut perf 14 and 16 and an 1862 rough cut perf 14 and 16. I was advised by a specialist in these stamps that identification and certification of the perforations proved too difficult, so it was decided that this was a distinction without a difference and the cheaper version became the new #1. A second example of catalogue confusion is Switzerland Scott #195c which is assumed to be a redrawing print variety of #195 and is priced at $3,100 mint and $7,500 used. The printing variety they are pricing, however, is something entirely different and is clearly illustrated in the Zumstein Swiss catalog. At least two dealers have jumped on this discrepancy and offer this $.75 stamp on eBay; one for $500, and a second for a mere $2,925 with 24 month financing available, but with interest. To top it off, both dealers were too cheap to buy the current Scott Catalogue since they show it at a previous $4,500 value versus the current $7,500. What is discouraging is that this discrepancy has existed for over two decade and no one alerted Scott. The lesson here is, when buying such high priced items, get them certified.

Expertizing settles the question of a stamp's legitimacy and should be done at the time of purchase or made a condition thereto. It costs upwards of $20 per item with fees scaled up base on appraised value. Note it is also important if you intend to keep the stamps at home and therefor need to consider insurance. For general items I recommend a firm called GradingMatters.com. For specialized material such as Mexico, you should use the Mexico Elmhurst Philatelic Society International (website mepsi.org).

Country Profiles - USA

The universe of investment grade stamps for the USA is one of the largest in philately. My analysis focused on over 3,000 listed items issued before 1950 and priced at $25 or more. Since our investment grade universe includes some 60,000 items, it means US stamps are the biggest single component country. In terms of aggregate investment value, it represents $13 million in mint and $11 million in used stamps; good to know in case you have as a goal a complete US collection. But then, wouldn't it be a lot more prudent putting that together than spending $9.5 million on a single British Guiana stamp?

Since the market for US stamps is so deep and mature, it cannot be expected to perform like that of say China which has only recently accumulated massive discretionary wealth. Still there are several areas and numerous individual USA stamps which continue to do well despite a slow growth in other categories of investment and the economy as a whole. For US mint stamps, those priced $25,000 and higher showed five and ten year growth of 16.47% and 169.33% respectively. These 105 stamps, though few in number, represent 78% of the $12 million investment value being measured and thus need to be considered separately. Stamps between $1,000 and $5,000 showed a respectable 7% and 40.22% appreciation for the 5 and 10 year period, but more importantly, demonstrated a major shift in collector focus. Looking at the 69 mint stamps which have appreciated more than 50% in the last five years, it is noteworthy that 29 were revenue issues and 19 were officials. Only 32% of the top appreciating stamps were regular issues. This rising prominence in back of the book stamps has no obvious reason. If I had to guess I would attribute it to the notion that US collectors are, as a group, mature and advanced collectors who have already bought most of the things they can afford in traditional stamps. They are therefore diversifying into revenue and official stamps because they are more affordable. In any case, the matter deserves some serious debate since it may have long term market consequences.

Note that I have done a separate analysis of the stamps and postmarks for the Confederate States. They have been stellar performers in the last 5 years with used stamps leading the way, appreciating 31.04% and 50.02% over the last 5 and 10 years with most of that appreciation in the last 5 years. Mint stamps appreciated 17.31% and 40.94% for the same periods. It was noted, however, that almost all the appreciation in both mint and used took place in only 53 of the mint and 143 of the used stamps out of a universe of about 400 items. Hence, those items that appreciated actually did so at twice the rates shown for the group; in short, it pays to know who the winners are and not just buy the group.

When evaluating buying a high priced stamp, an in depth review of its pricing history is essential. By way of example, albeit an extreme one, is an envelope cut square Scott # U447A which in 1995 was priced at $1500 unused. For subsequent years it went unpriced until in 2005 the price shot up to an astronomical $50,000 where it remained through 2009. In 2010, however, the price was dropped to $3,500 and now became the price for an entire envelope rather than a cut square. In 2011 the price dropped further to $1,500 and then rose again to $3,500 where it stands today. Was this a typo error by Scott, or maybe a rigged auction bid, or did someone actually take the kind of loss I thought only the stock market could deliver? In any case, it demonstrates the potential risks in buying pricy items without a good price history and provenance.

Investors should be aware that US stamps have brought the recognition of price premiums for never hinged stamps to a high art form. I have always been dubious of the concept that the state of the gum on the back of a stamp should garner more than a nominal premium. In US stamps, however, not only do they generally bring premiums of 40%-50%, it can run as much as 1000%! I suspect that investment minded buyers are at the heart of this price disparity since they want to minimize the degree of expertise needed to judge an individual stamp and protect its resale value. The offsetting risk is that no one knows just how rare an old stamp in never hinged condition may be, hence, the value premium is guesswork at best. Still and all, never hinged stamps as a rule will likely continue to lead hinged stamps in appreciation. It's only the degree of price premium that is the principal concern, i.e. it's an added element of risk.

Country Profiles – Australia

The analysis of Australian stamps covered some 2,000 issues by Australia and its states between 1840 and 1950 which had achieved a value of $25 and higher. The analysis evaluated each stamp's appreciation (mint or used) over the last 5 and 10 year time periods and compared this across various catalog systems. Since my focus is on the investment aspects of stamps, I hope collectors will not be offended by this singular focus. Stamps become an investment to the most ardent collectors once they get past the easy to get items and have to budget their funds among numerous items they would like but cannot afford all. For example, all the +$25 items for Australia will cost you over $2 million. Even the 400 or so items priced from $25 to $100 will cost you $27,000 and all 1200 items below $1000 will cost $300,000. And this for a country that doesn't even make the top 10 in collector interest. Investment buyers will be focused on which stamps have the best potential for appreciation, and every country has a few such. Who would have guessed the most valuable stamp comes from British Guiana!

Overall, Australia showed only a paltry 10.3% overall appreciation rate over the last 5 years, but the growth has been steady for at least 10 years and the data shows numerous candidates for substantial growth in the near future. Pricing was erratic in the early states' issues due in part to the attempt to assign values to a multitude of different perforations and color shades, many of which can be attributed to the primitive state of the printing art in these early years. Most countries have these problems, but some country dealers and collectors carry this to an extreme. I have tended to ignore such sub varieties since the investment potential for such items is limited. Weakness was also noted in the postal use of fiscal stamps. They have shown little upside in the last 10 years and a few are showing large declines. The investment potential lies mainly in the issues by the Australian states and I include a profile of each state in the Tables attached.

Country Profiles - China

The economy of China has had explosive growth the last 10 years and its stamp prices have reflected this to an astounding degree. My universe of investment rated stamps is slightly more than 1,000 stamps and includes only stamps issued to 1950 and cataloging at least $25 today. This excludes almost all issues of the Peoples Republic of China which was only founded in 1949. This leaves only about 3,000 Scott catalogued varieties of stamps. In short, almost one third of all the stamps issued in this time period have risen to above $25 which I doubt any other nation, with the possible exception of the USA, have achieved.

In terms of price appreciation, the numbers are even more impressive. The five year appreciation has averaged 164% and for ten years, 719%. These are astounding numbers and deserve a more detailed look since the aggregate value of these stamps is some $3.8 million. When one looks at stamps below $1000 the picture is quite a bit different. Mint stamps have a five year appreciation average of 45.1% and used, 27.8%. These are more reasonable numbers, but they leave open an obvious question, namely, what accounts for the 175% five year and 719% ten year appreciation by the 250 stamps cataloging over $1000? The answer may lie in what is going on in China today.

We see that the Chinese government is making a major effort to crack down on corruption by government officials. Several thousand have been caught up in an anti-corruption campaign and it may continue on for some time. What makes this campaign so successful there is that the banking system is wholly transparent to the government so it is easy to see who is on the take. Enter postage stamps, which is a way to bribe a government official without leaving a money trail. In fact, given their price appreciation and low visibility, they may well become the preferred method of bribery.

Given the crack down on monetary bribes it stands to reason that stamps will become an even more popular alternative currency for hiding payments and for wealth transport. Hence, I would expect that the appreciation of the priciest stamps will continue to outperform the market as a whole. But individuals in China are limited to $50,000 a year in foreign bank transfers, thus creating a great need for an alternative to cash.

Country Profiles - India

Those interested in stamps with investment and appreciation potential should look at India. Economic factors play a big role in the outlook for this nation. It has a population size next to China's with projections that it will overtake China by about 2050. It has a democratic form of government making it attractive to investors. And it has a rising middle class, who form the heart of any collector community. Its progress has not evolved as quickly as China's principally because it spent much of the 1980s allying itself with Russia and thinking this was a viable model for governance, a model which stalled their economy for a decade. Now they are seen as the counter-weight to China in an area where fear of Chinese dominance. Its stamps have not exploded in price as much as in China, but this is more a matter of timing than probability as I will soon clarify.

Indian stamps have shown mixed performance to date for a variety of reasons. The British Empire issues of India proper have had a significant rise in the last 5 years with appreciation of over 38% for both mint and used. Note that my analysis deals with stamps cataloging $25 or more and issued up to 1950. As I pointed out in a previous article, stamps are a bifurcated market where investor interest is focused on such higher priced stamps; which is why they consistently outperform the market as a whole.

When analyzing the performance of the convention and feudatory states, the picture becomes much more complicated. These stamps exist in smaller quantities and have already had a much higher appreciation rate, and for more stamps, than those of India proper. So, does this mean they will not rise as rapidly? The answer is a definite no but requires some explanation. First of all, the Scott catalogue has not revised the pricing for the Indian states in at least the last 5 years. The Stanley Gibbons catalog, which shows substantially higher prices is a better guide given recent auction results which equaled even those prices. Hence, serious collectors will need to see actual market prices of recent transactions to get a feel for the correct valuation. Indian states have already experienced significant appreciation, rising an average of 378% over the last 25 years, even with the lag in price updates by Scott. Since India's empire issues appreciated an average of 718% in this same time period, I think this is a good indicator of the future pricing for Indian states.

Since most USA dealers benchmark their pricing off Scott, look at their pricing as an opportunity to buy these stamps at a significant discount from future pricing. One caveat about the state issues, only buy the higher priced items certified. A certificate will only enhance a stamps value and avoid a costly mistake in a difficult area. There are many stamps with reprints, errors, color varieties and dubious provenance. Another complication is that many stamps were issued without gum and are imperforated and not well centered. While these impair pricing for most countries, they are of little consequence here since they are the rule rather than the exception.

We are likely to see explosive price appreciation for India and Indian States stamps in the coming decade for three additional reasons according to Sandeep Jaiswal of Stamps Inc, an Indian stamp specialist. Inheritance taxes in India provide an exemption for family heirlooms, something which stamps can easily provide. Also, stamps are subject to an antiquities law that bans the export of stamps over 100 years old. This thus includes most Indian states stamps. Sandeep also points out that Indians have an instinctual desire to collect things, something stamp collectors can relate to.

Country Profiles - Mexico

Few countries are, philatelically, as well documented or actively organized as Mexico. Its attraction is its rich and often violent history which is well represented in its postage stamps. It is also of high interest for stamp investors for a variety of reasons, the main one being that its early stamps are tremendously undervalued. But first, some background.

Mexico was a country that embraced the concept of revolution and took it to new levels. It suffered occupation by the French and ruled by Maximillian as emperor until he was overthrown. Then a variety of revolutionary leaders took power and had to fend off internal challenges to their leadership. The US was also a factor, primarily in its ambitions for Mexican territory. Governments came and went at a rapid pace, but not without leaving their footprint in philately. For example, most countries issued only about 200 different stamps from their inception in 1840 until 1916. For Mexico, the number of primary listings is some 600, and the varieties therefrom number in the thousands.

The early postal system was organized into 54 geographic districts and, as a way of controlling stamp theft by highway robbers, stamps were overprinted in Mexico City with each district's number and year before being shipped and then manually overprinted with the name of the district on safe arrival. Hence, if the stamps were stolen, they could be identified by the printed district number and determined to be invalid by the lack of the overprinted name. That was the plan, but actual execution fell well short. As a personal undertaking, I decided to determine just how rare one issue of such stamps was. I selected the two sets of stamps issued from 1879 to 1883 which were specifically printed to handle international mail.

In 1879, Mexico joined the Universal Postal Union and thus had to collect the rates set by the UPU, which rates were lower than those for Mexico's internal mail. To handle the rate difference two sets of stamps were printed; the first set picturing President Juarez and a later set with just the rate numeral. During this period 54 different district numbers and various year overprints from 1879 to 1883 resulted in the printing of some 2,000 different combinations of overprints for stamps, but are listed in the Scott catalog as only 26 varieties.

What really makes these stamps a good investment is their absolute rarity. Mexico in the 1880s was not a land of high literacy rates where few people traveled abroad or knew anyone outside their immediate vicinity. Most stamp usage was commercial. Postal authorities had to guess how many stamps would be needed in each district and they started modestly, by which I mean they printed only 50 to 100 stamps in 1879 for many districts and even those quantities proved excessive. Districts with higher demand had follow on printings dated 1880 and 1881. In 1882, a general recall of unused stamps was made and replaced with new stamps bearing that year. Postal records show that many districts and values had almost no usage during 1879-1882 and all were returned unused. All such supplies were eventually sold off to stamp dealers in 1889. They cancelled many of the unused stamps to fill collector requests for used stamps since mint stamps were not as popular. This led to many stamps which exist only as Cancelled To Order (CTO) with few if any surviving postally used examples. Many varieties of stamps and errors also exist. Chief among these are stamps which were returned and redirected to a different district, termed Habilitado issues. They bear two sets of district and date numbers, generally with the second district overprinted in red. These stamps are even rarer because they were prepared from returned or unneeded stocks, which were usually very small.

StampFinder created a catalog for these stamps and then priced the individual stamps based strictly on known or derived quantities without setting new highs for those stamps clearly recognized as rare, i.e. $300 with a few exceptions. Excluding the most metropolitan areas of Mexico, stamp quantities numbered only in the hundreds and that were quantities printed, not quantities that survived after 130 years.

What makes these stamps a compelling investment is that their pricing by dealers is totally out of touch with their rarity. Existing pricing guides are based on a historical lack of information rather than rarity. It's a classic case of underpricing based on perceived comparables without realizing that the only comparables are derived from trading in the issues from the half dozen large districts. I suspect most dealer pricing is based on what they paid for a collection without researching individual items. My catalog is thus a treasure map for picking up stamps for pennies, stamps which can only appreciate once their rarity becomes better known.

TABLE 1 – Market Overview

To begin our survey of the investment grade stamps market it will be helpful to see how well that market has performed over the last 25 years and which segments did the best. The 25 year time period is used because, unfortunately, catalogs are not truly updated on a predictable basis. Popular countries get an annual review, less popular maybe every 5 to 10 years. This is not always apparent since higher priced stamps have annual auction results and are not dependent on dealers to provide pricing guidance or objectivity. Hence, we can see short term price manipulations for certain countries or price swings tied to currency actions. The longer 25 year perspective also emphasizes the fact that stamps are more akin to long term investments like real estate, but with different characteristics.

Table 1 provides a snapshot of the most recent 25 year time period, an era in which stamps experienced the prosperity of the 1990s, the rise of the Internet as the principal marketplace for stamp sales, the financial crisis of 2008 and the declining demographics throughout. While stamp prices declined in most major collecting countries, investment grade stamps showed a remarkable resilience. As mentioned elsewhere in this book, this was due to greatly increased market participation by investment oriented collectors as well as outright investment buyers.

The results represent a refinement of my previous study of these stamps which now includes many items which have only been recognized in the last decade. This seems unusual given that these stamps were all issued at least 70 years ago or longer. We can attribute this to the fact that the Internet has vastly expanded the sources of information about stamps and thereby, much information known only at a local level has entered into the mainstream market via recognition by the major catalog companies. This recognition translated into new demand for relatively scarce items and thereby lifted the overall performance statistics. *It can thereby be concluded that new variety listings by major catalogs is, in and of itself, a driver of stamp prices.*

The Table 1 analysis of mint (unused) stamps demonstrates that all price categories of investment grade stamps showed appreciation rates which rival rates of return in the fixed income securities market during this same time period. The big variable, however, is that the transaction costs for the stamps is much higher, so short term gains of this magnitude are unlikely. The rates of return on the items above $25,000 are, likely, understated. These are trophy stamps of which only one or a handful exist and their appearance for sale is so infrequent that the price may be decades out of date.

The table's results for used stamps shows a much calmer market and relatively fewer items. This reflects that fact that used stamps represents the bulk of the collector market because it was the preferred form of collecting for almost a century and because used stamp quantities are generally greater than unused ones. Because of their preference by collectors, their market is more vulnerable to the negative demographics of the hobby. Hence, *we can expect over the coming decade that mint stamps will outperform used stamps because of lower supply and collector demographics.*

Again, Table 1 is the universe of investment grade stamps. The good news then is that, through the use of refined analysis, I expect to be able to provide recommendations of investment grade stamps which will exceed these average results, as I did with my 1994 guide.

TABLE 1 – Market Overview
25 Year History - Investment Grade Stamps

Individual Value Ranges	# Items	Initial Investment	Current Value	Appreciation % 25 Yrs	Appreciation % Rate
Mint Stamps					
$25 to $250	9,537	$917,388	$2,843,077	209.9%	8.4%
$250 to $500	1,675	$428,770	$2,135,762	398.1%	15.9%
$500 to $1,000	1,037	$600,912	$2,675,170	345.2%	13.8%
$1,000 to $2,500	897	$1,487,471	$4,689,582	215.3%	8.6%
$2,500 to $5,000	353	$1,266,600	$3,866,050	205.2%	8.2%
$5,000 to $10,000	233	$1,650,250	$5,698,950	245.3%	9.8%
10,000 to $25,000	98	$1,556,000	$5,453,250	250.5%	10.0%
$25,000 to $50,000	16	$534,500	$1,840,000	244.2%	9.8%
$50,000 to $100,000	7	$480,000	$1,124,500	134.3%	5.4%
>100,000	10	$1,740,000	$5,765,000	231.3%	9.3%
Totals	13,863	$10,661,891	$36,091,341	238.5%	9.5%
Used Stamps					
$25 to $250	8,162	$734,351	$2,132,265	190.4%	7.6%
$250 to $500	1,230	$457,503	$1,315,957	187.6%	7.5%
$500 to $1,000	791	$587,377	$1,619,780	175.8%	7.0%
$1,000 to $2,500	610	$989,450	$2,630,325	165.8%	6.6%
$2,500 to $5,000	276	$968,350	$2,872,587	196.6%	7.9%
$5,000 to $10,000	164	$1,113,750	$4,264,500	282.9%	11.3%
10,000 to $25,000	84	$1,291,250	$3,921,100	203.7%	8.1%
$25,000 to $50,000	21	$695,000	$1,513,500	117.8%	4.7%
$50,000 to $100,000	11	$695,000	$1,805,000	159.7%	6.4%
>100,000	7	$1,050,000	$2,270,000	116.2%	4.6%
Totals	11,356	$8,582,031	$24,345,014	183.7%	7.3%

TABLE 2 – Moneystamps
25 year Performance 1994-2019

Performance Range	Stars Rtng	# Mint	Mint %	# Used	Used %
Greater than 10%/Yr	*****	5,019	10.9%	3,624	10.1%
6% to 10% per Year	****	3,133	6.8%	2,409	6.7%
4% to 6% per Year	***	2,585	5.6%	1,981	5.5%
2% to 4% per Year	**	3,197	6.9%	2,166	6.0%
>0% to 2% per Year	*	3,289	7.1%	2,297	6.4%
Unrated		29,034	62.7%	23,503	65.3%
Totals		46,257	100.0%	35,980	100.0%

While we surveyed some 60,000 investment grade stamps based on their age and catalog price, some reached inclusion only through their mint only or used only price histories. Since price histories are independently calculated, it is possible for the mint and used stamps of any country to bear different star ratings or only one condition to be rated. It is worth noting that almost two-thirds of the stamps that qualify for inclusion based on their size and age did not qualify for ranking because they failed to show any price increase or actually declined in value. This may be due to a stamps rarity which means it doesn't trade often enough, or it may be due to dealers holding back on pricing information in order to exploit it. In either case, it implies that many unrated items are hidden gems and will need a more extensive effort on our part to flush them out.

The actual performance range numbers are translated into a star rating with 5 stars representing a return of 5% or more per year. Note that these are historic ratings and returns and aren't the basis for a stamp's rating going forward. Investor involvement has led to a preference for stamps that have never been hinged, variously described as mint never hinged (MNH) or post office fresh. Such stamps can command price premiums as high as 100% to 1,000% and have led to a problem in that stamps can be re-gummed in order to capture this premium. Hence, having stamp expertized becomes essential.

The table appears to demonstrate a similarity in the performance of mint and used stamps, but this is misleading. Used stamps are generally cheaper and there is a much larger supply of such stamps for most issues. The fact is that more mint stamps have star ratings than used stamps during the time period of 1840 to 1950 despite the quantities of the used stamps being vastly greater for almost all issues except for the trophy stamp category. This disparity demonstrates that mint investment grade stamps are more likely to appreciate in the future since they are fewer in number and are the preferred focus of investors but are still of interest to collectors.

TABLE 3 – Value of Investment Grade Stamps by Star Rating

Star Rating	Mint $(000)	% Mint	Average Size $	Used $(000)	% Used	Average Size $	
*****	$42,382	73.4%	$4,639	$21428	65.0%	$778	(1)
****	$4,263	7.4%	$200	$1,242	3.8%	$965	
***	$2,447	4.2%	$637	$1,772	5.4%	$1,376	
**	$2,946	5.1%	$1,558	$2,369	7.2%	$1,527	
*	$3,741	6.5%	$949	$4,609	14.1%	$1,568	
(*)	$1,712	3.0%	$826	$1,270	3.9%	$715	
(**)	$253	0.4%	$578	$132	0.4%	$809	
Total	$57,744	100.0%	$2,626	$32,690	100.0%	$1,027	

(1) Average Size $ Used excludes 3 unique stamps - British Guiana #13 ($9,500,000), Sweden 1A color error ($3,000,000) and USA # 85A Z grill ($3,000,000).

As can be seen in this table, 4 and 5 star ratings account for the bulk of of the money stamps. To translate, the star ratings represent the 25 year performance of a stamp with;

5 stars representing appreciation of 5% or more per year or 125% in 25 years.
4 stars representing appreciation of 4% or more per year or 100% in 25 years.
3 stars representing appreciation of 3% or more per year or 75% in 25 years.
2 stars representing appreciation of 2% or more per year or 50% in 25 years.
1 star representing appreciation of about 16% to 25% in 25 years.
A negative star (*) denotes a stamp which declined 15% or rose only up to 15% in 25 years.
Two negative stars (**) denotes stamps which declined more than15% in 25 years.

Note that the star ratings do not translate into the relative prospects of a specific stamps or an endorsement of the future. A specific endorsement is made after a considering a variety of other factors including how the country as a whole is performing and how long it has been since the catalogue prices were reviewed. A long delay may mean a sharp rise or drop is coming. This is where current market prices and demand come into play. Specific recommendations by stamp and country will be made via my Moneystamps Advisor newsletter at StampFinder.com.

TABLE 4 – Most Valuable Mint Moneystamps

Country	Subsection	Scott #	Issue Year	Value	Variety	Catalog Value	Star Rating
MAURITIUS	REGULAR ISSUES	1	1847	1p	Regular Issue	$1,250,000	*****
USA	REGULAR ISSUES	119b	1869	15c	Printing Variety	$1,000,000	*****
CHINA	REGULAR ISSUES	83	1897	$1/3ca	Regular Issue	$900,000	*****
USA	REGULAR ISSUES	120b	1869	24c	Printing Variety	$750,000	*****
FRANCE	REGULAR ISSUES	8b	1849	1fr	Multiple Tete-Beche	$750,000	*****
USA	REGULAR ISSUES	120b	1869	24c	Printing Variety	$750,000	*****
USA	REGULAR ISSUES	121b	1869	30c	Printing Variety	$750,000	*****
HAWAII	REGULAR ISSUES	1	1851	2c	Regular Issue	$660,000	*****
USA	PRE POSTAL/ FORERUNNERS	1X1a	1846	5c	Printing Variety	$625,000	*****
RUSSIA	AIR MAIL STAMPS	C68c	1935	1r	Overprint-inverted	$600,000	N/R
USA	NEWSPAPER STAMPS	PR53	1875	24d	Normal issue	$500,000	N/R
CHINA	REGULAR ISSUES	35b	1897	10c/9c	Inverted Overprint	$450,000	*****
USA	REGULAR ISSUES	181	1875	5c	Regular Issue	$450,000	*****
CHINA	REGULAR ISSUES	35b	1897	10c/9c	Inverted Overprint	$450,000	*****
FRANCE	REGULAR ISSUES	8d	1849	1fr	Multiple - Tete Beche	$450,000	*****
USA	REGULAR ISSUES	321	1908	2c	Regular Issue	$450,000	*****
USA	AIR MAIL STAMPS	C3a	1918	24c	Printing variety	$450,000	*****
GREAT BRITAIN	OFFICIAL STAMPS	O22	1902	6p	Regular Issue	$400,000	*****
ITALY	OFFICES ABROAD- CHINA-PEKING	11	1917	40c/lL	Regular Issue	$350,000	*****
USA	NEWSPAPER STAMPS	PR51	1875	$9	Normal issue	$350,000	*****
FRANCE	REGULAR ISSUES	19a	1853	80c	Multiple Tete-Beche	$340,000	****
CHINA	REGULAR ISSUES	274a	1925	3c/4c	Multiple Imperforate	$300,000	*****
USA	REGULAR ISSUES	321	1908	2c	Regular Issue	$250,000	**

TABLE 5 – Most Valuable Used Moneystamps

Country	Subsection	Scott #	Issue Year	Value	Variety	Catalog Value	Star Rating
BRITISH GUIANA	REGULAR ISSUES	13	1856	1c	Normal issue	$9,500,000	*****
USA	REGULAR ISSUES	85A	1868	1c	Normal issue	$3,000,000	*****
SWEDEN	REGULAR ISSUES	1a	1855	3s	Color-error	$3,000,000	N/R
USA	REGULAR ISSUES	85F	1867	15c	Printing Variety	$2,000,000	*****
MAURITIUS	REGULAR ISSUES	2	1847	2p	Regular Issue	$1,700,000	*****
BADEN	REGULAR ISSUES	4b	1851	9kr	Color Variety	$1,300,000	*****
MAURITIUS	REGULAR ISSUES	1	1847	1p	Regular Issue	$1,250,000	*****
TUSCANY	REGULAR ISSUES	14a	1857	4cr	Printing Variety	$1,100,000	N/R
BRAZIL	REGULAR ISSUES	1c	1843	30r/60r	Multiple-different stamps	$950,000	*****
USA	REGULAR ISSUES	82	1867	3c	Regular Issue	$900,000	*****
USA	REGULAR ISSUES	85D	1867	10c	Printing Variety	$600,000	*****
BERMUDA	PRE-POSTALSTAMPS	X2a	1856	1p	Color - variety(shade)	$400,000	*****
USA	REGULAR ISSUES	164	1873	24c	Normal issue	$357,500	N/R
VENEZUELA	REGULAR ISSUES	4d	1862	1/2r	Color-error	$350,000	N/R
BRITISH GUIANA	REGULAR ISSUES	1	1850	2c	Regular Issue	$325,000	*****
CHINA	REGULAR ISSUES	274a	1925	3c/4c	Multiple Imperfor	$275,000	*****
FRANCE	REGULAR ISSUES	2c	1849	15c	Multiple - Tete Beche	$260,000	*****
FRANCE	REGULAR ISSUES	7g	1950	40c on 20c	Cover-/w partial stamp	$260,000	*****
USA	REGULAR ISSUES	80a	1867	5c dk brn	Color Variety	$260,000	*****
CHINA	REGULAR ISSUES	81a	1897	4c/3c	Overprint Variety	$250,000	*****
BRITISH GUIANA	REGULAR ISSUES	5c	1850	12c	Printing variety	$250,000	*****
CANADA	REGULAR ISSUES	32	1868	2C	Regular Issue	$250,000	*****
USA	REGULAR ISSUES	321	1908	2c	Regular Issue	$250,000	**

Note that this table does not include stamps on envelopes (called entires) which also have numerous items in or near the million dollar range. For the most part these are unique items.

TABLE 6 - Appreciation Rankings - By Mint Stamps

COUNTRY	#	$ Total 2019	$ Total 2093	% Change	Ranking
ITALY	417	$1,685,348	$189,140	791.1%	1
INDIA	660	$1,675,890	$218,445	667.2%	2
RUSSIA	217	$647,437	$94,620	584.2%	3
INDIA CONVEN STATES	187	$353,437	$51,877	581.3%	4
CHINA	488	$4,254,812	$638,202	566.7%	5
IRAN	270	$522,345	$84,405	518.9%	6
AUSTRALIA	139	$369,746	$65,083	468.1%	7
AUSTRIA	140	$369,971	$65,258	466.9%	8
GREAT BRITAIN	295	$3,600,100	$689,775	421.9%	9
USA	943	$12,720,066	$2,684,109	373.9%	10
KOREA	80	$34,437	$8,824	290.3%	11
TURKEY	210	$46,285	$13,130	252.5%	12
CANADA	366	$1,020,535	$339,902	200.2%	13
NEW ZEALAND	251	$742,177	$253,571	192.7%	14
AUSTRALIAN STATES	733	$1,463,437	$502,256	191.4%	15
FRANCE	602	$4,112,437	$1,504,591	173.3%	16
ARGENTINA	179	$298,472	$124,993	138.8%	17
BELGIUM	152	$150,491	$65,570	129.5%	18
NORWAY	80	$52,847	$23,222	127.6%	19
GERMAN STATES	485	$462,420	$226,823	103.9%	20
GREECE	469	$145,519	$72,528	100.6%	21
MEXICO	531	$288,239	$148,425	94.2%	22
BRAZIL	154	$92,282	$48,813	89.1%	23
JAPAN	263	$154,991	$83,326	86.0%	24
PHILIPPINES	169	$179,982	$97,432	84.7%	25
COLUMBIA	139	$178,745	$98,666	81.2%	26
SWITZERLAND	195	$618,100	$345,256	79.0%	27
SPAIN	360	$445,777	$269,849	65.2%	28
GERMANY	195	$119,816	$75,124	59.5%	29
VENEZUELA	87	$56,982	$42,777	33.2%	30
TOTAL	9456	$36,863,123	$9,125,992	303.9%	

TABLE 7 - Appreciation Rankings - By Used Stamps

COUNTRY	#	$ Total 2019	$ Total 2093	% Change	Ranking
USA	538	$5,585,270	$554,811	906.7%	1
AUSTRALIA	89	$243,378	$28,693	748.2%	2
AUSTRIA	90	$243,465	$28,768	746.3%	3
CHINA	322	$1,668,542	$201,232	729.2%	4
INDIA CONVEN STATES	115	$117,930	$15,448	663.4%	5
RUSSIA	137	$771,402	$111,088	594.4%	6
ITALY	496	$1,015,050	$148,825	582.0%	7
INDIA	459	$1,803,788	$272,697	561.5%	8
IRAN	156	$231,680	$36,236	539.4%	9
BRAZIL	93	$992,840	$230,019	331.6%	10
GREAT BRITAIN	249	$870,592	$213,636	307.5%	11
KOREA	52	$13,407	$4,350	208.2%	12
TURKEY	135	$25,100	$9,740	157.7%	13
JAPAN	133	$146,558	$57,128	156.5%	14
CANADA	131	$617,677	$244,042	153.1%	15
GREECE	228	$103,747	$41,508	149.9%	16
AUSTRALIAN STATES	600	$539,624	$216,703	149.0%	17
PHILIPPINES	104	$83,235	$33,452	148.8%	18
COLUMBIA	123	$166,931	$67,919	145.8%	19
MEXICO	448	$482,707	$203,007	137.8%	20
ARGENTINA	118	$246,384	$108,754	126.6%	21
NEW ZEALAND	252	$407,552	$180,715	125.5%	22
VENEZUELA	71	$48,212	$22,066	118.5%	23
FRANCE	369	$1,151,681	$542,600	112.3%	24
BELGIUM	77	$28,226	$13,682	106.3%	25
GERMAN STATES	447	$772,685	$393,729	96.2%	26
SWITZERLAND	200	$762,355	$409,197	86.3%	27
SPAIN	224	$195,725	$111,050	76.2%	28
NORWAY	48	$37,132	$23,414	58.6%	29
GERMANY	135	$198,450	$128,636	54.3%	30
TOTALS	6639	$19,571,325	$4,653,145	320.6%	

Tables 6 and 7 provide the summary statistics for the moneystamps of the countries for which detailed information going back 25 years is provided in the appendix to this book. The top 30 countries are shown in the order of their performance ranking mint and used.

Note that the selection of countries was made to provide a cross section of the various types of countries and regions of the world. Because of demographics the European and North American markets are shrinking and the Asian, African and South American markets are growing. Hence, past performance is not always the best predictor of the future.

My recommendations of specific stamps will be part of an analysis of individual countries. That analysis will be more focused on the last five or ten years since picking what has done well in the short term has more promise than what did well the last 25 years, but not the last five years or the next five years. In this regard looking for which countries are overdue for a price uplift across the board seems to me the best starting point. However, if you want to begin building a portfolio of Moneystamps based on stamps from a top ten performance country, that too is likely to bring you favorable results. This year I will be publishing a list of stamps I consider BESTBUYS for a country which I have reviewed I detail. Again, these will be featured in my Moneystamps Advisor newsletter.

A Selection of Investment Grade Stamps by Country

The following selections by country represent the earliest investment grade stamps of that country with their 5 and 25year appreciation rates based on catalog values. Market values will generally be much lower, depending on a stamps condition, but this does not affect the appreciation percentages since dealers generally price their offerings as a percentage of such catalog values. You will find their pricing averages around 70% of catalog value for fine/very fine quality stamps. Anything lower is usually due to quality issues.

No catalog prices are shown as they are proprietary to Scott Catalogue. The best single source for catalog prices is the Scott Classic Specialized Catalogue 1840 to 1940 which is published annually. It is a must have resource for anyone serous about investment grade stamps. For market price information the best sources are on-line. For material below $250 go to the eBay.com stamp sales website. For higher priced material go to stampauctionnetwork.com. It has an auction price history service which greatly simplifies bid determination.

  Note that Scott does not revise its prices annually, except for the USA and a few others, and may not do so even every five years. This is the reason we show price appreciation for 5 and 25 years. It is for this reason that the five year appreciation numbers for many countries are zero and why, when they change, the changes are substantial. A good example of this are the Australian states where dramatic increases took place; but two states, Victoria and Western Australia show very little movement. Apparently, their pricing source did not get down to the end of the alphabet by publication time (some would call this a buying opportunity.) It also appears that some countries are not even reviewed every 5 years. This will be reflected in the ratings which will be updated in my *Moneystamps Advisor* newsletter when it becomes clear that market prices are running ahead of the catalog updates.

The star ratings are based on a variety of factors with 5 stars representing the stamps with the highest appreciation history and potential. The 5 star rating represents stamps that have averaged annual returns of 5% or higher over the last 25 years. 4 stars have averaged from 4% to 5% annually over that time period. 3 stars averaged 3% to 4% and 2 star averaged from

2% to 3%. The 1 star category returned from 0.6% to 2% a year. The (*) designates a stamp with no appreciation or actual decline up to 2% a year and (**) represents declines of over 2% a year. Note that the star ratings alone are only sufficient to determine a starting point for selecting stamps with future potential. Factors such as population and economic growth as well as political and financial stability come into play as well. For example, a five star Great Britain stamp is less attractive than a 5 star Indian stamp despite their similar appreciation profiles. British stamps are under pressure due to a weak economy, weak currency and negative demographics. Its stamp prices have not been updated by Scott in at least five years and probably would go down. India, on the other hand, has been updated and needs further updating for the Indian states because demand in India is so strong. Both will do well over a long horizon, but clearly India is the better buy today.

Stamps designated with bracketed stars, i.e. (*) and (**) have had poor performance which may also be due to pricing manipulation or erratic auction results. No ratings or history is supplied when we could not find a price for 25 years ago or when the item may not have previously been known to exist in that condition or has only been given a catalog number more recently. This is also the reason that certain items do not appear at all except in our shorter time period studies.

Note that more comprehensive ratings by country and time periods are available at www.stampfinder.com. It also features a look-up function for individual stamp profiles and ratings. It is important to note that before the publication of this book, moneystamps were being priced by dealers without understanding their added demand and value for investment. This is why you see significant negative growth in the 5 year appreciation for many European countries. **That is bound to change, albeit change comes slowly in this industry. It is an added reason for why acting today is important since readily available supplies of these items will rapidly disappear.**

A Selection of Investment Grade Stamps
by Country - USA

USA Scott #	Issue Year	Value	Rating Mint	5 Year Mint Appreciation %	25 Year Mint Appreciation %	Rating Used	5 Year Used Appreciation %	25 Year Used Appreciation %
1	1847	5c	**	-3.7%	62.5%	(*)	-6.3%	-11.8%
1a	1847	5c	****	0.0%	118.8%	*	-11.1%	28.0%
1b	1847	5c	(*)	0.0%	122.2%	*	-6.3%	7.1%
1c	1847	5c	***	0.0%	150.0%	980	0.0%	90.0%
1d	1847	5c				***	0.0%	90.5%
2	1847	10c	****	0.0%	100.0%	(**)	-5.9%	-20.0%
2b	1847	10c				**	0.0%	50.0%
3	1847	5c	*	0.0%	21.4%			
4	1847	10c	*	5.0%	16.7%			
5	1851	1c	(*)	0.0%	12.5%	*****	-3.6%	285.7%
5A	1851	1c	*****	0.0%	282.4%	*****	-16.7%	200.0%
6	1851	1c	****	0.0%	100.0%	**	-9.1%	53.8%
6b	1851	1c	*	0.0%	40.0%	*****	0.0%	132.1%
7	1851	1c	***	-4.8%	81.8%	*	-7.4%	25.0%
8	1851	1c	*****	0.0%	284.6%	(*)	-20.0%	20.0%
8A	1851	1c	*****	0.0%	140.0%	*	-11.1%	33.3%
9	1852	1c	***	-3.3%	93.3%	(*)	-15.8%	-5.9%
10	1851	3c	*****	0.0%	247.8%	*****	-5.0%	375.0%
11	1851	3c	****	0.0%	111.5%	(*)	0.0%	0.0%
11Ac	1851	3c				(*)	0.0%	0.0%
11Ad	1851	3c				(*)	0.0%	0.0%
11Ae	1851	3c				*****	0.0%	500.0%
12	1851	5c	*****	0.0%	252.9%	(**)	0.0%	-20.0%
13	1855	10c	****	0.0%	111.1%	*	-8.1%	47.8%
14	1855	10c	*****	0.0%	150.0%	(**)	-6.3%	-21.1%
15	1855	10c	*****	0.0%	150.0%	(**)	-6.3%	-21.1%
16	1855	10c	*****	7.1%	200.0%	*	3.0%	36.0%

A Selection of Investment Grade Stamps
by Country - USA

USA Scott #	Issue Year	Value	Rating Mint	5 Year Mint Appreciation %	25 Year Mint Appreciation %	Rating Used	5 Year Used Appreciation %	25 Year Used Appreciation %
17	1851	12c	*****	0.0%	150.0%	(*)	0.0%	0.0%
17a	1851	12c				(**)	-65.0%	0.0%
17b	1851	12c				(*)	0.0%	0.0%
17c	1855	12c				*****	0.0%	700.0%
18	1857	1c	*****	0.0%	180.0%	**	0.0%	69.2%
19	1857	1c	*****	0.0%	269.6%	*****	0.0%	227.3%
19b	1857	1c	*****	0.0%	183.3%	*****	10.0%	175.0%
20	1857	1c	****	0.0%	100.0%	**	-9.1%	66.7%
21	1857	1c	*****	0.0%	250.0%	*	-2.8%	40.0%
22	1857	1c	*****	0.0%	220.0%	***	0.0%	88.7%
23	1857	1c	*****	0.0%	263.6%	*****	11.1%	207.7%
24	1857	1c	(**)	0.0%	-20.0%	***	0.0%	77.8%
25	1857	3c	*****	0.0%	266.7%	*****	16.7%	483.3%
26	1857	3c	*	0.0%	44.4%	(*)	11.1%	0.0%
26b	1857	3c	*****	0.0%	250.0%			
26e	1857	3c				*****	500.0%	500.0%
27	1857	5c	*****	0.0%	788.9%	*****	0.0%	146.2%
28	1857	5c	*****	0.0%	4344.4%	*****	0.0%	340.0%
28A	1858	5c	****	0.0%	1358.3%	****	0.0%	100.0%
29	1859	5c	*****	0.0%	547.1%	***	-6.3%	87.5%
30	1861	5c	**	-4.0%	60.0%	*	0.0%	40.0%
30A	1860	5c	*****	0.0%	388.9%	**	-3.3%	65.7%
30Ab	1860	5c				*****	-22.2%	677.7%
31	1857	10c	*****	0.0%	418.5%	*****	0.0%	140.0%
32	1857	10c	*****	0.0%	140.0%	*	0.0%	33.3%
33	1857	10c	*****	0.0%	140.0%	*	0.0%	33.3%
34	1857	10c	*****	0.0%	185.7%	**	0.0%	50.0%

A Selection of Investment Grade Stamps
by Country - USA

USA Scott #	Issue Year	Value	Rating Mint	5 Year Mint Appreciation %	25 Year Mint Appreciation %	Rating Used	5 Year Used Appreciation %	25 Year Used Appreciation %
35	1857	10c	(*)	0.0%	12.5%	*	0.0%	44.4%
36	1857	12c	*****	-2.6%	393.3%	*****	-7.1%	282.4%
36B	1859	10c	****	0.0%	100.0%	*****	0.0%	175.0%
37	1860	24c	*****	-3.3%	141.7%	****	0.0%	100.0%
37a	1860	24c	*	3.6%	20.8%	*	6.7%	33.3%
38	1860	30c	*****	-7.0%	166.7%	*	0.0%	41.7%
39	1860	90c	*****	0.0%	160.9%	****	-9.1%	122.2%
40	1860	1c	*	4.3%	20.0%			
41	1860	3c	**	0.0%	50.0%			
42	1860	5c	*	4.2%	38.9%			
43	1860	10c	*	0.0%	42.9%			
44	1860	12c	**	9.1%	50.0%			
45	1860	24c	**	8.3%	62.5%			
46	1860	30c	**	8.3%	62.5%			
47	1860	90c	*	-3.7%	18.5%			
62B	1861	10c	*	3.1%	37.5%	*****	0.0%	255.6%
63	1861	1c	****	0.0%	114.3%	*****	0.0%	233.3%
63a	1861	1c	*****	0.0%	900.0%	*****	18.8%	280.0%
63b	1861	1c	*****	0.0%	321.1%	*****	6.3%	1445.5%
63e	1861	1c				*****	-30.0%	1400.0%
64	1861	3c	*****	0.0%	211.1%	***	-13.3%	85.7%

A Selection of Investment Grade Stamps
by Country - USA

USA Scott #	Issue Year	Value	Rating Mint	5 Year Mint Appreciation %	25 Year Mint Appreciation %	Rating Used	5 Year Used Appreciation %	25 Year Used Appreciation %
219D	1890	2c	*	0.0%	16.7%			
220a	1890	2c	*****	0.0%	328.6%			
220c	1890	2c	*****	0.0%	420.0%	*****	0.0%	337.5%
221	1890	3c	*	-7.7%	20.0%			
222	1890	4c	***	0.0%	80.0%			
223	1890	5c	*	-7.1%	30.0%			
224	1890	6c	(*)	-7.7%	9.1%	**	0.0%	66.7%
225	1893	8c	*	0.0%	25.0%			
226	1890	10c	***	0.0%	84.2%			
227	1890	15c	*	-11.1%	33.3%			
228	1890	30c	*	-7.7%	33.3%	***	0.0%	75.0%
229	1890	90c	*	0.0%	35.7%	**	0.0%	57.9%
232	1893	3c	(**)	0.0%	-25.0%			
233	1893	4c	(**)	0.0%	-21.4%			
234	1893	5c	(**)	0.0%	-26.7%			
235	1893	6c	(**)	0.0%	-21.4%	*	0.0%	38.9%
235a	1893	6c	(**)	0.0%	-21.4%	*	0.0%	38.9%
236	1893	8c	(*)	0.0%	-12.5%			
237	1893	10c	(*)	0.0%	-13.0%			
238	1893	15c	*	0.0%	18.4%	**	0.0%	65.0%
239	1893	30c	(*)	0.0%	-7.7%	*	0.0%	42.9%
240	1893	50c	*	0.0%	17.6%	**	0.0%	66.7%
241	1893	$1	(**)	0.0%	-18.5%	(*)	-8.3%	4.8%
242	1893	$2	(**)	0.0%	-17.9%	*	-8.3%	22.2%
243	1893	$3	(**)	0.0%	-37.5%	(*)	-3.0%	0.0%
243a	1893	$3	(**)	0.0%	-37.5%			
244	1893	$4	(**)	0.0%	-31.0%	(*)	-4.8%	0.0%
244a	1893	$4	(**)	0.0%	-31.0%			
245	1893	$5	(**)	0.0%	-26.2%	(*)	0.0%	0.0%

A Selection of Investment Grade Stamps
by Country - USA

USA Scott #	Issue Year	Value	Rating Mint	5 Year Mint Appreciation %	25 Year Mint Appreciation %	Rating Used	5 Year Used Appreciation %	25 Year Used Appreciation %
246	1894	1c	***	0.0%	87.5%	*****	0.0%	250.0%
247	1894	1c	**	0.0%	73.3%			
248	1894	2c	*****	0.0%	140.0%			
249	1894	2c	****	0.0%	100.0%			
250b	1894	2c	*	0.0%	33.3%			
251	1894	2c	*****	0.0%	200.0%			
252	1894	2c	***	0.0%	78.6%			
252b	1894	2c	*****	0.0%	270.4%			
252b	1894	2c	*****	0.0%	233.3%			
253	1894	3c	****	0.0%	120.0%			
254	1894	4c	*****	0.0%	216.7%			
255	1894	5c	*****	9.1%	152.6%			
255c	1894	5c	*****	-12.5%	250.0%			
256	1894	6c	***	0.0%	77.8%			
256a	1894	6c	*****	0.0%	252.9%			
257	1894	8c	****	0.0%	100.0%			
258	1894	10c	*****	0.0%	139.1%			
259	1894	15c	*	0.0%	48.6%	*****	0.0%	133.3%
260	1894	50c	****	0.0%	100.0%	*****	0.0%	150.0%
261	1894	$1	****	0.0%	100.0%	*****	0.0%	134.4%
261A	1894	$1	**	0.0%	61.5%	*****	0.0%	135.7%
262	1894	$2	**	0.0%	61.8%	*****	0.0%	212.5%
263	1894	$5	***	-5.6%	88.9%	*****	0.0%	266.7%
273	1895	10c	****	0.0%	111.1%			
274	1895	15c	**	0.0%	68.0%			
275	1895	50c	*	0.0%	48.6%	*****	0.0%	185.7%
275a	1895	50c	***	0.0%	79.5%			
276	1895	$1	*	0.0%	41.2%	****	0.0%	122.2%
276A	1895	$1	*	0.0%	42.9%	****	0.0%	121.1%

A Selection of Investment Grade Stamps
by Country - USA

USA Scott #	Issue Year	Value	Rating Mint	5 Year Mint Appreciation %	25 Year Mint Appreciation %	Rating Used	5 Year Used Appreciation %	25 Year Used Appreciation %
277	1895	$2	*	0.0%	33.3%	***	0.0%	88.9%
277a	1896	$2	(*)	0.0%	9.1%	***	0.0%	80.9%
278	1895	$5	*	0.0%	33.3%	****	0.0%	108.3%
279Bc	1898	2c	***	0.0%	83.3%	*****	10.0%	780.0%
279Bj	1898	2c	**	1328.6%	53.8%			
280	1898	4c	**	20.0%	50.0%			
280a	1898	4c	**	20.0%	50.0%			
280b	1898	4c	**	20.0%	50.0%			
281	1898	5c	*	0.0%	44.4%			
282	1898	6c	*	0.0%	38.5%			
282C	1898	10c	*	0.0%	40.0%			
282a	1898	6c	****	0.0%	114.3%	*****	33.3%	1112.1%
283	1898	10c	****	0.0%	100.0%	*****	0.0%	500.0%
284	1898	15c	**	0.0%	50.0%	*****	0.0%	188.9%
285	1898	1c	*	0.0%	19.0%	***	55.6%	75.0%
286	1898	2c	*	0.0%	31.6%	*****	0.0%	175.0%
287	1898	4c	(*)	0.0%	0.0%	**	0.0%	71.9%
288	1898	5c	*	0.0%	17.6%	***	0.0%	78.6%
289	1898	8c	(*)	0.0%	7.1%	**	0.0%	66.7%
289a	1898	8c	****	0.0%	103.7%			
290	1898	10c	(*)	0.0%	11.1%	****	0.0%	100.0%
291	1898	50c	**	0.0%	50.0%	*	0.0%	33.3%
292	1898	$1	*	0.0%	33.3%	***	0.0%	81.3%
293	1898	$2	(*)	0.0%	5.6%	**	0.0%	57.1%
296	1901	4c	(*)	0.0%	-3.4%			
296a	1901	4c	*****	0.0%	580.0%			
297	1901	5c	(*)	0.0%	-11.8%			
298	1901	8c	(*)	0.0%	-5.3%	*	0.0%	22.2%
299	1901	10c	(**)	0.0%	-23.3%	**	0.0%	62.5%

A Selection of Investment Grade Stamps
by Country - USA

USA Scott #	Issue Year	Value	Rating Mint	5 Year Mint Appreciation %	25 Year Mint Appreciation %	Rating Used	5 Year Used Appreciation %	25 Year Used Appreciation %
O1	1873	1c	*****	7.1%	233.3%	*****	0.0%	185.7%
O2	1873	2c	*****	14.6%	292.9%	*****	0.0%	471.4%
O3	1873	3c	*****	2.3%	221.4%	*****	0.0%	483.3%
O4	1873	6c	*****	5.8%	266.7%	*****	0.0%	380.0%
O5	1873	10c	*****	0.0%	250.0%	*****	0.0%	233.3%
O6	1873	12c	*****	0.0%	125.0%	*****	0.0%	205.9%
O7	1873	15c	*****	0.0%	183.3%	*****	0.0%	283.3%
O8	1873	24c	*****	0.0%	142.9%	*****	0.0%	316.7%
O9	1873	30c	*****	0.0%	144.4%	*****	0.0%	180.0%
O10	1873	1c	*****	5.9%	157.1%	*****	15.8%	214.3%
O11	1873	2c	*****	4.5%	155.6%	*****	8.3%	160.0%
O12	1873	3c	*****	0.0%	154.5%	*****	7.1%	164.7%
O13	1873	6c	*****	0.0%	125.0%	*****	9.1%	140.0%
O14	1873	10c	*****	0.0%	220.0%	*****	25.0%	400.0%
O15	1873	1c	*****	0.0%	275.0%			
O16	1873	2c	*****	0.0%	300.0%			
O17	1873	3c	*****	0.0%	190.9%			
O18	1873	6c	*****	0.0%	250.0%			
O19	1873	10c	*****	0.0%	268.4%			
O20	1873	12c	*****	0.0%	200.0%			
O21	1873	15c	*****	0.0%	300.0%	*****	0.0%	316.7%
O22	1873	24c	*****	0.0%	380.0%	*****	0.0%	300.0%
O23	1873	30c	*****	0.0%	480.0%	*****	0.0%	233.3%
O24	1873	90c	*****	0.0%	195.5%	*****	0.0%	400.0%
O25	1873	1c	*****	0.0%	316.7%	*****	0.0%	400.0%
O26	1873	2c	*****	0.0%	226.3%	*****	0.0%	450.0%
O27	1873	3c	*****	0.0%	236.8%	*****	0.0%	483.3%
O28	1873	6c	*****	0.0%	244.4%	*****	0.0%	350.0%

A Selection of Investment Grade Stamps
by Country - USA

USA Scott #	Issue Year	Value	Rating Mint	5 Year Mint Appreciation %	25 Year Mint Appreciation %	Rating Used	5 Year Used Appreciation %	25 Year Used Appreciation %
PR1	1865	5c	*****	0.0%	305.4%			
PR1a	1865	5c	*****	8.0%	629.7%			
PR2	1865	10c	*****	0.0%	252.9%			
PR2a	1865	10c	*****	0.0%	252.9%			
PR2b	1865	10c	*****	0.0%	220.0%			
PR3	1865	25c	*****	0.0%	220.0%			
PR3a	1865	25c	*****	0.0%	183.3%			
PR3b	1865	25c	*****	0.0%	260.0%			
PR4	1865	5c	*****	0.0%	1300.0%			
PR4a	1865	5c	*****	0.0%	1300.0%			
PR4b	1865	5c	*****	0.0%	1500.0%			
PR5	1875	5c	*****	0.0%	221.4%			
PR6	1875	10c	*****	0.0%	400.0%			
PR6a	1875	10c	*****	0.0%	142.9%			
PR7	1875	25c	*****	0.0%	275.0%			
PR8	1880	5c	*****	0.0%	420.0%			
PR9	1875	2c	*****	0.0%	2042.9%	*****	0.0%	263.6%
PR10	1875	3c	*****	0.0%	1614.3%	*****	0.0%	210.3%
PR11	1875	4c	*****	0.0%	1900.0%	*****	0.0%	220.0%
PR12	1875	6c	*****	0.0%	1400.0%	*****	0.0%	164.7%
PR13	1875	8c	*****	0.0%	1172.7%	*****	0.0%	188.9%
PR14	1875	9c	*****	0.0%	900.0%	*****	0.0%	150.0%
PR15	1875	10c	*****	0.0%	1263.6%	*****	0.0%	200.0%
PR16	1875	12c	*****	0.0%	1130.8%	*****	0.0%	150.0%
PR17	1875	24c	*****	0.0%	930.3%	*****	0.0%	177.8%
PR18	1875	36c	*****	0.0%	818.9%	*****	0.0%	200.0%
PR19	1875	48c	*****	0.0%	657.6%	*****	0.0%	370.6%
PR20	1875	60c	*****	0.0%	1415.2%	*****	0.0%	155.6%

A Selection of Investment Grade Stamps
by Country - USA

USA Scott #	Issue Year	Value	Rating Mint	5 Year Mint Appreciation %	25 Year Mint Appreciation %	Rating Used	5 Year Used Appreciation %	25 Year Used Appreciation %
R1a	1862	1c				**	0.0%	50.0%
R1b	1862	1c				***	0.0%	83.3%
R1d	1862	1c				*****	133.3%	366.7%
R2a	1862	1c				*****	7.7%	288.9%
R2b	1862	1c				*****	12.5%	309.1%
R3a	1862	2c				****	0.0%	108.3%
R3b	1862	2c				*****	0.0%	175.0%
R3d	1862	2c				*****	4.3%	445.5%
R4a	1862	2c				*****	0.0%	166.7%
R5e	1862	2c				****	0.0%	100.0%
R6b	1862	2c				*	0.0%	20.0%
R6d	1862	2c				**	0.0%	57.1%
R6e	1862	2c				****	0.0%	100.0%
R9b	1862	2c				*****	0.0%	133.3%
R10d	1862	2c				*****	25.0%	400.0%
R11b	1862	2c				*****	0.0%	182.6%
R13a	1862	2c				*****	0.0%	300.0%
R13b	1862	2c				*****	0.0%	250.0%
R13d	1862	2c				*****	42.9%	809.1%
R13e	1862	2c				****	0.0%	100.0%
R15e	1864	2c				*****	33.3%	344.4%
R16b	1862	3c				*****	0.0%	442.9%
R16d	1862	3c				*****	14.3%	566.7%
R17a	1862	3c				*****	0.0%	400.0%
R18b	1862	3c				*****	0.0%	525.0%
R18d	1862	3c				*****	20.0%	650.0%
R18e	1862	3c				*	25.0%	-21.9%
R19a	1862	3c				****	0.0%	122.2%

A Selection of Investment Grade Stamps
by Country - Argentina

Argentina Scott #	Issue Year	Value	Rating Mint	5 Year Mint Appreciation %	25 Year Mint Appreciation %	Rating Used	5 Year Used Appreciation %	25 Year Used Appreciation %
1a	1858	5c				****	-7.1%	195.5%
1b	1858	5c				****	-7.1%	195.5%
2	1858	10c				***	0.0%	89.5%
2a	1858	10c				*****	222.2%	281.6%
3	1858	15c				****	0.0%	100.0%
4	1860	5c	(*)	0.0%	8.3%	**	0.0%	60.0%
4B	1860	15c	*****	0.0%	361.5%			
5	1862	5	*	0.0%	22.5%	(*)	0.0%	0.0%
5a	1862	5c	**	0.0%	71.4%	(*)	0.0%	0.0%
6	1862	10c	*	0.0%	25.0%	*	0.0%	23.1%
6b	1862	10c				**	0.0%	64.7%
7	1862	15c	*	0.0%	27.3%	(*)	0.0%	0.0%
7Cd	1863	5c	****	0.0%	100.0%	*****	0.0%	127.3%
7Co	1863	5c	*	0.0%	25.0%	*****	0.0%	281.0%
7F	1863	10c	*****	0.0%	185.7%	*	0.0%	42.9%
7Fg	1863	10c	*****	0.0%	200.0%	**	0.0%	60.0%
7H	1864	5c	*	0.0%	40.6%	(*)	0.0%	0.0%
7a	1864	15c	*	0.0%	45.5%	*****	0.0%	233.3%
7b	1864	15c	*****	0.0%	233.3%	*****	0.0%	336.4%
7i	1864	15c	*	0.0%	17.6%	(*)	0.0%	7.7%
8	1864	5c	***	0.0%	92.3%	**	0.0%	56.3%
8a	1864	5c	**	0.0%	66.7%	*****	0.0%	127.3%
9	1864	10c	****	0.0%	114.3%	***	0.0%	94.4%
10	1864	15c	***	0.0%	86.2%	****	0.0%	116.7%
11B	1864	5c	*	0.0%	29.0%			
12	1864	10c	****	0.0%	114.3%	*****	0.0%	133.3%
12a	1864	10c				*****	0.0%	166.7%
13	1864	15c	*****	0.0%	221.4%	*****	0.0%	150.0%

A Selection of Investment Grade Stamps
by Country - Argentina

Argentina Scott #	Issue Year	Value	Rating Mint	5 Year Mint Appreciation %	25 Year Mint Appreciation %	Rating Used	5 Year Used Appreciation %	25 Year Used Appreciation %
14	1867	5c	***	0.0%	75.0%	***	0.0%	81.8%
15	1867	5c	***	0.0%	75.0%	(*)	0.0%	14.3%
15A	1867	10c	(**)	0.0%	-29.4%	(**)	0.0%	-24.7%
16	1867	15c	**	0.0%	71.4%	**	0.0%	54.3%
17	1867	5c	*****	0.0%	185.7%			
18	1867	5c	(*)	0.0%	12.5%			
18A	1872	10c	**	0.0%	66.7%			
18Ab	1867	10c				*****	0.0%	376.2%
19	1867	15c	****	0.0%	122.2%			
21	1867	15c	*	0.0%	29.7%			
24	1873	30c	*	0.0%	40.0%	***	0.0%	66.7%
25	1873	60c	**	0.0%	60.0%			
26	1873	90c	(**)	0.0%	-40.0%			
27	1873	10c	*****	0.0%	1200.0%	****	0.0%	103.1%
30	1877	1c/5c	**	0.0%	57.9%	**	0.0%	66.7%
30a	1877	1c/5c	*****	0.0%	185.7%	**	0.0%	50.0%
31	1877	2c/5c	*	0.0%	35.1%	*	0.0%	25.0%
31a	1877	2c/5c	**	0.0%	71.4%	**	0.0%	50.0%
32	1877	8c/10c	*	0.0%	28.0%	*	0.0%	33.3%
32b	1877	8c/10c	*****	0.0%	400.0%	*****	0.0%	135.3%
33	1876	5c	*	0.0%	33.3%	*	0.0%	41.7%
34	1877	8c	*	0.0%	40.0%			
37	1878	24c	***	0.0%	76.5%			
39a	1880	8c	***	0.0%	90.9%			
40	1878	25c	*	0.0%	33.3%			
41a	1882	1.5c/5c	*****	0.0%	300.0%	*	0.0%	614.3%
41b	1882	0.5c/5c	*****	0.0%	185.7%	******	0.0%	257.1%
41c	1882	1.5c/5c	*****	0.0%	214.3%	*****	0.0%	214.3%
41d	1882	1.5c/5c	*****	0.0%	300.0%			

A Selection of Investment Grade Stamps
by Country - Argentina

Argentina Scott #	Issue Year	Value	Rating Mint	5 Year Mint Appreciation %	25 Year Mint Appreciation %	Rating Used	5 Year Used Appreciation %	25 Year Used Appreciation %
41e	1882	0.5c/5c	*****	0.0%	471.4%	*****	0.0%	471.4%
41f	1882	1.5c/5c	*****	0.0%	185.7%			
42a	1882	0.5c/5c	*****	0.0%	316.7%	*****	0.0%	316.7%
43a	1882	1/2c	*****	0.0%	300.0%	*****	0.0%	220.0%
45	1882	12c	**	0.0%	63.6%			
45A	1882	12c	*	0.0%	44.4%			
46	1882	12c	***	0.0%	80.0%			
47a	1884	1.5c/15c	*****	0.0%	140.0%	***	0.0%	80.0%
47b	1884	0.5c/15c	*****	0.0%	133.3%	*****	0.0%	138.1%
48b	1884	1c/15c	*****	0.0%	135.3%	***	0.0%	78.6%
48c	1884	Ic/15c	*****	0.0%	212.5%	*****	0.0%	185.7%
48d	1884	1c/15c	*	0.0%	23.1%			
49a	1884	1.5c/5c	****	0.0%	128.6%	****	0.0%	114.3%
49b	1884	1.5c/5c	*****	0.0%	515.4%			
49c	1884	1.5c/5c	*****	0.0%	354.5%			
50a	1884	0.5c/15c	****	0.0%	122.2%	****	0.0%	100.0%
50b	1884	0.5c/15c	*****	0.0%	300.0%	*****	0.0%	233.3%
51a	1884	4c/5c	*****	0.0%	150.0%	*****	0.0%	166.7%
51b	1884	4c/5c	*****	0.0%	180.0%	*****	0.0%	133.3%
51c	1884	4c/5c	*****	0.0%	294.7%	*****	0.0%	550.0%
53a	1884	1c	*****	0.0%	566.7%			
54	1884	12c	(**)	0.0%	-22.2%			
54a	1884	12c	****	0.0%	100.0%			
54b	1884	12c	*****	0.0%	566.7%			

A Selection of Investment Grade Stamps
by Country - Australia

Australia Scott #	Issue Year	Value	Rating Mint	5 Year Mint Appreciation %	25 Year Mint Appreciation %	Rating Used	5 Year Used Appreciation %	25 Year Used Appreciation %
3	1913	2p	*****	0.0%	337.5%	*****	0.0%	150.0%
4	1913	2 1/2p	*****	0.0%	300.0%	*****	0.0%	291.3%
5	1913	3p	*****	0.0%	409.1%	*****	0.0%	288.9%
6	1913	4p	*****	0.0%	275.0%	*****	0.0%	150.0%
7	1913	5p	*****	-10.0%	285.7%	*****	0.0%	177.8%
8	1913	6p	*****	-10.7%	257.1%	*****	0.0%	215.8%
9	1913	9p	*****	0.0%	357.1%	*****	0.0%	212.5%
10	1913	1sh	*****	0.0%	205.9%	****	-22.4%	125.0%
11	1913	2sh	****	0.0%	100.0%	****	0.0%	115.4%
12	1913	5sh	*****	0.0%	144.4%	***	0.0%	92.6%
13	1913	10sh	*****	0.0%	178.3%	****	0.0%	100.0%
14	1913	1L	*****	-18.8%	160.0%			
15	1913	2L	*****	-29.4%	166.7%	*****	-9.3%	172.0%
17a	1913	1p	*	-15.4%	37.5%			
18	1914	6p	**	-13.0%	53.8%	***	-10.7%	92.3%
19a	1915	0.5p	*****	-10.0%	1185.7%	*****	8.7%	792.9%
21a	1914	1p	*****	66.7%	400.0%			
21b	1918	1p	*	-9.1%	33.3%			
21c	1918	1p	*	-5.9%	45.5%	***	0.0%	75.0%
30	1924	3p	***	-10.8%	123.1%	*****	0.0%	287.5%
31	1915	4p	*****	-11.1%	185.7%			
33	1922	4p	***	-11.1%	87.5%			
34	1924	4p	****	-7.1%	103.1%			
35	1924	4 1/2p	**	-9.1%	56.3%			
37	1920	1sh/4p	**	-28.6%	73.9%	**	-14.3%	66.7%
38	1915	2p	*****	-43.8%	157.1%			
39	1915	2.5p	*****	-42.9%	128.6%	*****	-13.3%	132.1%

A Selection of Investment Grade Stamps
by Country - New South Wales

New South Wales Scott #	Issue Year	Value	Rating Mint	5 Year Mint Appreciation %	25 Year Mint Appreciation %	Rating Used	5 Year Used Appreciation %	25 Year Used Appreciation %
1	1850	1p	*****	15.8%	131.6%	(**)	-51.7%	0.0%
1b	1850	1p	*****	15.8%	131.6%	(*)	-37.9%	0.0%
2c	1850	1p	*****	28.6%	260.0%	*****	13.3%	261.7%
2f	1850	1p	*****	28.6%	237.5%	*****	0.0%	293.6%
2g	1850	1p	*****	28.6%	237.5%	*****	0.0%	293.6%
2h	1850	1p	*****	28.6%	237.5%	*****	0.0%	293.6%
3	1850	2p	****	50.0%	575.0%	***	-25.0%	104.5%
3a	1850	2p	*****	44.0%	300.0%	*****	13.6%	127.3%
4	1850	2p	*****	46.2%	245.5%	**	0.0%	60.0%
5	1850	2p	*****	61.1%	530.4%	(*)	9.1%	2.9%
5F	1850	2p	*****	58.3%	427.8%	**	0.0%	50.0%
5Fg	1850	2p				**	0.0%	72.7%
5Fi	1850	2p				***	-56.7%	136.4%
5a	1850	2p				(*)	9.1%	2.9%
5b	1850	2p				(*)	9.1%	2.9%
5e	1850	2p	*****	53.8%	455.6%	*	0.0%	30.0%
5h	1850	2p	*****	47.1%	212.5%	**	0.0%	66.7%
6	1850	2p	*****	41.7%	507.1%	**	0.0%	71.4%
6a	1850	2p				****	0.0%	116.7%
6b	1850	2p				**	-15.0%	70.0%
6c	1850	2p				***	0.0%	90.0%
7	1851	2p	*****	45.5%	384.8%	**	0.0%	66.7%
7a	1851	2p	*****	28.6%	318.6%	***	0.0%	83.3%
7b	1851	2p	*****	39.1%	384.8%	**	-9.1%	66.7%
8	1851	2p	*****	45.5%	384.8%	****	0.0%	100.0%
8a	1851	2p	*****	11.8%	192.3%	*	-11.8%	36.4%
8b	1851	2p				****	0.0%	122.2%

A Selection of Investment Grade Stamps
by Country - Queensland

Queensland Scott #	Issue Year	Value	Rating Mint	5 Year Mint Appreciation %	25 Year Mint Appreciation %	Rating Used	5 Year Used Appreciation %	25 Year Used Appreciation %
1	1860	1p	****	46.7%	120.0%	*****	0.0%	180.0%
2	1860	2p	*****	35.4%	160.0%			
3	1860	6p	*****	20.6%	141.2%	*****	0.0%	281.8%
4	1860	1p	**	0.0%	57.1%	*****	0.0%	177.8%
5	1860	2p	*****	38.1%	205.3%	****	0.0%	107.4%
6	1860	6p	*****	38.1%	205.3%	*****	0.0%	214.3%
6A	1860	2p	***	5.4%	85.7%	**	0.0%	68.8%
6Ab	1860	2p				*****	187.5%	1603.7%
6D	1861	3p	*****	40.9%	244.4%	*****	0.0%	144.4%
6E	1860	6p	*****	35.0%	145.5%	****	0.0%	111.1%
6F	1860	1sh	*****	38.1%	205.3%	*****	0.0%	152.6%
6H	1860	1p	***	0.0%	80.0%	*****	0.0%	150.0%
6I	1860	2p	***	0.0%	92.3%	*****	0.0%	180.0%
7	1860	1p	***	0.0%	91.7%	*****	0.0%	130.0%
8	1860	2p	*****	62.2%	233.3%	*****	0.0%	200.0%
9	1861	3p	*****	0.0%	180.0%	*****	0.0%	242.9%
9a	1861	3p	*****	95.2%	412.5%			
10	1860	6p	*****	109.1%	228.6%	*****	0.0%	162.5%
11	1860	1sh	*****	43.8%	187.5%	*****	0.0%	180.0%
12	1862	1p	***	0.0%	76.9%	*****	0.0%	130.0%
13	1863	1p	*****	0.0%	133.3%			
13a	1867	1p	*****	0.0%	255.6%	*****	0.0%	183.3%
13c	1859	1sh				*	25.0%	42.9%
14	1862	2p	*****	0.0%	150.0%			
14a	1862	2p	****	0.0%	122.2%	*****	0.0%	130.8%
14b	1867	2p	**	0.0%	66.7%	***	0.0%	96.4%
14c	1862	2p				*****	37.5%	1471.4%

A Selection of Investment Grade Stamps
by Country - South Australia

South Australia Scott #	Issue Year	Value	Rating Mint	5 Year Mint Appreciation %	25 Year Mint Appreciation %	Rating Used	5 Year Used Appreciation %	25 Year Used Appreciation %
6	1856	2p	****	44.4%	116.7%	**	0.0%	63.6%
7	1856	2p	*	-3.1%	10.7%	*	0.0%	22.2%
7a	1856	2p				*	0.0%	38.5%
8	1857	6p	***	17.3%	76.0%	*	-4.8%	33.3%
9	1857	1sh	*****	50.0%	136.8%	**	0.0%	53.8%
13c	1863	1p				*****	50.0%	114.3%
14	1860	1p	*****	40.0%	211.1%	*****	-4.3%	175.0%
14a	1860	1p	*****	9.5%	130.0%	*	-2.7%	38.5%
15	1860	1p	*****	26.9%	127.6%	*****	-4.3%	175.0%
16	1862	2p	*****	37.5%	450.0%			
16a	1862	2p	*****	29.0%	566.7%	***	19.2%	93.8%
16b	1862	2p				*	27.3%	0.0%
16c	1862	2p				*	-23.3%	15.0%
18	1867	4p	*****	34.6%	268.4%	*****	12.5%	246.2%
19	1863	6p	*****	96.4%	400.0%			
20	1867	6p	*****	75.0%	311.8%			
20a	1867	6p	****	37.5%	120.0%			
20b	1867	6p	*	-4.5%	40.0%	*	-36.1%	15.0%
20c	1867	6p				*****	62.5%	282.4%
21	1869	9p	*****	65.0%	230.0%			
22	1869	10p/9p	*****	42.9%	471.4%	*****	-20.0%	150.0%
23	1867	10p/9p	*****	20.0%	354.5%	**	-26.3%	66.7%
24	1869	10p/9p	***	33.9%	87.5%	*****	24.1%	227.3%
24a	1869	10p/9p				*****	50.0%	172.7%
26a	1864	1sh	*****	29.3%	200.0%			
27	1867	2sh	*****	57.1%	233.3%	***	-28.6%	87.5%
27a	1867	2sh				*****	71.9%	175.0%

A Selection of Investment Grade Stamps
by Country - Tasmania

Tasmania Scott #	Issue Year	Value	Rating Mint	5 Year Mint Appreciation %	25 Year Mint Appreciation %	Rating Used	5 Year Used Appreciation %	25 Year Used Appreciation %
1	1853	1p	*****	53.3%	228.6%	*****	18.5%	220.0%
2	1853	4p	*****	66.7%	190.7%	**	0.0%	57.1%
2a	1853	4p	****	64.3%	155.6%	****	-5.6%	112.5%
4	1855	1p	***	16.7%	75.0%	*	0.0%	21.2%
5	1855	2p	*****	43.8%	219.4%	*	-9.1%	42.9%
5a	1855	2p	*****	43.8%	1050.0%	**	-4.0%	60.0%
6	1855	4p	*****	53.8%	300.0%	****	16.0%	176.2%
7	1856	1p	*****	28.6%	125.0%	***	-6.7%	75.0%
8	1857	2p	*****	26.9%	127.6%	**	-9.1%	53.8%
9	1857	4p	*****	55.9%	253.3%	*****	3.7%	154.5%
10	1856	1p	*****	13.8%	243.8%	**	-13.5%	100.0%
11	1857	1p	*****	108.3%	435.7%	*****	-55.2%	225.0%
11a	1857	1p	*****	15.4%	400.0%	*****	-34.8%	275.0%
11b	1857	1p	**	-3.8%	56.3%	****	-19.0%	102.4%
11c	1857	1p				***	0.0%	81.8%
12	1857	2p	*****	45.5%	207.7%	*****	-17.4%	171.4%
12a	1857	2p	*****	26.7%	280.0%	*****	-21.9%	212.5%
12b	1857	2p				****	-28.9%	125.0%
13	1857	4p	*****	54.5%	226.9%	*****	-29.4%	150.0%
14	1858	6p	*****	100.0%	650.0%	*****	11.8%	375.0%
14a	1858	6p	***	31.4%	91.7%	**	5.6%	52.0%
14b	1858	6p				*****	0.0%	500.0%
15	1858	6p	*****	64.3%	820.0%	*****	11.1%	328.6%
16	1858	1sh	*****	22.2%	153.8%	*****	0.0%	125.0%
17	1864	1p	*****	26.7%	153.3%	*****	18.2%	160.0%
17a	1864	1p				*****	17.6%	177.8%
18	1864	2p				*****	0.0%	354.5%
19	1864	4p				*****	18.8%	163.9%
21	1864	6p				*****	10.5%	133.3%
22	1864	1sh				****	3.8%	116.0%

A Selection of Investment Grade Stamps
by Country - Victoria

Victoria Scott #	Issue Year	Value	Rating Mint	5 Year Mint Appreciation %	25 Year Mint Appreciation %	Rating Used	5 Year Used Appreciation %	25 Year Used Appreciation %
1	1850	1p	*****	6.7%	357.1%	*****	0.0%	275.0%
1a	1850	1p	*****	10.0%	816.7%	*****	0.0%	733.3%
2	1850	1p	*****	0.0%	833.3%	*****	0.0%	669.2%
2a	1850	1p	*****	0.0%	326.8%	*****	0.0%	630.8%
3	1850	3p	*****	8.3%	983.3%	*****	0.0%	1630.8%
3a	1850	3p	*****	7.1%	309.1%	*****	0.0%	300.0%
4	1850	3p	*****	0.0%	380.0%	*****	0.0%	263.6%
5	1850	2p	*****	0.0%	150.0%	*****	0.0%	155.8%
5a	1850	2p	***	0.0%	86.7%	**	0.0%	69.2%
6	1850	2p	*****	0.0%	185.7%	*****	0.0%	233.3%
6a	1850	2p	*****	0.0%	548.6%	*****	0.0%	166.7%
7	1850	2p	*****	0.0%	728.6%	*****	0.0%	233.3%
7a	1850	2p	*****	0.0%	1157.1%	*****	0.0%	614.3%
7b	1850	2p				*****	0.0%	600.0%
8	1850	2p	*****	0.0%	361.5%	*****	0.0%	400.0%
9	1850	1p				*****	0.0%	168.0%
10	1850	3p				***	0.0%	78.6%
10a	1850	3p	**	0.0%	56.3%	**	0.0%	57.9%
12	1850	3p	(*)	0.0%	0.0%	*	0.0%	40.0%
12a	1850	3p	(*)	0.0%	0.0%	*	0.0%	40.0%
14	1852	2p	*****	0.0%	150.0%	*****	0.0%	181.3%
15	1854	2p	****	0.0%	104.5%	*****	0.0%	221.4%
16	1854	2p	**	0.0%	50.0%	*****	0.0%	220.0%
16a	1854	2p				*****	0.0%	167.9%
17	1854	6p	*****	0.0%	150.0%	*****	0.0%	182.6%
17a	1854	6p	****	0.0%	108.3%	*****	0.0%	170.8%
18	1854	1sh	*****	0.0%	358.3%	*****	0.0%	133.3%

A Selection of Investment Grade Stamps
by Country - Western Australia

Western Australia Scott #	Issue Year	Value	Rating Mint	5 Year Mint Appreciation %	25 Year Mint Appreciation %	Rating Used	5 Year Used Appreciation %	25 Year Used Appreciation %
1	1854	1p	****	0.0%	116.0%	**	0.0%	57.1%
2	1857	2p	*****	0.0%	247.8%	*****	0.0%	128.6%
2a	1857	2p	*****	0.0%	226.9%	*****	0.0%	175.0%
2b	1854	2p	*****	0.0%	254.2%	*	0.0%	46.2%
3	1854	4p	**	0.0%	50.0%	****	0.0%	120.0%
3a	1854	4p				**	0.0%	58.3%
3b	1854	4p	*****	0.0%	341.2%	*****	0.0%	184.2%
4	1857	6p	****	0.0%	100.0%	*****	0.0%	125.0%
5	1854	1sh	*	0.0%	37.5%	*****	0.0%	128.6%
5a	1854	1sh	*	0.0%	40.0%	*	0.0%	20.0%
5b	1854	1sh	*****	0.0%	181.3%	*****	0.0%	150.0%
5c	1854	1sh				****	0.0%	122.2%
6	1854	1p	***	0.0%	82.9%	**	0.0%	50.0%
7	1857	2p	*****	0.0%	192.3%	**	0.0%	58.3%
8	1854	4p				(*)	0.0%	12.5%
9	1857	6p	*****	0.0%	257.1%	****	0.0%	122.2%
10	1857	1sh	*****	5.3%	150.0%	*	0.0%	21.2%
14	1860	2p	*	0.0%	40.0%	*	0.0%	48.6%
14a	1860	2p	*	0.0%	47.4%	****	0.0%	116.7%
15	1860	4p	***	0.0%	75.7%	*****	0.0%	150.0%
16	1860	6p	*****	38.1%	222.2%	****	0.0%	118.8%
17	1860	2p	*	0.0%	33.3%	*	0.0%	38.9%
17a	1860	2p	(*)	0.0%	8.3%	*	0.0%	38.9%
18	1860	4p	****	0.0%	100.0%			
19	1860	6p				***	0.0%	87.5%
20	1861	1p	****	0.0%	112.1%	*****	0.0%	166.7%
21	1861	2p	****	0.0%	115.4%	****	0.0%	100.0%

A Selection of Investment Grade Stamps
by Country - Austria

Austria Scott #	Issue Year	Value	Rating Mint	5 Year Mint Appreciation %	25 Year Mint Appreciation %	Rating Used	5 Year Used Appreciation %	25 Year Used Appreciation %
1	1850	1kr	****	0.0%	153.8%	****	0.0%	109.1%
1a	1850	1kr	*	0.0%	37.9%	(*)	0.0%	7.1%
1b	1850	1kr	****	0.0%	123.8%	*****	0.0%	150.0%
1c	1950	1kr	***	0.0%	82.9%	****	0.0%	108.3%
1d	1850	1kr	***	0.0%	81.3%	*****	0.0%	150.0%
2	1850	2kr	*****	0.0%	161.9%	***	0.0%	83.3%
2a	1850	2kr				*****	0.0%	237.0%
2b	50	2kr	*****	0.0%	135.0%	*****	0.0%	140.0%
2c	1850	2kr	*****	0.0%	159.3%	****	0.0%	113.3%
3	1850	3kr	*****	0.0%	200.0%			
3a	1850	3kr	*****	0.0%	166.7%	*****	0.0%	255.6%
3b	1850	3kr				*****	0.0%	153.3%
3c	1850	3kr				*	0.0%	33.3%
3e	1850	3kr	***	0.0%	90.0%			
3ef	1850	3kr	*****	0.0%	165.7%	*****	0.0%	425.0%
4	1850	6KR	*****	0.0%	233.3%			
4a	1850	6KR				****	0.0%	113.0%
4b	1850	6KR	*****	0.0%	200.0%			
5	1850	9KR	*****	0.0%	261.5%			
5a	1850	9KR	***	0.0%	95.7%			
5b	1950	9KR				*	0.0%	25.0%
5c	1850	9KR				*****	0.0%	140.0%
5d	1850	9KR				*	0.0%	23.3%
5e	1850	9KR	****	0.0%	105.0%			
6	1858	2KR	*****	0.0%	206.3%	*****	0.0%	292.9%
6a	1858	2KR	*****	0.0%	233.3%	*	0.0%	23.1%
6b	1858	2KR	*****	0.0%	316.7%	*****	0.0%	125.0%
7	1858	3KR	***	0.0%	85.2%	***	0.0%	75.0%

A Selection of Investment Grade Stamps
by Country - Austria

Austria Scott #	Issue Year	Value	Rating Mint	5 Year Mint Appreciation %	25 Year Mint Appreciation %	Rating Used	5 Year Used Appreciation %	25 Year Used Appreciation %
7a	1858	3KR	*****	0.0%	344.4%	***	0.0%	92.0%
8	1859	3KR	*****	0.0%	260.0%	****	0.0%	124.0%
9	1858	5KR	*****	0.0%	280.0%			
9a	1858	5KR	*****	0.0%	1233.3%			
9b	1858	5KR	*****	0.0%	375.0%	*****	0.0%	160.0%
10	1858	10KR	*****	0.0%	191.7%			
10a	1858	10KR	*****	0.0%	700.0%			
11	1858	15KR	*****	0.0%	220.0%			
11a	1858	15KR	*****	0.0%	336.4%			
12	1860	2KR	****	0.0%	100.0%	*****	0.0%	133.3%
13	1860	3KR	***	0.0%	87.5%	*****	0.0%	150.0%
14	1860	5KR	*****	0.0%	132.0%			
15	1860	10KR	***	0.0%	85.7%			
16	1860	15KR	*****	0.0%	227.6%			
17	1863	2KR	****	0.0%	107.7%	****	0.0%	100.0%
18	1863	3KR	*****	0.0%	133.3%	****	0.0%	100.0%
19	1863	5KR	*****	0.0%	346.4%			
20	1863	10KR	*****	0.0%	247.4%			
21	1863	15KR	*****	0.0%	200.0%			
22	1863	2KR	*****	0.0%	153.3%			
23	1863	3KR	*****	0.0%	153.3%			
24	1863	5kr	***	0.0%	83.3%			
25	1863	10KR	*****	-13.8%	257.1%			
26	1863	15KR	*****	0.0%	200.0%			
27	1867	2KR	*	0.0%	41.2%			
28	1867	3KR	***	0.0%	75.0%			
29	1867	5KR	***	0.0%	84.2%			
29a	1867	5KR	****	0.0%	111.1%			

A Selection of Investment Grade Stamps
by Country - Austria

Austria Scott #	Issue Year	Value	Rating Mint	5 Year Mint Appreciation %	25 Year Mint Appreciation %	Rating Used	5 Year Used Appreciation %	25 Year Used Appreciation %
29b	1867	5KR	****	0.0%	123.5%			
29c	1867	3KR				**	0.0%	50.0%
30	1867	10KR	*****	0.0%	222.2%			
31	1867	15KR	*****	0.0%	205.3%			
32	1867	25kr	*****	0.0%	525.0%			
32b	1867	25KR	*****	0.0%	400.0%	*****	0.0%	209.5%
33	1867	50KR	****	0.0%	100.0%	*****	0.0%	205.9%
33a	1867	50KR	*****	0.0%	488.2%	*****	0.0%	300.0%
33b	1867	50KR	***	0.0%	81.8%	*****	0.0%	242.1%
33c	1867	50KR	****	0.0%	107.1%	****	0.0%	106.1%
34a	1876	2KR	*****	0.0%	150.0%	*****	0.0%	490.9%
34c	1874	2KR	***	0.0%	83.3%	*****	0.0%	276.5%
34d	1874	2KR	*****	0.0%	182.6%	*****	0.0%	380.0%
35	1876	3kr	*****	0.0%	188.9%			
35a	1874	3KR	*****	0.0%	136.8%	*****	0.0%	200.0%
35b	1874	3KR	*****	0.0%	263.6%			
35c	1874	3KR	****	0.0%	117.4%	*****	0.0%	511.1%
35d	1874	3KR	*****	0.0%	136.8%			
36a	1874	5KR	***	0.0%	94.4%			
36c	1874	5kr	**	0.0%	71.4%			
36d	1874	5KR	*****	0.0%	136.4%			
37	1875	10KR	*****	0.0%	220.0%			
37a	1874	10KR	*****	0.0%	144.4%	*****	0.0%	218.2%
37b	1874	10KR	*****	0.0%	373.7%	*****	0.0%	120.0%
37c	1874	10KR	*****	0.0%	133.3%	*****	0.0%	160.0%

A Selection of Investment Grade Stamps
by Country - Belgium

Belgium Scott #	Issue Year	Value	Rating Mint	5 Year Mint Appreciation %	25 Year Mint Appreciation %	Rating Used	5 Year Used Appreciation %	25 Year Used Appreciation %
1	1849	10c	****	0.0%	108.0%	**	0.0%	53.8%
1a	1849	10c	****	0.0%	138.9%	****	0.0%	112.5%
2	1849	20c	**	0.0%	51.4%	(*)	0.0%	9.5%
2a	1949	20C	***	0.0%	94.7%	*	0.0%	28.0%
3	1850	10c	*****	0.0%	150.0%	***	0.0%	81.8%
4	1850	20c	***	0.0%	76.0%	*	0.0%	31.6%
5	1849	40c	****	0.0%	100.0%	*****	0.0%	162.5%
6	1849	10c	*	0.0%	47.1%			
7	1849	20c	***	0.0%	88.2%			
7a	1854	20c	**	0.0%	53.8%	***	0.0%	92.3%
8	1849	40c	*****	0.0%	400.0%	**	0.0%	51.7%
8a	1854	40c	*****	0.0%	284.6%	***	0.0%	92.6%
9	1861	1c	(*)	0.0%	0.0%	(**)	0.0%	-30.6%
10	1858	10c	*	0.0%	35.7%			
11	1858	20c	*	0.0%	42.9%			
12	1858	40c	****	0.0%	120.6%	*****	0.0%	140.0%
13	1863	1c	*	0.0%	19.0%	(**)	0.0%	-42.2%
14	1863	10c	(*)	0.0%	6.7%			
15	1863	20c	(*)	0.0%	0.0%			
16	1863	40c	(*)	0.0%	-14.3%	(**)	0.0%	-37.5%
17	1865	1fr	*****	0.0%	150.0%	(*)	0.0%	-8.3%
18	1866	10c	****	0.0%	117.6%			
19	1866	20c	*****	0.0%	190.0%			
19a	1865	20c	*****	0.0%	360.0%			
20	1865	30c	*****	0.0%	212.5%			
20a	1865	30c	(*)	0.0%	3.7%			
21	1866	40c	*****	0.0%	158.3%			
22	1865	1fr	*****	0.0%	166.7%	(*)	0.0%	-18.8%
23	1866	1c	(*)	0.0%	0.0%	(*)	0.0%	0.0%

A Selection of Investment Grade Stamps
by Country - Belgium

Belgium Scott #	Issue Year	Value	Rating Mint	5 Year Mint Appreciation %	25 Year Mint Appreciation %	Rating Used	5 Year Used Appreciation %	25 Year Used Appreciation %
24	1866	1c	**	0.0%	53.3%			
25	1867	2c	*	0.0%	40.7%	(*)	0.0%	0.0%
25a	1867	2c	*	0.0%	33.3%	(*)	0.0%	-9.1%
26	1866	5c	***	0.0%	77.8%	(*)	0.0%	0.0%
29	1870	2c	*****	0.0%	163.2%			
30	1870	5c	**	0.0%	66.7%			
31	1870	8c	(*)	0.0%	-10.0%	(*)	0.0%	0.0%
32	1870	10c	**	0.0%	57.1%			
33	1870	20c	***	0.0%	78.6%			
34	1870	30c	(*)	0.0%	14.3%			
35	1870	40c	***	0.0%	92.9%			
36	1870	1fr	****	0.0%	100.0%			
36a	1869	1fr	*****	0.0%	132.6%			
37	1875	25c	*****	0.0%	200.0%			
37a	1869	25c	*****	0.0%	236.4%			
38	1870	50c	*	0.0%	37.5%			
38a	1869	50c	(*)	0.0%	0.0%	(*)	0.0%	-9.1%
39	1875	5fr	**	0.0%	70.0%	*****	0.0%	190.0%
39a	1878	5fr	****	0.0%	120.6%	*****	0.0%	480.0%
42	1881	5c	*	0.0%	37.5%			
42a	1881	5c	*	0.0%	37.5%			
43	1881	10c	(*)	0.0%	-8.3%			
44	1881	25c	**	0.0%	72.7%			
45	1883	10c	(*)	0.0%	0.0%			
46	1883	20c	**	0.0%	52.2%			
47	1883	25c	**	-5.3%	60.0%	*	0.0%	27.3%
48	1883	50c	**	0.0%	62.5%	(*)	0.0%	0.0%
51	1884	5c	*****	0.0%	167.9%			

A Selection of Investment Grade Stamps
by Country - Belgium

Belgium Scott #	Issue Year	Value	Rating Mint	5 Year Mint Appreciation %	25 Year Mint Appreciation %	Rating Used	5 Year Used Appreciation %	25 Year Used Appreciation %
52c	1884	10c	*****	0.0%	350.0%			
54	1884	1fr	**	0.0%	50.0%			
56	1886	20c	****	0.0%	110.5%			
59	1886	2fr	(*)	0.0%	-19.4%	(*)	0.0%	16.7%
68a	1893	25c	(*)	0.0%	0.0%			
69a	1893	35C	(*)	0.0%	-17.6%			
70	1893	50c	(*)	0.0%	-8.0%			
71	1897	50c	(*)	0.0%	8.7%			
72	1893	1fr	(*)	0.0%	6.7%			
73	1900	1fr	(*)	0.0%	-4.8%			
74	1893	2fr	(**)	0.0%	-27.3%	(*)	0.0%	-15.2%
75	1900	2fr	(*)	0.0%	6.7%			
86	1905	20c	****	0.0%	116.7%			
88	1905	35c	**	0.0%	52.8%			
89	1905	50c	****	0.0%	100.0%			
90	1905	1fr	***	0.0%	76.0%			
91	1905	2fr	*	0.0%	20.0%			
102	1912	5fr	(*)	0.0%	-11.1%	*	0.0%	4.2%
119	1915	1fr	*****	0.0%	150.0%			
121	1915	5fr	***	0.0%	83.3%	****	0.0%	100.0%

A Selection of Investment Grade Stamps
by Country - Brazil

Brazil Scott #	Issue Year	Value	Rating Mint	5 Year Mint Appreciation %	25 Year Mint Appreciation %	Rating Used	5 Year Used Appreciation %	25 Year Used Appreciation %
1	1843	30r	*****	0.0%	172.7%	*	0.0%	22.2%
1c	1843	30r				*****	0.0%	375.0%
2	1843	60r	**	37.5%	43.5%	*	-8.3%	37.5%
3	1843	90r	*	0.0%	45.5%	*	-7.1%	18.2%
7	1844	10r	***	0.0%	92.3%	(*)	0.0%	11.1%
8	1844	30r	***	-9.4%	75.8%	(*)	0.0%	0.0%
9	1844	60r	***	0.0%	92.3%	(*)	0.0%	11.1%
10	1844	90r	****	0.0%	100.0%	(*)	0.0%	-14.3%
11	1844	180r	*	0.0%	28.6%	*	0.0%	28.6%
12	1844	300r	*	0.0%	23.8%	(*)	0.0%	11.1%
13	1844	600r	*	0.0%	20.0%	(*)	0.0%	10.0%
21	1850	10r	*	0.0%	25.0%	****	-17.6%	133.3%
22	1850	20r	*	0.0%	42.3%	*	0.0%	26.3%
25	1850	90r	*	10.0%	37.5%	*	0.0%	26.1%
26	1850	180r	*	15.0%	43.8%	*	0.0%	23.8%
27	1850	300r	**	0.0%	53.8%	(*)	0.0%	-3.3%
28	1850	600r	*	0.0%	42.9%	*	0.0%	15.8%
38	1854	30r	*	0.0%	23.1%	(*)	8.3%	8.3%
39	1861	280r	*	-8.6%	14.3%	(*)	-8.3%	0.0%
40	1861	430r	(*)	-20.0%	-11.1%	*	-8.6%	28.0%
42	1866	10r	*****	140.0%	400.0%	**	0.0%	57.9%
43	1866	20r	*****	0.0%	193.3%	***	0.0%	92.3%
44	1866	30r	****	0.0%	112.1%	****	0.0%	100.0%
45	1866	30r	***	0.0%	77.8%	**	0.0%	60.9%
46	1866	60r	*****	114.3%	400.0%	**	0.0%	71.4%
47	1866	90r	****	0.0%	141.7%	****	0.0%	112.1%
48	1866	180r	*****	0.0%	208.3%	****	0.0%	112.1%
49	1866	280r	*****	0.0%	128.6%	**	6.3%	70.0%

A Selection of Investment Grade Stamps
by Country - Brazil

Brazil Scott #	Issue Year	Value	Rating Mint	5 Year Mint Appreciation %	25 Year Mint Appreciation %	Rating Used	5 Year Used Appreciation %	25 Year Used Appreciation %
50	1866	300r	***	46.7%	91.3%	**	6.3%	63.5%
51	1866	430r	****	0.0%	107.1%	*	0.0%	30.8%
52	1866	600r	****	0.0%	107.1%	***	0.0%	81.8%
53a	1866	10r	**	0.0%	60.0%	(*)	0.0%	11.1%
54a	1866	20r	**	0.0%	52.4%	*	0.0%	20.0%
54b	1866	20r	**	0.0%	52.0%	**	16.7%	40.0%
56a	1866	50r	***	-10.0%	80.0%	*****	0.0%	140.0%
57	1866	80r	*****	0.0%	131.3%	*	0.0%	41.2%
57a	1866	80r	***	0.0%	81.8%	*	0.0%	40.0%
58	1866	100r	*****	0.0%	133.3%			
59	1866	200r	(*)	0.0%	-14.3%	*****	20.0%	182.4%
60	1866	500r	(*)	0.0%	-13.2%	(*)	-17.6%	-4.8%
61	1877	10r	*****	0.0%	141.7%	*	-17.6%	27.3%
62	1877	20r	****	0.0%	100.0%	*	-14.3%	42.9%
63	1877	50r	****	0.0%	112.5%			
64	1877	80r	****	0.0%	121.1%	**	-20.0%	60.0%
65	1876	100r	*****	0.0%	300.0%			
66	1877	200r	*****	0.0%	185.7%			
67	1876	500r	***	0.0%	80.0%	**	-15.0%	70.0%
70	1878	50r	*****	0.0%	172.7%			
71	1878	80r	*****	0.0%	180.0%			
72	1878	100r	*****	0.0%	180.0%			
73	1878	200r	****	0.0%	118.8%			
74	1878	260r	****	0.0%	100.0%	**	0.0%	61.8%
75	1878	300r	****	0.0%	100.0%	**	0.0%	70.6%
76	1878	700r	**	0.0%	72.7%	*	0.0%	25.0%
77	1878	1000r	**	0.0%	60.7%	*	0.0%	46.2%
78	1878	300r	****	0.0%	100.0%	**	0.0%	66.7%
79	1881	50r	***	7.1%	87.5%	**	9.5%	64.3%

A Selection of Investment Grade Stamps
by Country - Brazil

Brazil Scott #	Issue Year	Value	Rating Mint	5 Year Mint Appreciation %	25 Year Mint Appreciation %	Rating Used	5 Year Used Appreciation %	25 Year Used Appreciation %
80	1881	100r	****	0.0%	118.2%	**	35.7%	72.7%
81	1881	200r	*	0.0%	41.2%	**	0.0%	60.0%
82	1882	10r				*****	0.0%	127.3%
83	1882	100r	*****	17.6%	138.1%			
83b	1882	100r	*****	70.0%	286.4%			
84	1882	200r	***	0.0%	81.8%	**	9.1%	50.0%
85	1882	200r	****	0.0%	111.5%			
85a	1882	200r				*****	0.0%	6685.7%
87	1884	20r	*****	0.0%	536.4%			
87a	1884	20r	*****	0.0%	600.0%			
88	1884	50r	*****	0.0%	150.0%			
90	1884	100r	*****	0.0%	185.7%			
91	1884	100r	***	0.0%	81.8%			
92	1885	100r	*****	12.0%	460.0%			
93	1887	50r	*****	0.0%	150.0%			
94	1887	300r	*****	-8.0%	162.9%	***	0.0%	87.5%
95	1887	500r	*****	0.0%	133.3%	*	0.0%	40.0%
96	1888	100r	*****	0.0%	281.6%			
96a	1888	100r	*****	0.0%	140.0%	****	0.0%	100.0%
97	1888	700r	***	0.0%	88.2%	***	0.0%	76.0%
98	1888	1000r	***	-8.3%	96.4%	***	0.0%	76.0%
101	1890	100r	*****	5.6%	150.0%			
102	1890	100r	**	0.0%	71.4%			
102a	1890	100r	*****	0.0%	163.2%	*	0.0%	31.0%
103b	1890	200r	*	0.0%	31.0%			
104	1890	300r	*****	0.0%	176.9%			
104a	1890	300r	*****	0.0%	157.1%			

A Selection of Investment Grade Stamps
by Country - Canada

Canada Scott #	Issue Year	Value	Rating Mint	5 Year Mint Appreciation %	25 Year Mint Appreciation %	Rating Used	5 Year Used Appreciation %	25 Year Used Appreciation %
1	1851	3P	*****	14.3%	300.0%	*****	0.0%	185.7%
2	1851	6P	*****	0.0%	300.0%	*****	-5.7%	200.0%
3	1851	12P	*****	0.0%	169.2%	*****	-3.6%	170.0%
4	1852	3P	****	0.0%	50.0%	****	0.0%	104.5%
4a	1852	3P	**	0.0%	61.9%	*****	0.0%	127.3%
4b	1852	3P				(*)	0.0%	8.3%
4c	1852	3P	****	12.5%	125.0%	****	4.5%	109.1%
4d	1852	3P	**	0.0%	60.0%	**	0.0%	60.7%
5	1855	6P	*****	0.0%	300.0%	*****	-20.0%	200.0%
5a	1855	6P	*****	0.0%	344.4%	*****	-12.5%	150.0%
5b	1855	6P	*****	0.0%	300.0%	***	-20.0%	84.6%
5c	1852	6p				*	0.0%	16.7%
5d	1855	6P	*****	0.0%	233.3%	*****	0.0%	275.0%
7	1855	10P	*****	9.1%	200.0%	*****	-5.7%	135.7%
7a	1855	10P	****	8.3%	116.7%	*****	0.0%	125.0%
8	1857	1/2P	*****	0.0%	144.4%	*****	0.0%	164.2%
8a	1857	1/2P	*****	0.0%	233.3%	***	0.0%	85.2%
8b	1857	1/2P	****	0.0%	166.7%	****	0.0%	114.3%
9	1857	7.5P	****	0.0%	100.0%	*****	0.0%	288.9%
10	1857	6P	*****	0.0%	195.5%	*****	0.0%	233.3%
10a	1857	6P				*	-16.7%	25.0%
11	1858	1/2 P	*****	21.4%	203.6%	*****	0.0%	347.1%
12	1859	3P	*****	0.0%	600.0%	*****	3.8%	390.9%
13	1859	6P	*****	0.0%	309.1%	*****	0.0%	233.3%
13a	1859	6P	*****	0.0%	309.1%	*****	0.0%	233.3%
14	1859	1C	****	0.0%	123.7%	****	0.0%	300.0%
14a	1859	1C	****	10.0%	120.0%			
15	1859	5C	*****	9.5%	228.6%	*****	0.0%	275.0%

A Selection of Investment Grade Stamps
by Country - Canada

Canada Scott #	Issue Year	Value	Rating Mint	5 Year Mint Appreciation %	25 Year Mint Appreciation %	Rating Used	5 Year Used Appreciation %	25 Year Used Appreciation %
15a	1859	5C	*****	7.1%	150.0%			
15b	1859	5C				(*)	4.2%	13.6%
16	1859	10C	*****	11.1%	316.7%	*****	0.0%	261.1%
16a	1859	10C				*	14.7%	30.0%
17	1859	10C	*****	-30.0%	211.1%	*****	16.7%	438.5%
17a	1859	10C	*****	-20.0%	300.0%	*****	0.0%	392.3%
17b	1859	10C	*****	-30.0%	194.7%	*****	0.0%	330.8%
17c	1859	10C	*****	0.0%	144.4%			
17d	1859	10C				***	25.0%	78.6%
18	1859	12.5C	*****	2.9%	300.0%	*****	25.0%	566.7%
18a	1859	12.5C	*****	4.8%	238.5%	*****	8.0%	390.9%
18b	1859	12.5C	*****	15.0%	130.0%			
19	1859	17C	*****	0.0%	150.0%	*****	5.3%	300.0%
19a	1859	17C	*****	4.0%	126.1%	*****	7.1%	275.0%
19b	1859	17C	***	10.5%	75.0%			
20	1859	2C	***	-18.8%	100.0%	*****	0.0%	140.0%
20a	1859	2C	***	-11.8%	87.5%	*****	0.0%	133.3%
20b	1859	2C	****	0.0%	100.0%			
21	1868	1/2 C	*****	0.0%	340.0%	*****	0.0%	220.0%
21a	1868	1/2 C	*****	0.0%	500.0%	*****	0.0%	260.0%
21b	1868	1/2 C	*	21.6%	36.4%	**	0.0%	57.1%
21c	1868	1/2 C	*****	0.0%	400.0%	*****	0.0%	190.9%
22	1868	1C	*****	-11.1%	255.6%	*****	0.0%	392.3%
22a	1868	1C	***	0.0%	85.7%	*****	0.0%	233.3%
22b	1868	1C	*****	0.0%	216.7%	*****	0.0%	330.8%
23	1869	1C	*****	0.0%	311.8%	*****	28.9%	480.0%
23a	1869	1C	*****	0.0%	455.6%	*****	0.0%	372.7%
24	1868	2C	*****	11.1%	344.4%	*****	0.0%	344.4%
24a	1868	2C	***	0.0%	85.7%	*****	0.0%	183.3%

A Selection of Investment Grade Stamps
by Country - Canada

Canada Scott #	Issue Year	Value	Rating Mint	5 Year Mint Appreciation %	25 Year Mint Appreciation %	Rating Used	5 Year Used Appreciation %	25 Year Used Appreciation %
24b	1868	2C	*****	0.0%	280.0%	*****	0.0%	266.7%
24c	1868	2C				*	0.0%	33.3%
25	1868	3C	*****	0.0%	462.5%	*****	0.0%	300.0%
25a	1868	3C	*****	0.0%	162.5%	*****	0.0%	280.0%
25b	1868	3C	*****	0.0%	455.6%	*****	15.8%	358.3%
26	1875	5C	*****	0.0%	300.0%	*****	0.0%	429.4%
27	1868	6C	*****	0.0%	462.5%	*****	0.0%	366.7%
27a	1868	6C	*****	0.0%	433.3%	*****	-10.7%	354.5%
27b	1868	6C	*****	0.0%	860.0%	*****	0.0%	194.1%
27c	1868	6C	*****	0.0%	281.8%	*****	-8.6%	255.6%
27d	1868	6C				*	0.0%	20.0%
28	1868	12.5C	*****	0.0%	400.0%	*****	0.0%	316.7%
28a	1868	12.5C	*****	-6.7%	366.7%	*****	0.0%	240.0%
28b	1868	12.5C	*****	0.0%	336.4%	*****	0.0%	200.0%
29	1874	15C	*****	-18.2%	200.0%	*****	0.0%	261.1%
29a	1874	15C	*****	0.0%	233.3%	*****	0.0%	431.3%
29b	1874	15C	**	-4.8%	66.7%	*****	-3.8%	194.1%
29c	1874	15C	*****	0.0%	316.7%	*****	0.0%	150.0%
29d	1874	15C	**	-20.0%	71.4%			
29e	1874	15C	***	0.0%	77.8%	*****	0.0%	172.7%
30	1873	15C	*****	-18.2%	200.0%	*****	0.0%	261.1%
30a	1873	15C	*****	29.6%	191.7%	*****	0.0%	431.3%
30b	1873	15C	*****	3.8%	390.9%	*****	0.0%	233.3%
30c	1873	15C	***	0.0%	75.0%	****	0.0%	100.0%
30d	1873	15C	*****	0.0%	284.6%	*****	0.0%	300.0%
31	1868	1C	*****	0.0%	300.0%	*****	-10.0%	350.0%
32	1868	2C				*****	25.0%	316.7%
33	1868	3C	*****	0.0%	163.2%	*****	0.0%	462.5%

A Selection of Investment Grade Stamps
by Country - China

China Scott #	Issue Year	Value	Rating Mint	5 Year Mint Appreciation %	25 Year Mint Appreciation %	Rating Used	5 Year Used Appreciation %	25 Year Used Appreciation %
1	1878	1c	*****	-28.6%	185.7%	*****	0.0%	511.1%
1a	1878	1c	****	-3.1%	106.7%	*****	4.3%	263.6%
2	1878	3c	*****	-18.2%	170.0%	*****	-5.3%	800.0%
2a	1878	3c	***	2.8%	94.7%	*****	0.0%	300.0%
3	1878	5c	*****	-13.9%	287.5%	*****	0.0%	700.0%
4	1882	1c	*****	-22.6%	200.0%	*****	0.0%	300.0%
4a	1882	1c	*****	-5.9%	128.6%	*****	-10.5%	183.3%
5	1882	3c	*****	-18.5%	214.3%	*****	0.0%	525.0%
6	1882	5c	*****	0.0%	150.0%	*****	0.0%	200.0%
7	1883	1c	*****	-12.9%	350.0%	*****	-9.6%	533.3%
7c	1883	1c	****	-13.9%	106.7%			
8	1883	3c	*****	-14.8%	360.0%	*****	-14.8%	1011.1%
8b	1883	3c				*****	0.0%	1433.3%
9	1883	5c	*****	-15.9%	3600.0%	*****	-10.3%	1200.0%
10a	1885	1c	****	0.0%	100.0%			
11	1885	3c	*****	-10.0%	1185.7%	*****	-7.2%	1200.0%
11a	1885	3c				***	0.0%	94.4%
11b	1885	3c				*****	0.0%	140.0%
12	1885	5c	*****	-11.1%	627.3%	*****	-7.2%	881.1%
12a	1885	5c	*****	-3.4%	1066.7%	*****	-5.9%	1042.9%
12b	1885	5c	*****	0.0%	140.0%	****	0.0%	100.0%
12c	1885	5c				*****	0.0%	425.0%
13	1888	1c	****	-15.0%	400.0%	*****	9.1%	400.0%
14	1888	3c	*****	10.0%	1275.0%	*****	11.1%	1900.0%
14b	1888	3c				**	0.0%	57.1%
15	1888	5c	*****	11.1%	1566.6%	*****	7.1%	900.0%
15b	1888	5c				*****	4.2%	1011.0%
15c	1888	5c	*****	0.0%	214.3%	*****	0.0%	214.3%

A Selection of Investment Grade Stamps
by Country - China

China Scott #	Issue Year	Value	Rating Mint	5 Year Mint Appreciation %	25 Year Mint Appreciation %	Rating Used	5 Year Used Appreciation %	25 Year Used Appreciation %
16	1894	1c	*****	-7.7%	1042.8%	*****	5.3%	400.0%
16a	1894	1c	*	0.0%	25.0%	*	0.0%	16.7%
16b	1894	1c	*****	0.0%	872.2%	*****	0.0%	566.7%
16c	1894	1c	****	0.0%	116.7%	****	0.0%	116.7%
16n	1897	1c	*****	79.3%	642.9%			
17	1894	2c	*****	-7.1%	2066.7%	*****	22.2%	1733.0%
17a	1894	2c	*****	0.0%	1263.6%			
17n	1897	2c	*****	8.3%	550.0%			
18a	1894	3c	****	0.0%	133.3%	*****	0.0%	133.3%
18np	1894	3c	**	10.0%	29.4%			
19	1894	4c	*****	-16.7%	566.7%	*****	0.0%	1011.0%
19a	1894	4c	*****	0.0%	677.8%			
19n	1897	4c	*****	5.7%	428.6%			
20	1894	5c	****	-22.2%	600.0%	*****	-20.0%	742.1%
20n	1897	5c	*****	14.3%	700.0%			
21	1894	6c	*****	-21.1%	1150.0%	*****	0.0%	900.0%
21a	1894	6c	*****	0.0%	433.3%			
21b	1894	6c	*****	0.0%	177.8%			
21n	1897	6c	*****	10.0%	340.0%			
22	1894	9c	****	-46.2%	536.4%	*****	0.0%	900.0%
22a	1894	9c	*****	0.0%	275.0%			
22b	1894	9c	*****	0.0%	608.3%			
22c	1894	9c	****	0.0%	112.5%			
22d	1894	9c	***	0.0%	90.0%			
22e	1894	9c	*****	21.2%	344.4%	*****	0.0%	260.0%
22f	1894	9c	***	0.0%	83.3%			
22g	1894	9c	***	0.0%	83.3%			
22h	1894	9c	***	0.0%	83.3%			

A Selection of Investment Grade Stamps
by Country - China

China Scott #	Issue Year	Value	Rating Mint	5 Year Mint Appreciation %	25 Year Mint Appreciation %	Rating Used	5 Year Used Appreciation %	25 Year Used Appreciation %
22i	1894	9c	**	0.0%	50.0%	*	0.0%	23.8%
22n	1897	9c	*****	4.0%	1200.0%			
23	1897	12c	*****	-3.7%	1268.4%	*****	-28.6%	1150.0%
23n	1897	12c	*****	60.0%	1400.0%			
24	1897	24c	*****	-11.1%	742.1%	*****	20.0%	823.1%
24a	1894	24c	*****	0.0%	566.7%			
24n	1897	24c	*****	77.3%	1014.3%			
25	1897	1c/1c	*****	0.0%	213.0%	*****	0.0%	580.0%
25a	1897	1c/1c	***	0.0%	66.7%	**	0.0%	70.0%
26	1897	2c/3c	*****	-7.7%	500.0%	*****	0.0%	500.0%
27	1897	5c/5c	*****	0.0%	185.7%	*****	0.0%	475.0%
28	1897	2c/3c	*****	0.0%	542.8%	*****	7.7%	465.2%
28a	1897	1/2c/3c	*****	28.6%	200.0%	*****	28.6%	200.0%
28b	1897	1/2c/3c	*****	95.0%	509.4%			
28c	1897	1/2c/3c	*****	80.0%	462.5%	****	0.0%	100.0%
28d	1897	1/2c/3c	*****	0.0%	140.0%			
28e	1897	1/2c/3c	*****	80.0%	462.5%			
28f	1897	1/2c/3c	****	0.0%	84.6%	****	0.0%	100.0%
29	1897	1c/1c	*****	63.6%	650.0%	*****	20.0%	400.0%
29a	1897	1c/1c	*****	100.0%	2677.8%	*****	90.5%	455.6%
29b	1897	1c/1c	*	0.0%	36.4%	**	0.0%	66.7%
30	1897	2c/2c	*****	23.1%	566.7%	*****	0.0%	542.9%
30a	1897	2c/2c	*****	50.0%	445.5%			
30b	1897	2c/2c	*****	50.0%	300.0%			
30c	1897	2c/2c	*****	0.0%	180.0%			
31	1897	4c/4c	*****	28.6%	1025.0%	*****	0.0%	685.7%
31a	1897	4c/4c	*****	0.0%	650.0%	*****	0.0%	400.0%

A Selection of Investment Grade Stamps
by Country - Colombia

Colombia Scott #	Issue Year	Value	Rating Mint	5 Year Mint Appreciation %	25 Year Mint Appreciation %	Rating Used	5 Year Used Appreciation %	25 Year Used Appreciation %
1	1859	2 1/2C	**	0.0%	71.4%	**	0.0%	54.8%
1a	1859	2 1/2C	**	0.0%	71.4%	**	0.0%	54.8%
2	1859	5C	*	86.7%	47.4%	*	16.7%	40.0%
2a	1859	5C	**	0.0%	63.6%	**	37.9%	73.9%
3	1859	5C	****	0.0%	114.3%	**	0.0%	50.0%
4	1859	10C	***	-6.7%	75.0%	*	-20.0%	39.1%
4a	1859	10C	***	0.0%	75.0%	*	0.0%	39.1%
6	1859	20C	**	9.1%	50.0%	*	-3.6%	35.0%
6a	1859	20C	**	0.0%	50.0%	*	0.0%	35.0%
6c	1859	20C	**	0.0%	60.0%	*	0.0%	30.0%
7	1859	1P	*	0.0%	45.0%	*	0.0%	41.2%
7a	1859	1P	*****	0.0%	120.0%	***	0.0%	76.5%
8	1859	1P	*	0.0%	40.0%			
9	1860	5c	**	0.0%	62.5%	*	0.0%	40.0%
10	1860	5C	**	0.0%	54.5%	*	0.0%	44.4%
10a	1860	5C	**	0.0%	54.5%	*	0.0%	44.4%
11	1860	10C	***	5.9%	80.0%	*****	63.6%	125.0%
11a	1860	10C	(**)	-28.6%	-9.1%			
12	1860	20c	**	0.0%	68.0%	*	0.0%	40.0%
13	1861	2 1/2C	**	0.0%	65.7%	**	0.0%	60.0%
14	1861	5c	**	0.0%	60.0%	(*)	0.0%	0.0%
14a	1861	5c	**	0.0%	60.0%	(*)	0.0%	0.0%
16	1861	10c	**	0.0%	66.7%	*	0.0%	40.0%
17	1861	20c	*	0.0%	42.9%	*****	0.0%	171.4%
18	1861	1p	**	0.0%	66.7%	*	0.0%	36.4%
19	1862	10c	**	0.0%	66.7%	*	0.0%	47.1%
20	1862	20c	**	25.0%	63.6%	*	20.8%	45.0%
21	1862	50C	**	0.0%	66.7%	**	0.0%	59.1%
22	1862	1p	**	0.0%	50.0%	**	0.0%	59.1%

A Selection of Investment Grade Stamps
by Country - Colombia

Colombia Scott #	Issue Year	Value	Rating Mint	5 Year Mint Appreciation %	25 Year Mint Appreciation %	Rating Used	5 Year Used Appreciation %	25 Year Used Appreciation %
23	1862	1P	**	0.0%	69.2%	*	0.0%	34.6%
24	1863	5C	**	0.0%	66.7%	*	0.0%	44.4%
24a	1863	5C	**	0.0%	57.1%	*	0.0%	38.1%
25	1863	10C	*	0.0%	25.0%	*	0.0%	37.1%
25a	1863	10C	*	0.0%	33.3%	**	0.0%	50.0%
26	1863	20C	**	0.0%	60.7%	*	0.0%	36.4%
26a	1863	20C	**	0.0%	66.7%	*	0.0%	37.5%
26b	1863	20C	*	0.0%	32.1%	*	0.0%	22.2%
28	1863	10C	***	0.0%	75.0%	*	0.0%	30.0%
28a	1863	10C	**	0.0%	72.7%	*	0.0%	34.6%
29	1863	50C	**	0.0%	68.0%	*	0.0%	36.4%
29a	1863	50C	**	0.0%	61.5%	*	0.0%	29.2%
30	1864	5C	*	0.0%	33.3%	*	0.0%	36.4%
30a	1864	5C	*	0.0%	35.7%	*	0.0%	23.1%
31	1864	10C	**	0.0%	57.1%			
31a	1864	10C	**	0.0%	57.1%			
32	1864	20C	**	0.0%	66.7%	*	0.0%	37.5%
33	1864	50C	**	0.0%	70.0%	*	0.0%	37.5%
34	1864	1P	***	14.3%	77.8%	*	-14.3%	20.0%
35a	1865	1C	**	0.0%	71.4%			
37	1865	5C	**	0.0%	72.7%			
37a	1865	5C	**	0.0%	72.7%			
38	1865	10C	**	0.0%	68.8%			
39	1865	20C	**	0.0%	68.8%			
40	1865	50C	**	0.0%	71.4%	*	0.0%	40.0%
41	1865	50C	**	0.0%	71.4%	*	0.0%	40.0%
42	1865	1P	**	0.0%	61.3%			
42a	1865	1P	**	0.0%	61.3%			
42b	1865	1P	***	0.0%	76.5%			

A Selection of Investment Grade Stamps
by Country - Colombia

Colombia Scott #	Issue Year	Value	Rating Mint	5 Year Mint Appreciation %	25 Year Mint Appreciation %	Rating Used	5 Year Used Appreciation %	25 Year Used Appreciation %
45	1866	5C	**	0.0%	70.6%	*	0.0%	37.5%
47	1866	20c	**	0.0%	70.0%			
47a	1866	20C	**	0.0%	68.8%	**	0.0%	61.5%
49	1866	1P	**	0.0%	60.9%	*	0.0%	44.4%
49a	1866	1P	**	0.0%	60.9%	*	0.0%	44.4%
51	1866	5P	**	0.0%	66.7%	*	0.0%	40.0%
52	1866	10P	**	0.0%	55.6%	*	0.0%	42.9%
53	1868	5C	**	0.0%	58.8%	*	0.0%	40.0%
57a	1868	1P	*	0.0%	40.0%	(*)	0.0%	17.6%
57b	1868	1p	**	0.0%	71.4%	*	0.0%	37.5%
59a	1869	2 1/2C	**	0.0%	71.1%	*	0.0%	31.6%
59b	1870	2.5c	**	0.0%	71.4%	*	0.0%	37.1%
64	1870	5P	**	0.0%	66.7%	*	0.0%	42.1%
65	1870	10P	**	0.0%	71.4%	*	0.0%	42.1%
69d	1874	10C	**	0.0%	64.7%	**	0.0%	64.7%
69e	1874	10C	**	0.0%	64.7%	**	0.0%	64.7%
75a	1877	20c	*****	0.0%	376.2%			
77	1877	10P	**	0.0%	71.4%	*	0.0%	35.0%
78	1877	5P	**	0.0%	70.0%	*	0.0%	30.0%
80	1876	5C	**	0.0%	70.0%	*	0.0%	30.0%
81	1876	10c	**	0.0%	72.7%			
82	1876	20C	**	0.0%	66.7%	*	0.0%	35.0%
83	1879	50C	**	0.0%	56.0%	*	0.0%	36.8%
84	1879	1P	**	0.0%	56.3%			
89	1879	25c	*	0.0%	35.4%	*	0.0%	30.0%
114b	1883	5c	*	0.0%	25.0%	(*)	0.0%	14.3%
119a	1883	10c	*	0.0%	33.3%	*	0.0%	30.0%

A Selection of Investment Grade Stamps
by Country - Cuba

Cuba Scott #	Issue Year	Value	Rating Mint	5 Year Mint Appreciation %	25 Year Mint Appreciation %	Rating Used	5 Year Used Appreciation %	25 Year Used Appreciation %
1	1855	1/2r	*****	-20.0%	207.7%			
3	1855	2r p	*****	23.1%	433.3%			
4	1855	2r p	*****	36.4%	809.1%			
5	1855	0.25r/2r	****	25.0%	122.2%	**	42.9%	66.7%
6	1855	0.25r/2r				*****	18.5%	190.9%
7	1855	0.25r/2r	****	37.5%	120.0%	*****	50.0%	233.3%
7a	1855	0.25r/2r				*****	20.0%	361.5%
8	1855	0.25r/2r	*****	50.0%	166.7%	*****	60.0%	242.9%
10	1856	1r p	*****	4.2%	257.1%	*****	66.7%	185.7%
10a	1856	1r	*****	25.0%	337.5%	*****	100.0%	669.2%
11	1856	2r	*****	40.0%	211.1%	*****	150.0%	185.7%
14	1857	2r p	**	35.1%	66.7%			
15	1860	0.25r/2r	**	25.0%	71.4%	**	17.6%	66.7%
15a	1860	0.25r/2r	*****	42.9%	138.1%	**	33.3%	60.0%
16	1862	1/4r p	*	87.5%	42.9%	*****	100.0%	500.0%
17	1864	1/4r p	*	66.7%	42.9%	*****	100.0%	500.0%
20a	1864	1r				*****	140.0%	200.0%
21	1864	2r p	*	20.0%	9.1%	(*)	33.3%	3.2%
22	1866	0.25r	*	6.3%	30.8%	*****	20.0%	433.3%
23	1866	5c	(*)	-13.0%	5.3%	*****	20.0%	166.7%
26	1866	40c	*****	122.2%	354.5%	*****	328.6%	566.7%
27	1867	5c	(*)	-27.3%	14.3%	*****	16.7%	169.2%
28	1867	10c	*****	20.7%	483.3%			
28a	1867	10c	*****	0.0%	511.1%			
29a	1867	20c	*****	0.0%	175.0%	*	7.1%	15.4%
30	1867	40c				*****	100.0%	300.0%
32a	1868	10c				*****	25.0%	150.0%
33a	1868	20c				****	37.5%	120.0%
34	1868	40c	***	61.3%	78.6%			

A Selection of Investment Grade Stamps
by Country - Cuba

Cuba Scott #	Issue Year	Value	Rating Mint	5 Year Mint Appreciation %	25 Year Mint Appreciation %	Rating Used	5 Year Used Appreciation %	25 Year Used Appreciation %
35	1868	5c	*	0.0%	36.4%	*	0.0%	30.0%
35A	1868	10c	*	0.0%	36.4%	*	0.0%	30.0%
36	1868	20c	*	0.0%	36.4%	*	0.0%	30.0%
37	1868	40c	*	0.0%	36.4%	*	0.0%	30.0%
38	1869	5c	(*)	-25.9%	11.1%	*****	60.0%	233.3%
39a	1869	10c				***	0.0%	86.7%
41	1869	40c	(*)	-20.0%	14.3%	*****	50.0%	263.6%
42	1869	5c	(**)	-39.4%	-28.6%	*	-5.9%	23.1%
43	1869	10c	*****	90.5%	90.5%	****	23.1%	100.0%
44	1869	20c	*****	122.2%	135.3%	*	23.1%	45.5%
45	1869	40c	**	37.9%	53.8%	*	23.1%	45.5%
46	1870	5c	*****	-25.0%	125.0%	*****	38.9%	212.5%
47a	1870	10c				*****	25.0%	177.8%
48a	1870	20c				*****	25.0%	233.3%
49	1870	40c	***	20.0%	100.0%	*****	100.0%	300.0%
50a	1871	12c	***	17.6%	81.8%			
51a	1871	25c	*****	25.0%	1900.0%			
52a	1871	50c	***	57.9%	76.5%			
52b	1871	50c				****	25.0%	100.0%
53	1871	1p	**	-20.0%	60.0%	***	66.7%	87.5%
53a	1871	1p	*****	25.0%	194.1%		-100.0%	-100.0%
54	1873	12 1/2c	(*)	14.3%	14.3%	*****	20.0%	140.0%
55a	1873	25c				**	26.3%	60.0%
56a	1873	50c	****	36.4%	100.0%			
56b	1873	50c				*****	122.2%	166.7%
57	1873	1p	****	28.6%	125.0%	***	42.9%	87.5%
57a	1873	lp				*****	172.7%	275.0%
58	1874	12 1/2c	*****	33.3%	130.8%	*****	35.1%	316.7%
59a	1874	25c				*	0.0%	33.3%

A Selection of Investment Grade Stamps
by Country - Cuba

Cuba Scott #	Issue Year	Value	Rating Mint	5 Year Mint Appreciation %	25 Year Mint Appreciation %	Rating Used	5 Year Used Appreciation %	25 Year Used Appreciation %
61a	1874	50c				*****	59.1%	133.3%
62	1874	1p	*****	7.7%	366.7%	*****	566.7%	1233.3%
62a	1874	lp	*****	16.7%	300.0%	*	19.0%	42.9%
63a	1875	12.5c	*****	33.3%	185.7%			
64a	1875	25c	*****	33.3%	185.7%			
64b	1875	25c				*	42.9%	33.3%
65a	1875	50c	*****	33.3%	185.7%			
65b	1875	50c				***	0.0%	77.8%
66b	1875	lp				**	8.0%	58.8%
68a	1876	25c				*	11.1%	33.3%
70	1876	1p	***	0.0%	87.5%	*****	150.0%	614.3%
70a	1876	1p	*	0.0%	45.5%			
71	1877	10c	*	66.7%	23.1%			
72a	1877	12 1/2c	*****	207.7%	400.0%			
73a	1877	25c	*****	207.7%	400.0%			
74a	1877	50c	*****	207.7%	400.0%			
74b	1877	50c				*	37.9%	33.3%
75	1877	1p	*	25.0%	33.3%	***	108.3%	66.7%
76a	1878	5c						
77	1878	10c	***	0.0%	81.8%			
77a	1878	10c	*****	90.5%	166.7%			
79a	1878	25c	*****	185.7%	400.0%			
79b	1878	25c				**	66.7%	66.7%
81a	1878	lp	*****	36.4%	275.0%			
83	1879	10c	**	33.3%	60.0%	*	0.0%	15.4%
85a	1879	25c				*	25.0%	33.3%
85b	1879	25c	****	66.7%	87.5%			
86a	1879	50c				*	25.0%	33.3%
89	1880	10c	****	-37.5%	108.3%			

A Selection of Investment Grade Stamps
by Country - Egypt

Egypt Scott #	Issue Year	Value	Rating Mint	5 Year Mint Appreciation %	25 Year Mint Appreciation %	Rating Used	5 Year Used Appreciation %	25 Year Used Appreciation %
1	1866	5pa	*****	8.7%	127.3%	*****	0.0%	212.5%
1a	1866	5pa	(*)	0.0%	11.1%			
1b	1866	5pa	*	0.0%	45.5%			
1c	1866	5pa	*****	6.5%	135.7%	***	8.7%	78.6%
1d	1866	5pa	*	0.0%	18.2%	(*)	0.0%	12.3%
2	1866	10pa	****	0.0%	114.3%	*****	0.0%	150.0%
2a	1866	10pa	*	0.0%	31.3%			
2b	1866	10pa	*****	16.7%	228.1%			
2c	1866	10pa	***	20.8%	81.3%			
2d	1866	10pa	*	35.4%	44.4%	*	34.6%	40.0%
3	1866	20pa	*****	0.0%	200.0%	**	0.0%	90.5%
3a	1866	20pa	(*)	0.0%	9.1%			
3b	1866	20pa	*	0.0%	25.0%			
3c	1866	20pa	***	12.0%	75.0%	*	0.0%	18.8%
3d	1866	20pa	*	15.0%	43.8%	**	15.4%	50.0%
4	1866	2pi	****	0.0%	108.3%	****	0.0%	110.0%
4a	1866	2pi	***	0.0%	87.5%	*****	0.0%	233.3%
4b	1866	2pi	****	0.0%	122.2%	***	0.0%	88.9%
4c	1866	2pi	****	10.5%	110.0%			
4d	1866	2pi				*****	0.0%	200.0%
4e	1866	2pi	*****	21.2%	150.0%	*****	11.1%	200.0%
5	1866	5pi	***	0.0%	80.6%	*****	0.0%	150.0%
5a	1866	5pi	****	0.0%	112.5%	*****	0.0%	150.0%
5b	1866	5pi	***	0.0%	92.3%			
5d	1866	5pi	*****	-12.0%	214.3%			
5e	1866	5pi	***	0.0%	75.0%	***	0.0%	83.3%
5f	1866	5pi	*****	0.0%	162.5%	*****	0.0%	233.3%

A Selection of Investment Grade Stamps
by Country - Egypt

Egypt Scott #	Issue Year	Value	Rating Mint	5 Year Mint Appreciation %	25 Year Mint Appreciation %	Rating Used	5 Year Used Appreciation %	25 Year Used Appreciation %
6	1866	10pi	*****	0.0%	150.0%	*****	0.0%	160.0%
6a	1866	10pi	*****	0.0%	266.7%	*****	0.0%	221.4%
6b	1866	10pi	***	0.0%	78.6%			
6c	1866	10pi	**	0.0%	57.1%	****	0.0%	120.0%
6d	1866	10pi	*	0.0%	42.9%			
7	1866	1 piaster	*****	0.0%	128.6%			
7a	1866	1pi	***	0.0%	92.3%			
7b	1866	1pi	****	0.0%	122.2%			
7c	1866	1pi	****	0.0%	120.0%	*	0.0%	25.0%
7d	1866	1pi	****	12.5%	100.0%	*****	20.0%	200.0%
8	1867	5pa	*****	0.0%	372.2%			
8a	1867	5pa	*****	0.0%	614.3%			
8b	1867	5pa	*	0.0%	35.7%			
9	1869	10pa	*****	0.0%	154.5%			
9a	1867	10pa	*****	0.0%	375.0%			
9b	1867	10pa				*****	0.0%	183.3%
11	1867	20pa	*****	0.0%	500.0%			
11a	1867	20pa	*****	0.0%	440.0%			
13	1867	1pi	*****	0.0%	746.2%			
13a	1867	1pi	*****	0.0%	275.0%			
13b	1867	1pi	****	0.0%	114.3%			
13d	1867	1pi	****	-76.7%	100.0%			
14	1867	2pi	*****	0.0%	200.0%			
14a	1867	2pi	*****	0.0%	225.0%			
14b	1867	2pi	*	0.0%	42.9%			
14d	1867	2pi	**	-45.0%	57.1%			
15	1867	5pi	****	0.0%	114.3%	*****	0.0%	166.7%
19a	1872	5pa	****	0.0%	120.0%			
20bg	1872	10pa	**	0.0%	60.7%	*****	0.0%	125.0%

A Selection of Investment Grade Stamps
by Country - Egypt

Egypt Scott #	Issue Year	Value	Rating Mint	5 Year Mint Appreciation %	25 Year Mint Appreciation %	Rating Used	5 Year Used Appreciation %	25 Year Used Appreciation %
20c	1874	10pa	*****	0.0%	837.5%			
20ci	1872	10pa	**	0.0%	60.7%	*****	0.0%	125.0%
21	1872	20pa	*****	0.0%	321.9%			
21a	1872	20pa	*****	0.0%	216.7%			
21b	1875	20pa	*****	0.0%	320.0%			
21ch	1872	20pa	****	0.0%	118.8%			
21m	1872	20pa	****	0.0%	100.0%			
21n	1872	20pa	***	0.0%	78.6%	**	0.0%	62.5%
22	1872	1pi	*****	0.0%	222.2%			
22a	1872	1pi	*****	0.0%	171.4%			
22bg	1872	1pi	*****	0.0%	200.0%	*****	0.0%	212.5%
22c	1875	1pi	*****	0.0%	1185.7%			
22ci	1872	1pi	(**)	-55.0%	-25.0%			
22h	1875	1pi				*****	0.0%	400.0%
22m	1872	1pi	*****	0.0%	243.8%			
23	1872	2pi	*****	0.0%	185.7%			
23b	1875	2pi	*****	0.0%	350.0%			
23bi	1872	2pi	**	0.0%	71.4%	*****	0.0%	140.0%
23cg	1872	2pi	*	0.0%	25.0%	*	0.0%	25.0%
23d	1875	2pi	*****	0.0%	540.0%			
24	1872	2½pi	*****	0.0%	216.7%	*****	0.0%	733.3%
24a	1872	2½pi	**	0.0%	60.0%			
24bf	1872	2 1/2pi	*****	0.0%	140.0%	*****	0.0%	200.0%
24di	1872	2 1/2pi	****	0.0%	155.6%	****	0.0%	100.0%
25	1872	5pi	*****	0.0%	132.1%	****	0.0%	112.5%
25a	1872	5pi	*	0.0%	30.0%	**	0.0%	56.3%
25b	1872	5pi	*****	0.0%	188.9%			
25be	1872	5pi	*****	0.0%	2400.0%			
25d	1875	5pi	*****	0.0%	134.4%	*****	0.0%	252.9%

A Selection of Investment Grade Stamps
by Country - France

France Scott #	Issue Year	Value	Rating Mint	5 Year Mint Appreciation %	25 Year Mint Appreciation %	Rating Used	5 Year Used Appreciation %	25 Year Used Appreciation %
1	1850	10c	**	-25.0%	50.0%	(*)	-23.6%	-6.7%
1a	1849	10c	**	-20.7%	58.7%	(*)	-31.5%	-12.7%
1b	1849	10c	*	-14.5%	23.7%	**	41.2%	60.0%
1c	1849	10c	*****	-1.3%	107.9%	***	-10.0%	80.0%
1d	1850	10c	*****	-26.1%	112.5%	****	-28.0%	111.8%
1e	1849	10c	**	-26.1%	66.7%	****	-24.5%	123.5%
1g	1862	10c	*****	-21.0%	148.6%			
2	1849	15c	*****	-6.5%	152.9%	(*)	-11.2%	-8.6%
2a	1850	15c	****	-11.1%	110.5%	(**)	-22.3%	-22.2%
2c	1849	15c				****	-16.1%	173.6%
2d	1862	15c	*****	-20.0%	148.6%			
3	1849	20c	**	-15.0%	70.0%	(*)	-24.5%	-9.3%
3a	1849	20c	(*)	-21.1%	7.1%	*	-9.1%	17.6%
3b	1849	20c	(*)	-21.4%	-4.3%	(**)	-40.0%	-55.0%
3c	1849	20c	*****	-7.5%	131.3%	**	-1.5%	62.5%
3d	1862	20c	*****	-16.7%	134.4%			
4	1849	20c	*****	-15.8%	128.6%			
4a	1849	20c	***	-6.8%	78.3%			
4b	1849	20c	***	-21.4%	96.4%			
4c	1849	20c	*****	-14.3%	172.7%			
4d	1862	20c	****	-24.4%	112.5%			
4e	1849	20c	*****	-12.0%	161.9%			
4f	1849	20c	*****	-15.0%	304.7%			
6	1850	25c	****	-20.0%	107.7%	(*)	-25.0%	9.1%
6a	1849	25c	**	-20.0%	68.8%	(*)	-25.0%	-14.3%
6b	1849	25c	*****	-2.3%	140.4%	(*)	-20.0%	6.7%
6c	1849	25c	*****	-22.5%	158.3%	***	-21.9%	100.0%
6d	1862	25c	*****	-20.0%	150.0%			

A Selection of Investment Grade Stamps
by Country - France

France Scott #	Issue Year	Value	Rating Mint	5 Year Mint Appreciation %	25 Year Mint Appreciation %	Rating Used	5 Year Used Appreciation %	25 Year Used Appreciation %
7	1850	40c	***	-21.3%	84.4%	(*)	-24.2%	-4.0%
7a	1849	40c	***	-17.6%	84.2%	(*)	-9.5%	0.0%
7c	1849	40c	***	-22.5%	93.8%	****	-5.7%	123.2%
7d	1862	40c	*****	-17.9%	130.0%			
7e	1849	40c	**	-4.3%	57.1%			
8	1849	1fr	*****	2.8%	340.5%	*	-11.3%	44.7%
8a	1849	1fr	*****	5.6%	146.8%	*	-12.8%	21.4%
8c	1849	1fr	**	-24.5%	60.0%			
8d	1862	1fr	*****	-18.2%	181.2%			
9	1849	1fr	***	-27.1%	84.2%	(*)	-25.7%	4.0%
9a	1849	1fr	*****	-14.9%	185.7%	**	-1.1%	55.0%
9b	1849	1fr	**	-24.5%	60.0%	(**)	-27.3%	-15.8%
9c	1849	1fr	*****	6.5%	145.0%	**	30.3%	53.6%
9d	1862	1fr	*****	-20.0%	130.8%			
10	1852	10c	***	-23.1%	87.5%	*	-21.7%	38.5%
10a	1852	10c	**	-25.0%	71.4%	*	-19.2%	16.7%
10b	1862	10c	*****	-25.0%	162.5%	*	-19.3%	16.7%
10c	1862	10c	*****	-11.8%	114.3%	(*)	-27.3%	0.0%
11	1862	25c	*	-21.0%	40.0%	(*)	-18.8%	-7.1%
11a	1862	25c	****	-22.2%	112.1%			
11b	1852	25c	****	-21.6%	112.1%			
12a	1853	1c	*	-22.5%	24.0%	*	-28.9%	22.7%
13	1854	5c	*	-21.3%	48.2%	*	-26.5%	25.0%
14a	1853	10c	(*)	-20.0%	-4.0%	(**)	-26.7%	-52.2%
14b	1853	10c	*	-18.2%	38.5%	(*)	-26.0%	0.0%
14c	1860	10c	*	-18.2%	38.5%			
15a	1853	20c	*	-20.0%	25.7%			
15b	1853	20c	*	-18.2%	18.4%			
15c	1853	20c	**	-22.7%	70.0%	(*)	-24.2%	0.0%

A Selection of Investment Grade Stamps
by Country - France

France Scott #	Issue Year	Value	Rating Mint	5 Year Mint Appreciation %	25 Year Mint Appreciation %	Rating Used	5 Year Used Appreciation %	25 Year Used Appreciation %
15d	1860	20c	(*)	-12.3%	9.6%			
16a	1853	20c	**	-15.0%	54.5%	(**)	-20.0%	-37.5%
17	1853	25c	**	-18.0%	51.9%	(**)	-34.0%	-13.2%
17c	1862	25c	*****	0.0%	157.1%			
18	1853	40c	*	-20.0%	48.1%			
18a	1853	40c	****	3.6%	103.6%			
19	1854	80c	*****	-22.2%	166.7%	(*)	-51.5%	14.3%
19a	1853	80c	*****	-15.0%	195.7%	****	-21.4%	100.0%
19b	1854	80c				**	25.0%	42.9%
20	1860	80c	*****	-21.9%	141.9%	*	-10.5%	21.4%
20a	1853	80c	*****	-22.7%	135.7%	***	-56.5%	78.6%
21	1853	1fr	*****	-21.6%	170.9%	*	-23.8%	17.9%
21a	1853	1fr	*****	-20.0%	140.0%	*****	-20.6%	125.0%
21c	1862	1fr	*****	-20.0%	140.0%			
22	1862	1c	****	-12.5%	100.0%	(*)	-25.0%	9.1%
22a	1862	1c	****	-12.5%	100.0%	*	-12.5%	16.7%
23	1862	5c	***	-49.3%	81.0%			
23a	1862	5c	**	-10.0%	73.1%			
24	1871	5c	*****	-7.7%	188.0%	****	10.0%	109.5%
25	1862	10c	****	-15.6%	116.0%			
25a	1862	10c	*****	-12.5%	150.0%			
26	1862	20c	***	-11.1%	81.8%			
26a	1862	20c	***	-20.0%	77.8%	*	-23.1%	42.9%
27	1862	40c	**	-14.3%	71.4%			
28	1862	80c	***	-15.4%	83.3%	(*)	-20.0%	0.0%
28a	1862	80c	***	-13.3%	85.7%	(**)	-39.2%	-22.2%
28c	62	80c	*****	-32.3%	125.8%	****	-6.1%	158.3%
30	1863	2c	*****	-12.5%	162.5%	*	0.0%	31.6%

A Selection of Investment Grade Stamps
by Country - Germany

Germany Scott #	Issue Year	Value	Rating Mint	5 Year Mint Appreciation %	25 Year Mint Appreciation %	Rating Used	5 Year Used Appreciation %	25 Year Used Appreciation %
1	1872	1/4gr	*	-11.1%	42.9%	**	-10.5%	54.5%
2	1872	1/3gr	**	-9.5%	58.3%	*	-10.0%	44.0%
3	1872	1/2gr	*	-9.5%	11.8%	*	-11.1%	45.5%
3a	1872	1/2gr	**	-12.0%	63.0%	**	-9.5%	58.3%
4	1872	1gr	*	-10.8%	45.0%			
5a	1872	2gr				(*)	-10.5%	0.0%
6	1872	16pf	***	-8.3%	94.1%	*	-10.5%	47.8%
6a	1872	5gr				*	-9.1%	17.6%
7	1872	1kr	***	-10.3%	85.7%	*	-9.1%	25.0%
8	1872	24pf	*	-12.5%	40.0%	**	-8.6%	60.0%
8a	1872	2kr	***	-9.2%	81.5%	***	-12.3%	90.0%
9	1872	45pf	*****	-10.5%	325.0%	****	-9.4%	107.1%
10	1872	7kr	****	-9.6%	113.6%	**	-10.5%	54.5%
11	1872	18kr	*	-9.5%	18.8%	*	-10.0%	30.9%
12	1872	10gr	(**)	-9.1%	-33.3%	*	-10.3%	30.0%
13	1872	30gr	(*)	-13.6%	-13.6%	(*)	-9.1%	0.0%
14	1872	1/4gr	**	-3.3%	70.6%	***	-15.4%	91.3%
15	1872	1/3gr	**	-7.1%	62.5%	**	-10.0%	50.0%
15a	1872	1/3gr	*	-7.7%	33.3%	*	-8.3%	46.7%
16	1872	1/2gr	*	-6.7%	27.3%	*****	0.0%	140.0%
17	1872	1gr	*****	-10.0%	170.0%	*****	-8.3%	266.7%
17a	1872	1gr				***	-9.1%	76.5%
17b	1872	1gr				**	0.0%	58.8%
19	1872	2 1/2gr	*	-10.0%	33.3%	***	-10.0%	80.0%
19a	1872	2 1/2gr	(*)	-9.5%	-9.5%	****	-10.0%	116.0%
20	1872	5gr	*	-8.3%	37.5%	**	-8.3%	96.4%
20a	1872	5gr	(*)	0.0%	0.0%	(*)	-9.1%	-3.2%
21	1872	1kr	**	-9.3%	51.1%	**	-7.1%	62.5%
21a	1872	1kr	***	8.3%	85.7%	*****	-9.5%	216.7%

A Selection of Investment Grade Stamps
by Country - Germany

Germany Scott #	Issue Year	Value	Rating Mint	5 Year Mint Appreciation %	25 Year Mint Appreciation %	Rating Used	5 Year Used Appreciation %	25 Year Used Appreciation %
22	1872	2kr	*	-10.0%	28.6%	(*)	-6.3%	-10.0%
24	1872	7kr	*	-7.7%	33.3%	*	-11.1%	20.0%
25	1872	9kr	*****	-11.1%	128.6%	*****	-8.5%	200.0%
25a	1872	9kr	(*)	-10.0%	-3.6%	*	-20.0%	23.1%
26	1872	18kr	*	-7.1%	25.0%	*	-9.5%	18.8%
27	1874	2 1/2gr/2 1/	*	6.7%	45.5%	***	0.0%	77.1%
28	1874	9kr on 9k	**	0.0%	50.0%	*****	-5.6%	150.0%
29	1875	3pf	*	0.0%	27.8%	**	0.0%	50.0%
30	1875	5pf	*	0.0%	21.9%	*****	0.0%	275.0%
31	1875	10pf	*	0.0%	41.7%			
32	1875	20pf	*****	0.0%	157.1%			
33	1875	25pf	**	0.0%	53.8%			
34	1875	50pf	*****	0.0%	214.3%			
35	1877	50pf	(*)	0.0%	-5.0%			
36	1890	2M	*	0.0%	25.0%			
36a	1890	2M	*****	0.0%	484.6%	*****	0.0%	3677.8%
36b	1890	2M	*****	0.0%	316.7%	****	0.0%	118.2%
39a	1880	10pf	(*)	-7.7%	-14.3%			
41a	1883	25pf	*	-12.5%	16.7%			
45a	1900	2pf	(**)	0.0%	-20.0%	**	0.0%	47.4%
46b	1889	3pf	*****	0.0%	361.5%			
46c	1889	3pf	(*)	0.0%	5.0%			
48a	1889	10pf	(*)	0.0%	-10.0%			
49a	1889	20pf	*****	0.0%	542.9%	*****	0.0%	155.6%
50a	1889	25pf	**	0.0%	57.6%			
51	1889	50pf	*	0.0%	25.0%			
51a	1889	50pf	**	0.0%	50.0%			
52a	1900	2pf	*	0.0%	27.0%			

A Selection of Investment Grade Stamps
by Country - Germany

Germany Scott #	Issue Year	Value	Rating Mint	5 Year Mint Appreciation %	25 Year Mint Appreciation %	Rating Used	5 Year Used Appreciation %	25 Year Used Appreciation %
53a	1900	3pf	**	0.0%	60.0%			
55a	1900	10pf	(*)	0.0%	-4.0%			
57a	1900	25pf	*	0.0%	46.2%	*****	-9.7%	160.0%
58a	1899	30pf	*	0.0%	46.2%	**	-11.5%	70.0%
59	1900	40pf	*	0.0%	30.0%			
59a	1899	40P	*	0.0%	46.2%	**	-11.5%	70.0%
60	1900	50pf	*	0.0%	37.5%			
60a	1900	50P	*	0.0%	46.2%	**	-11.5%	70.0%
61	1900	80pf	*	0.0%	36.4%			
61a	1800	80P	*	0.0%	46.2%	**	-11.5%	70.0%
62	1900	1 M	**	-9.1%	66.7%			
62a	1900	1 M	***	-10.7%	92.3%			
63	1900	2 M	**	-9.1%	66.7%			
64	1900	3 M	*	-8.3%	22.2%	**	-10.0%	50.0%
65	1900	5 M	**	-11.1%	71.4%	*****	-6.7%	320.0%
65A	1900	5 M	*	-6.7%	27.3%	*	-10.0%	44.0%
65B	1901	3pf on 5p	*	-7.7%	38.5%	(*)	-6.7%	-12.5%
66a	1921	3P				*	0.0%	30.8%
69	1902	20pf	*	0.0%	15.4%			
70	1902	25pf	(*)	0.0%	-14.3%			
71	1902	30pf	*	0.0%	26.3%			
72	1902	40pf	*	0.0%	38.5%			
73	1902	50pf	(*)	0.0%	7.7%			
74	1902	80pf	****	0.0%	100.0%			
75	1902	1 M	*	0.0%	45.5%			
75a	1902	1M	(*)	0.0%	-2.7%			

A Selection of Investment Grade Stamps
by Country - Baden

Baden Scott #	Issue Year	Value	Rating Mint	5 Year Mint Appreciation %	25 Year Mint Appreciation %	Rating Used	5 Year Used Appreciation %	25 Year Used Appreciation %
1	1852	1K	**	-5.2%	57.1%	****	0.0%	100.0%
1a	1851	1K	*****	0.0%	247.8%	*	0.0%	28.0%
2	1852	3K	**	0.0%	55.6%	*	0.0%	23.1%
3	1852	6K	(*)	0.0%	10.0%	**	0.0%	60.7%
3a	1851	6K	**	0.0%	60.7%	*	0.0%	38.5%
4	1851	9K	**	0.0%	50.0%	***	4.0%	85.7%
4a	1851	9K	**	0.0%	64.7%	*	0.0%	45.5%
6	1853	1K	*	-8.6%	18.5%	**	0.0%	52.8%
7	1853	3K	*	0.0%	28.0%	*****	75.0%	180.0%
8	1858	3K	*****	0.0%	237.5%	**	0.0%	50.0%
9	1853	6K	*	0.0%	31.6%	***	0.0%	96.4%
10	1860	1K	*	-2.8%	45.8%	*	0.0%	25.0%
12a	1860	3K	*	-8.3%	22.2%	*****	-9.4%	559.1%
13	1861	6K	(*)	-5.0%	5.6%	***	-9.4%	90.8%
14	1861	9K	*	0.0%	31.6%	**	0.0%	59.1%
15	1862	1K	*	0.0%	44.4%	**	2.9%	65.1%
16	1862	6K	*	-10.7%	42.0%	*****	224.1%	389.6%
17	1862	9K	(*)	-11.1%	6.7%	*	0.0%	36.8%
17a	1862	9K	*****	-7.1%	242.1%	*****	-9.1%	150.0%
18	1862	3K	****	-10.0%	104.5%	(*)	-3.3%	-3.3%
22a	1865	6K	****	0.0%	109.1%	*	0.0%	20.7%
23a	1863	9K	*****	0.0%	127.3%	*****	0.0%	400.0%
24	1862	18K	**	0.0%	60.0%	*	0.0%	15.0%
25	1862	30K	**	0.0%	54.8%	***	0.0%	80.0%
LJ1	1862	1K				*	0.0%	44.4%
LJ1a	1862	1kr blk; Yel	(*)	0.0%	12.0%	*	0.0%	33.3%
LJ2	1862	3K				*	0.0%	25.0%

A Selection of Investment Grade Stamps
by Country - Bavaria

Bavaria Scott #	Issue Year	Value	Rating Mint	5 Year Mint Appreciation %	25 Year Mint Appreciation %	Rating Used	5 Year Used Appreciation %	25 Year Used Appreciation %
1	1849	1K	****	0.0%	122.2%	**	0.0%	66.7%
1a	1849	1K	**	0.0%	60.0%	*	0.0%	33.3%
1b	1849	1K	*****	0.0%	257.1%			
2	1849	3kr	*	0.0%	41.2%			
2a	1854	3kr	**	0.0%	71.4%			
2b	1857	3kr	**	0.0%	71.4%			
3	1849	6K	*	0.0%	27.3%	***	0.0%	77.8%
4	1849	1K	(*)	0.0%	-5.0%			
5	1850	6kr	*	0.0%	42.9%			
5a	1849	3K				****	0.0%	100.0%
6	1852	9K	*	0.0%	16.7%			
6a	1853	9K	*****	0.0%	214.3%	*****	0.0%	140.0%
7	1858	12K	**	0.0%	57.9%	**	0.0%	55.6%
8	1854	18K	*	0.0%	40.0%	**	0.0%	52.0%
9	1862	1K	**	0.0%	60.0%	**	0.0%	66.7%
10	1862	3K	****	0.0%	122.2%			
10a	1862	3kr	***	0.0%	75.0%			
11	1862	6K	*	0.0%	40.0%			
11a	1862	10K	*	0.0%	37.1%			
11b	1862	3K				**	0.0%	66.7%
12	1862	9K	**	0.0%	57.1%			
13	1862	12K	*	0.0%	26.7%	*	0.0%	32.1%
13a	1862	6K				***	0.0%	77.8%
14	1862	18K	**	0.0%	71.4%	***	0.0%	86.7%
14a	1862	18K	**	0.0%	52.0%	****	0.0%	100.0%
15	1867	1K	(*)	0.0%	8.3%			
15a	1867	1K	**	0.0%	62.2%	*****	0.0%	162.5%
16	1867	3K	**	0.0%	55.6%			

A Selection of Investment Grade Stamps
by Country - Bergdorf, Bremen, Brunswick

Scott #	Issue Year	Value	Rating Mint	5 Year Mint Appreciation %	25 Year Mint Appreciation %	Rating Used	5 Year Used Appreciation %	25 Year Used Appreciation %
Bergdorf								
1	1861	1/2S	(*)	0.0%	4.7%	***	0.0%	93.3%
1a	1867	1/2S	*	0.0%	38.9%	***	0.0%	90.0%
2	1861	1S	(*)	0.0%	4.7%	***	0.0%	97.4%
3	1861	1.5S	(*)	0.0%	-13.0%	*****	0.0%	190.9%
4	1861	3S	(*)	0.0%	-10.7%	****	0.0%	100.0%
5	1861	4S	(*)	0.0%	-10.7%	***	0.0%	80.0%
Bremen								
1	1855	3G	(*)	0.0%	14.3%	*	0.0%	16.0%
2	1856	5G	*	0.0%	20.0%	**	0.0%	71.4%
3	1860	7G	**	0.0%	60.0%	**	0.0%	52.6%
4	1863	5G	*****	0.0%	300.0%	*	0.0%	33.3%
5	1863	2G	*****	0.0%	166.7%	*	0.0%	25.0%
6	1862	5G	*****	0.0%	288.9%	*****	0.0%	150.0%
7	1861	10G	****	0.0%	100.0%	*	0.0%	22.6%
8	1864	5G	*****	0.0%	175.0%	**	0.0%	60.0%
9	1864	3G	****	0.0%	100.0%	***	0.0%	93.3%
10	1866	3G	(*)	0.0%	0.0%	****	0.0%	116.7%
11	1866	2G	*	0.0%	35.7%	**	0.0%	62.5%
12	1866	5G	*	0.0%	25.0%	*****	0.0%	195.5%
Brunswick								
1	1852	1G	*	0.0%	46.7%	*	0.0%	20.0%
2	1852	2G	**	0.0%	61.1%	**	0.0%	66.7%
3	1852	3G	**	0.0%	61.1%	****	0.0%	100.0%
4	1856	1/4G	*****	0.0%	300.0%	**	0.0%	51.5%
5	1856	1/3G	*	0.0%	40.0%	*	0.0%	30.0%
6	1863	1/2G	*****	0.0%	127.3%	*	0.0%	45.5%
7	1853	1G	*****	0.0%	344.4%	**	0.0%	66.7%
7a	1853	1G	*****	0.0%	344.4%	***	0.0%	97.0%

A Selection of Investment Grade Stamps
by Country - Hamburg, Hanover

Scott #	Issue Year	Value	Rating Mint	5 Year Mint Appreciation %	25 Year Mint Appreciation %	Rating Used	5 Year Used Appreciation %	25 Year Used Appreciation %
Hamburg								
1	1859	1/2S	****	0.0%	122.2%	*	0.0%	20.0%
2	1859	1S	**	0.0%	66.7%	**	0.0%	72.7%
3	1859	2S	***	0.0%	81.8%	(*)	0.0%	11.1%
4	1859	3S	****	0.0%	122.2%	*	0.0%	25.0%
5	1859	4S	**	0.0%	60.0%	*	0.0%	20.8%
Hanover								
1	1850	1G	(*)	0.0%	8.3%	*	0.0%	25.0%
2	1850	1g	****	0.0%	300.0%			
2a	1855	1G	*****	0.0%	475.8%	***	0.0%	80.6%
3	1851	1/30T	***	0.0%	82.7%	**	0.0%	51.5%
3a	1855	1/30T	***	0.0%	90.0%	**	0.0%	51.5%
5	1851	1/15T	****	0.0%	113.3%	****	0.0%	110.5%
6	1851	1/10T	*****	0.0%	220.0%	**	0.0%	57.9%
7	1853	3P	***	0.0%	77.8%	**	0.0%	50.0%
8	1855	1/10T	**	0.0%	60.0%	***	0.0%	77.8%
8a	1855	1/10T	*****	0.0%	185.7%	*****	0.0%	150.0%
9	1856	3P	*	0.0%	37.5%	*	0.0%	31.0%
9a	1856	3P	***	0.0%	77.8%	***	0.0%	75.0%
11	1856	1g	****	0.0%	120.0%			
12	1856	1/30T	***	0.0%	92.3%	*	0.0%	41.3%
12a	1856	1/60T				*****	0.0%	285.7%
13	1856	1/15T	***	0.0%	90.0%	*	0.0%	45.0%
14	1856	1/10T	*	0.0%	45.0%	(*)	0.0%	0.0%
16	1859	3P	*****	0.0%	133.3%	*	0.0%	33.3%
16a	1859	3P	**	0.0%	60.0%	*	0.0%	28.6%
17	1863	3P	***	0.0%	77.8%	*	0.0%	18.8%
18	1860	1/2G	****	0.0%	118.2%	***	0.0%	81.8%

A Selection of Investment Grade Stamps
by Country - Lubeck, Mecklenberg, N German Confed

Scott #	Issue Year	Value	Rating Mint	5 Year Mint Appreciation %	25 Year Mint Appreciation %	Rating Used	5 Year Used Appreciation %	25 Year Used Appreciation %
Lubeck								
1	1859	1/2S	*	0.0%	18.8%	**	0.0%	60.0%
2	1859	1S	*	0.0%	18.8%	**	0.0%	60.0%
3	1859	2S	***	0.0%	83.3%	*	0.0%	20.0%
3a	1859	2S	*	0.0%	45.5%	*	0.0%	15.2%
4	1859	2.5S	**	0.0%	66.7%	**	0.0%	60.0%
5	1859	4S	***	0.0%	83.3%	*****	0.0%	140.0%
11	1863	2.5S	*****	0.0%	212.5%	***	0.0%	90.5%
Mecklenberg-Streliz								
1	1864	1/4G	*	0.0%	40.0%	(*)	0.0%	9.1%
2	1864	1/3G	*	0.0%	33.3%	(*)	0.0%	12.5%
3	1864	1S	**	0.0%	65.7%	(*)	0.0%	-14.7%
4	1864	1G	*****	1900.0%	3633.3%	*****	900.0%	955.6%
5	1864	2G	**	0.0%	60.0%	(*)	0.0%	-5.9%
6	1864	3sg	*****	250.0%	300.0%	(*)	25.5%	6.7%
Mecklenberg-Schwerin								
6a	1867	2S	*	0.0%	20.0%	(*)	0.0%	6.7%
7	1867	3S	*	0.0%	28.6%	**	0.0%	50.0%
7a	1865	3S	(*)	0.0%	6.7%	**	0.0%	66.7%
8	1864	5S	(*)	0.0%	6.7%	*	0.0%	45.5%
8a	1864	5S	*	0.0%	20.0%	(*)	0.0%	13.3%
N German Confederation								
1a	1868	1/4G	***	0.0%	90.5%			
2	1868	1/3gr	*****	0.0%	300.0%			
2a	1868	1/3G	***	0.0%	97.9%			
3	1868	1/2gr	****	0.0%	100.0%			
3a	1868	1/2G	****	0.0%	105.9%			

A Selection of Investment Grade Stamps
by Country - Oldenberg, Prussia

Scott #	Issue Year	Value	Rating Mint	5 Year Mint Appreciation %	25 Year Mint Appreciation %	Rating Used	5 Year Used Appreciation %	25 Year Used Appreciation %
Oldenberg								
1	1854	1/30T	***	0.0%	75.0%	***	0.0%	83.3%
2	1852	1/15th	****	0.0%	100.0%	*	0.0%	33.3%
3	1852	1/10T	***	0.0%	77.8%	*	0.0%	35.7%
4	1855	1/3 sgr	***	0.0%	82.1%	**	0.0%	69.2%
5	1859	1/3G	**	0.0%	73.3%	(*)	0.0%	-3.3%
6	1859	1G	**	0.0%	70.6%	*****	0.0%	125.0%
7	1859	2G	***	0.0%	90.9%	*	0.0%	33.3%
8	1859	3G	**	0.0%	61.5%	(*)	0.0%	9.1%
9	1861	1/4G	****	0.0%	100.0%	*	0.0%	17.6%
10	1861	1/3g	**	0.0%	58.3%	*	0.0%	16.7%
10a	1861	1/3G	**	0.0%	72.7%	*	0.0%	34.6%
10b	1861	1/3G	**	0.0%	60.0%	*	0.0%	47.4%
Prussia								
1	1856	4P	**	0.0%	61.8%	**	0.0%	51.0%
2	1850	1/2G	**	0.0%	50.0%	*****	0.0%	128.3%
3	1850	1G	*	0.0%	33.3%	*****	0.0%	133.3%
4	1850	2sg	**	0.0%	63.0%	*****	0.0%	128.6%
5	1850	3G	**	0.0%	57.1%	****	0.0%	100.0%
6	1857	1G	(*)	0.0%	8.3%	***	0.0%	75.0%
7	1857	2G	*	0.0%	21.9%	****	0.0%	109.3%
8	1857	3G	**	0.0%	52.4%	*	0.0%	33.3%
12	1858	2G	*	0.0%	37.5%	**	0.0%	59.1%
13	1858	3G	**	0.0%	58.3%	***	0.0%	77.8%
21	1866	10G	*****	0.0%	171.4%	***	0.0%	75.0%
22	1866	30G	****	0.0%	120.0%	***	0.0%	80.0%
23	1867	1K	*	0.0%	42.9%	*****	0.0%	221.4%
24	1867	2K	*	0.0%	18.4%	*****	0.0%	216.7%

A Selection of Investment Grade Stamps
by Country - Saxony, Schleswig-Holstein

Scott #	Issue Year	Value	Rating Mint	5 Year Mint Appreciation %	25 Year Mint Appreciation %	Rating Used	5 Year Used Appreciation %	25 Year Used Appreciation %
Saxony								
1	1850	3P	*	0.0%	45.5%	*	0.0%	30.0%
1a	1850	3P	*	0.0%	20.0%	*	0.0%	36.0%
2	1851	3P	***	0.0%	78.6%	*****	0.0%	150.0%
2a	1851	3P	****	0.0%	118.8%	****	0.0%	100.0%
5	1851	1G	*****	0.0%	137.5%			
6	1851	2G	*	0.0%	42.9%	***	0.0%	75.0%
7	1852	2G	*	0.0%	20.8%	(*)	0.0%	3.8%
11a	1855	2G	*****	0.0%	245.2%	*****	0.0%	691.7%
13	1856	5G	**	0.0%	50.0%	*****	0.0%	170.8%
13a	1860	5G	***	0.0%	97.0%	*****	0.0%	195.5%
13b	1857	5G	(*)	0.0%	-3.3%	(*)	0.0%	-12.5%
14	1856	10G	(*)	0.0%	-10.0%	(*)	0.0%	12.5%
20a	1867	5G	***	0.0%	77.8%	*****	0.0%	718.2%
Schleswig- Holstein								
1	1850	1S	*	0.0%	30.0%	**	0.0%	60.0%
2	1850	2S	**	0.0%	60.0%	*	0.0%	37.1%
2a	1850	2S	**	0.0%	61.1%			
5	1865	1.33S	(*)	0.0%	12.5%	*	0.0%	25.0%
6	1865	2S	****	0.0%	100.0%	*	0.0%	45.5%
7	1865	4S	*	0.0%	30.0%	*	0.0%	30.0%
9	1864	4S	**	0.0%	58.3%	*	0.0%	38.5%
10	1865	1/2S	*	0.0%	30.0%	(*)	0.0%	10.0%
11	1865	1.25S	***	0.0%	77.4%	*****	0.0%	150.0%
12	1865	1.33S	(*)	0.0%	10.0%	*	0.0%	20.0%
13	1865	2S	**	0.0%	71.9%	***	0.0%	87.5%
14	1865	4S	*	0.0%	30.0%	*	0.0%	45.5%
15	1864	1.25S	*	0.0%	16.7%	**	0.0%	66.7%

A Selection of Investment Grade Stamps
by Country - Thurin & Taxis, Wurttemberg

Scott #	Issue Year	Value	Rating Mint	5 Year Mint Appreciation %	25 Year Mint Appreciation %	Rating Used	5 Year Used Appreciation %	25 Year Used Appreciation %
Thurin & Taxis								
1	1854	1/4G	****	0.0%	112.0%	(*)	0.0%	9.1%
2	1858	1/3G	*****	0.0%	135.8%	(*)	0.0%	11.1%
3	1852	1/2G	*****	0.0%	262.5%	**	0.0%	73.9%
4	1852	1G	*****	0.0%	307.7%	*****	0.0%	154.5%
5	1853	1G	****	0.0%	100.0%	***	0.0%	87.5%
6	1852	2G	*****	0.0%	183.3%	*****	0.0%	132.1%
7	1852	3G	*****	0.0%	300.0%	*****	0.0%	150.0%
8	1860	1/4sgr	*****	0.0%	125.0%	***	0.0%	92.9%
9	1860	1/2G	*****	0.0%	140.0%	**	0.0%	50.8%
10	1860	1G	*****	0.0%	140.0%	***	0.0%	95.7%
Wurttemberg								
1	1851	1K	*****	0.0%	324.5%	****	0.0%	120.9%
1a	1851	1K	*****	0.0%	288.9%	***	0.0%	81.8%
2	1851	3K	***	0.0%	83.3%	*****	0.0%	141.7%
2a	1851	3K	*****	0.0%	140.0%	****	0.0%	100.0%
4	1851	6K	*****	0.0%	141.7%	***	0.0%	80.6%
4a	1851	6K	****	0.0%	100.0%	**	0.0%	51.5%
5	1851	9K	*	0.0%	28.0%	****	-60.5%	108.3%
6	1852	18K	*****	0.0%	191.7%	*	0.0%	45.0%
7	1857	1K	*****	0.0%	344.4%	*	0.0%	33.3%
7a	1857	1K	*****	0.0%	158.8%	(*)	0.0%	0.0%
9	1857	3K	****	0.0%	100.0%	*****	0.0%	133.3%
10	1857	6K	*****	0.0%	166.7%	*****	0.0%	132.1%
11	1857	9K	*****	0.0%	266.7%	*****	0.0%	133.3%
12	1857	18K	*****	0.0%	346.7%	*****	0.0%	134.8%
13	1859	1K	*****	0.0%	160.0%	****	0.0%	100.0%

A Selection of Investment Grade Stamps
by Country - Great Britain

Great Britain Scott #	Issue Year	Value	Rating Mint	5 Year Mint Appreciation %	25 Year Mint Appreciation %	Rating Used	5 Year Used Appreciation %	25 Year Used Appreciation %
1	1940	1p	*****	0.0%	478.9%	*****	0.0%	190.9%
2	1940	2p	*****	0.0%	508.7%	*****	0.0%	211.1%
2a	1940	2p	*****	0.0%	500.0%	*****	0.0%	157.1%
3	1941	1p	*****	0.0%	681.3%	*****	0.0%	350.0%
3a	1841	1p				*****	0.0%	214.3%
3b	1841	1p				*****	0.0%	450.0%
3c	1941	1p	*****	0.0%	550.0%			
3d	1941	1p				*****	0.0%	354.5%
4	1941	2p	*****	0.0%	400.0%	***	0.0%	81.8%
4a	1941	2p	*****	0.0%	471.4%	**	0.0%	66.7%
5	1847	1sh	*****	0.0%	627.3%	*****	0.0%	350.0%
5a	1847	1sh	*****	0.0%	627.3%	*****	0.0%	362.5%
6	1848	10p	*****	0.0%	411.1%	*****	0.0%	275.0%
7	1854	6p	*****	0.0%	800.0%	*****	0.0%	471.4%
7a	1854	6p	*****	0.0%	800.0%	*****	0.0%	471.4%
7b	1854	6p	*****	0.0%	1200.0%	*****	0.0%	2328.6%
8	1854	1p	*****	0.0%	242.1%	*****	0.0%	2300.0%
8a	1969	1p	*****	0.0%	240.9%	*****	0.0%	1025.0%
9	1854	1p	*****	0.0%	286.4%	*****	0.0%	380.0%
10	1854	2p	*****	0.0%	344.4%	*****	0.0%	260.0%
10a	1854	2p	*****	0.0%	200.0%	*****	0.0%	150.0%
11	1854	1p	****	0.0%	108.3%	*****	0.0%	357.1%
12	1854	1p	*****	0.0%	242.9%	*****	0.0%	237.5%
12a	1854	1p	****	0.0%	300.0%	****	0.0%	100.0%
13	1854	2p	*****	0.0%	506.1%	*	0.0%	40.0%
14	1855	1p	*****	0.0%	471.4%	*****	0.0%	266.7%
15	1855	2p	*****	0.0%	700.0%	*****	0.0%	200.0%

A Selection of Investment Grade Stamps
by Country - Great Britain

Great Britain Scott #	Issue Year	Value	Rating Mint	5 Year Mint Appreciation %	25 Year Mint Appreciation %	Rating Used	5 Year Used Appreciation %	25 Year Used Appreciation %
15a	1855	2p				*****	0.0%	528.6%
16	1855	1p	*****	0.0%	150.0%	*****	0.0%	2700.0%
16a	1855	1p	*****	0.0%	225.0%	*****	0.0%	316.7%
16b	1855	1p	*****	0.0%	195.5%	*****	0.0%	525.0%
16c	1855	1p	*****	0.0%	540.0%	*****	0.0%	460.0%
17	1855	2p	*****	0.0%	244.8%	*****	0.0%	314.3%
18	1856	1p	*****	0.0%	464.7%	*****	0.0%	302.8%
19	1856	2p	*****	0.0%	354.5%	*****	0.0%	275.0%
20a	1856	1p	*****	0.0%	1025.0%	*****	0.0%	775.0%
20b	1856	1p	*****	0.0%	1042.9%	*****	0.0%	2400.0%
21	1856	2p	*****	0.0%	300.0%	*****	0.0%	154.5%
22	1855	4p	*****	0.0%	386.1%	*****	0.0%	300.0%
23	1855	4p				*****	0.0%	360.0%
24	1856	4p	*****	0.0%	309.1%	*****	0.0%	227.3%
25	1856	4p	*****	0.0%	528.6%	*****	0.0%	166.7%
26	1857	4p	*****	0.0%	250.0%	*****	0.0%	525.0%
27	1856	6p	*****	0.0%	211.1%	*****	0.0%	185.7%
27a	1856	6p	*****	0.0%	270.0%	*****	0.0%	180.0%
28	1856	1sh	*****	0.0%	400.0%	*****	0.0%	300.0%
28a	1856	1sh	*****	0.0%	421.7%	*****	0.0%	275.0%
29	1858	2p	*****	0.0%	218.2%	*****	0.0%	455.6%
29a	1858	2p	*****	0.0%	218.2%			
29b	1858	2p				*****	0.0%	257.1%
30	1858	2p	*****	0.0%	250.0%	*****	0.0%	1081.8%
30a	1858	2p	*****	0.0%	813.0%			
31	1860	1.5p	*****	0.0%	400.0%			

A Selection of Investment Grade Stamps
by Country - Great Britain

Great Britain Scott #	Issue Year	Value	Rating Mint	5 Year Mint Appreciation %	25 Year Mint Appreciation %	Rating Used	5 Year Used Appreciation %	25 Year Used Appreciation %
32	1860	1.5p	*****	0.0%	400.0%	*****	0.0%	642.9%
32a	1860	1.5p	*****	0.0%	300.0%	*****	0.0%	271.4%
33	1864	1p	*****	0.0%	354.5%			
34	1862	4p	*****	0.0%	280.0%	*****	0.0%	400.0%
34a	1862	4p	*****	0.0%	342.1%	*****	0.0%	516.7%
34b	1862	4p	*****	0.0%	152.9%			
37	1862	3p	*****	0.0%	426.3%	*****	0.0%	300.0%
37a	1862	3p	*****	0.0%	400.0%	*****	0.0%	320.0%
37b	1862	3p				*****	0.0%	433.3%
39	1862	6p	*****	0.0%	400.0%	*****	0.0%	600.0%
39a	1862	6p				*****	0.0%	3011.1%
39b	1862	6p				*****	0.0%	525.0%
40	1862	9p	*****	0.0%	500.0%	*****	0.0%	400.0%
40e	1862	9p	*****	0.0%	150.0%	*****	0.0%	409.1%
42	1862	1sh	*****	0.0%	342.9%	*****	0.0%	420.0%
42a	1862	1sh	*****	0.0%	533.3%	*****	0.0%	500.0%
43	1865	4p	*****	0.0%	242.9%	*****	0.0%	420.8%
43a	1865	4p	*****	0.0%	214.3%	*****	0.0%	650.0%
44	1865	3p	*****	0.0%	526.7%	*****	0.0%	855.6%
44a	1865	3p	*****	0.0%	400.0%	*****	0.0%	354.5%
46	1865	9p	*****	0.0%	400.0%	*****	0.0%	342.3%
46a	1865	9p				*****	0.0%	429.4%
47	1865	10p				*****	0.0%	155.8%
48	1865	1sh	*****	0.0%	316.7%	*****	0.0%	500.0%
48b	1865	1sh				*****	0.0%	275.0%
48c	1865	1sh				*****	0.0%	164.0%
49	1867	3p	*****	0.0%	162.5%	*****	0.0%	525.0%
49a	1867	3p	*****	0.0%	266.7%	*****	0.0%	825.0%
50	1867	6p	*****	0.0%	289.5%	*****	0.0%	362.5%

A Selection of Investment Grade Stamps
by Country - Great Britain

Great Britain Scott #	Issue Year	Value	Rating Mint	5 Year Mint Appreciation %	25 Year Mint Appreciation %	Rating Used	5 Year Used Appreciation %	25 Year Used Appreciation %
50a	1867	6p	*****	0.0%	268.4%	*****	0.0%	400.0%
51	1867	6p	****	0.0%	116.7%	*****	0.0%	500.0%
51a	1867	6p	*****	0.0%	125.0%	*****	0.0%	516.7%
51b	1867	6p	*****	0.0%	1718.2%	*****	0.0%	1025.0%
52	1867	9p	*****	0.0%	336.4%	*****	0.0%	361.5%
53	1867	10p	*****	0.0%	311.8%	*****	0.0%	250.0%
53a	1867	10p	*****	0.0%	316.7%	*****	0.0%	531.6%
54	1867	1sh				*****	0.0%	300.0%
54a	1867	1sh	*****	0.0%	163.2%	*****	0.0%	600.0%
54b	1867	1sh	*****	0.0%	660.9%	*****	0.0%	633.3%
55	1867	2sh	*****	0.0%	341.2%	*****	0.0%	233.3%
55a	1867	2sh	*****	0.0%	331.8%	*****	0.0%	220.0%
56	1867	2sh	*****	0.0%	358.3%	*****	0.0%	435.7%
57	1867	5sh	*****	0.0%	340.0%	*****	0.0%	500.0%
57a	1867	5sh	*****	0.0%	238.5%	*****	0.0%	300.0%
57b	1867	5sh	*****	0.0%	347.1%			
59	1872	6p	*****	0.0%	190.9%	*****	0.0%	292.9%
59a	1872	6p	*****	0.0%	372.7%	*****	0.0%	685.7%
60	1872	6p	*****	0.0%	375.0%	*****	0.0%	400.0%
60a	1872	6p	*****	0.0%	669.2%			

A Selection of Investment Grade Stamps
by Country - Greece

Scott #	Issue Year	Value	Rating Mint	5 Year Mint Appreciation %	25 Year Mint Appreciation %	Rating Used	5 Year Used Appreciation %	25 Year Used Appreciation %
1	1861	1l	*****	0.0%	300.0%	****	0.0%	100.0%
1a	1861	1l	****	0.0%	339.4%	****	0.0%	100.0%
2	1861	2l	*****	0.0%	221.4%	*****	0.0%	150.0%
2a	1861	2l	*****	0.0%	175.0%	*****	0.0%	130.8%
3	1861	5l	*****	0.0%	366.7%	**	0.0%	50.0%
4	1861	20l	*****	0.0%	142.1%	***	0.0%	81.0%
4a	1861	20l	****	0.0%	120.0%	****	0.0%	112.5%
4b	1861	20l				(*)	0.0%	10.0%
5	1861	40l	***	0.0%	97.0%	*	0.0%	30.0%
6	1861	80l	*****	0.0%	127.3%	**	0.0%	71.4%
6a	1861	80l	*****	0.0%	127.3%	**	0.0%	71.4%
7	1861	10l	*****	0.0%	278.2%	***	0.0%	81.8%
7c	1861	10l				*****	0.0%	174.1%
7d	1861	10l				*****	0.0%	254.8%
8	1861	1l	*	0.0%	30.7%	*****	0.0%	117.8%
8a	1862	1l	***	0.0%	92.6%	*****	0.0%	209.6%
9	1861	2l	****	0.0%	114.3%	*****	0.0%	131.6%
10	1861	20l				**	0.0%	50.0%
11	1861	5l	**	0.0%	71.4%	****	0.0%	107.7%
11a	1861	5l	**	0.0%	74.4%	*****	0.0%	192.3%
11b	1861	5l				*****	0.0%	500.0%
12	1862	10l	**	0.0%	50.0%	*	0.0%	33.3%
12a	1861	10l	*****	0.0%	169.0%	*****	0.0%	242.9%
13b	1861	20l	*	0.0%	40.0%	****	0.0%	100.0%
13a	1861	20l	*****	0.0%	145.5%	*****	0.0%	206.3%
14	1861	40l	*****	0.0%	250.0%	*****	0.0%	150.0%

A Selection of Investment Grade Stamps
by Country - Greece

Scott #	Issue Year	Value	Rating Mint	5 Year Mint Appreciation %	25 Year Mint Appreciation %	Rating Used	5 Year Used Appreciation %	25 Year Used Appreciation %
14a	1861	40l	*****	0.0%	525.0%	*****	0.0%	200.0%
15	1862	80l	****	0.0%	118.2%	**	0.0%	65.0%
15a	1862	80l	****	0.0%	118.2%	**	0.0%	65.0%
16	1862	1l	**	0.0%	71.4%	*****	0.0%	150.0%
16a	1862	1l	(*)	0.0%	7.1%	*****	0.0%	114.3%
16b	1862	1l	*****	0.0%	200.0%	*****	0.0%	200.0%
17	1862	2l	*****	0.0%	658.6%	*****	0.0%	823.1%
18	1862	5l	****	0.0%	100.0%	*****	0.0%	200.0%
18a	1862	5l	****	0.0%	100.0%			
19	1864	10l	*****	0.0%	166.7%	*****	0.0%	442.9%
19a	1864	10l	****	0.0%	100.0%	*****	0.0%	500.0%
19b	1862	10l				*****	0.0%	327.3%
19c	1865	10l	****	0.0%	116.7%	*****	0.0%	175.0%
19d	1862	10l				(**)	0.0%	-65.0%
20	1862	20l	****	0.0%	100.0%	*****	0.0%	336.4%
20a	1862	20l	*****	0.0%	200.0%	**	0.0%	71.4%
20b	1862	20l	*****	0.0%	433.3%	*****	0.0%	382.1%
20c	1862	20l	**	0.0%	70.0%	*****	0.0%	275.0%
20d	1862	20l				***	0.0%	88.5%
20e	1862	20l				*****	0.0%	757.1%
20f	1862	20l				*****	0.0%	292.9%
21	1862	40l	*****	0.0%	144.4%	*****	0.0%	212.5%
21a	1862	40l	*****	0.0%	677.8%	****	0.0%	212.5%
21b	1862	40l	**	0.0%	50.0%	*****	0.0%	239.3%
21c	1862	40l				*****	0.0%	611.1%
22	1862	80l	**	0.0%	60.0%	*****	0.0%	140.0%
22a	1862	80l	*	0.0%	45.5%	*****	0.0%	140.0%
22b	1862	80l				*****	0.0%	214.3%
22d	1862	80l				*****	0.0%	278.4%

A Selection of Investment Grade Stamps
by Country - Greece

Scott #	Issue Year	Value	Rating Mint	5 Year Mint Appreciation %	25 Year Mint Appreciation %	Rating Used	5 Year Used Appreciation %	25 Year Used Appreciation %
23	1868	1l	*****	0.0%	170.0%	*****	0.0%	233.3%
23a	1868	1l	*****	0.0%	200.0%	*****	0.0%	200.0%
24	1868	2l	*****	0.0%	170.8%	*****	0.0%	331.8%
25	1868	5l	*****	0.0%	490.9%	*****	0.0%	275.0%
26	1868	10l	***	0.0%	83.3%	*****	0.0%	344.4%
27	1868	20l	**	0.0%	50.0%	*****	0.0%	242.9%
27a	1868	20l				*****	0.0%	190.0%
28	1868	40l	*	0.0%	44.4%	****	0.0%	120.6%
28a	1868	40l				*****	0.0%	358.3%
29	1868	80l	**	0.0%	52.0%	*****	0.0%	244.8%
30	1870	1l	*****	0.0%	191.7%	*****	0.0%	185.7%
30a	1870	1l	*****	0.0%	150.0%	*****	0.0%	152.6%
31	1870	20l	*	0.0%	26.7%	***	0.0%	84.6%
31a	1870	20l	*	0.0%	25.0%	*****	0.0%	150.0%
31b	1870	20l				*****	0.0%	444.4%
31c	1870	20l				*****	0.0%	255.3%
32	1870	1l	*****	0.0%	465.2%	*****	0.0%	712.5%
32a	1870	1l	*****	0.0%	584.2%	*****	0.0%	828.6%
33	1870	2l	*****	0.0%	137.5%	*****	0.0%	462.5%
34	1870	5l	*****	0.0%	200.0%	*****	0.0%	300.0%
35	1870	10l				*****	0.0%	772.7%
36	1870	20l	*	0.0%	40.0%	*****	0.0%	231.0%
36a	1870	20l				*****	0.0%	215.8%
36b	1870	20l				*****	0.0%	587.5%
37	1870	40l	**	0.0%	73.7%	****	0.0%	106.3%
38	1872	1l	**	0.0%	69.2%	*****	0.0%	150.0%

A Selection of Investment Grade Stamps
by Country - India

India Scott #	Issue Year	Value	Rating Mint	5 Year Mint Appreciation %	25 Year Mint Appreciation %	Rating Used	5 Year Used Appreciation %	25 Year Used Appreciation %
1	1854	0.5a	*****	170.8%	490.9%			
2	1854	0.5a	*****	17.6%	233.3%	*****	0.0%	313.8%
2a	1854	0.5a	*****	26.3%	220.0%	*****	7.1%	305.4%
2b	1854	0.5a				*****	172.7%	500.0%
4	1854	1a	*****	20.0%	328.6%	*****	-8.3%	144.4%
4a	1854	1a	*****	128.6%	1042.9%	*****	-7.1%	136.4%
5	1854	2a	*****	108.3%	376.2%	*****	23.1%	185.7%
6	1854	4a	*****	66.7%	167.9%	*****	15.0%	130.0%
6a	1854	4a	*****	77.8%	300.0%	****	17.4%	107.7%
6c	1854	4a				*****	0.0%	246.2%
6e	1854	4a				(*)	20.0%	-14.3%
7	1855	1a	****	53.8%	150.0%	****	28.6%	104.5%
9	1855	4a	*****	106.9%	971.4%	*****	0.0%	190.3%
9a	1855	4a	*****	0.0%	2400.0%	*****	218.2%	2400.0%
9b	1855	4a				*****	66.7%	381.9%
10	1855	8a	*****	76.9%	820.0%	*****	0.0%	130.3%
10a	1855	8a	*****	200.0%	1284.6%			
10b	1855	8a				*****	56.3%	2531.6%
11	1855	0.5a	*****	118.8%	3788.9%			
11a	1855	0.5a	*****	131.6%	201.4%	*****	142.9%	900.0%
12a	1855	1a	*****	150.0%	207.7%	*****	150.0%	685.7%
12c	1855	1a				*****	47.1%	1823.1%
13	1855	2a	*****	73.3%	1525.0%	*****	40.0%	162.5%
13a	1855	2a	*****	50.0%	1150.0%	*****	2400.0%	8233.3%
14	1855	2a	*****	175.9%	207.7%			
14a	1855	2a	*****	1100.0%	2809.1%			
15	1855	2a	*****	100.0%	3650.0%	*****	0.0%	500.0%
15a	1855	2a	*****	114.3%	3650.0%	*****	0.0%	620.0%
15b	1855	2a	*****	185.7%	669.2%	*****	146.2%	1042.9%

A Selection of Investment Grade Stamps
by Country - India

India Scott #	Issue Year	Value	Rating Mint	5 Year Mint Appreciation %	25 Year Mint Appreciation %	Rating Used	5 Year Used Appreciation %	25 Year Used Appreciation %
16	1855	4a	*****	100.0%	2669.2%			
16a	1855	4a	*****	227.3%	1400.0%	*****	154.5%	1020.0%
16b	1855	4a				*****	42.9%	1150.0%
17	1855	4a	*****	166.7%	2566.7%	*****	11.1%	185.7%
18	1855	8a	*****	50.0%	3500.0%	*****	9.1%	361.5%
18a	1855	8a				*****	50.0%	1746.2%
19	1860	8p	*****	72.7%	1166.7%			
19C	1860	8p	*****	127.3%	594.4%	*****	50.0%	275.0%
19a	1860	8p				*****	0.0%	1354.5%
19b	1860	8p	*****	275.0%	2207.7%	*****	80.0%	1185.7%
20a	1865	0.5a				*****	56.3%	614.3%
23b	1865	2a				*****	52.9%	900.0%
24	1865	4a	****	126.1%	1385.7%	****	9.1%	100.0%
25	1865	8a	*****	150.0%	852.4%	**	11.8%	52.0%
26	1866	4a	*****	15.8%	1275.0%			
26B	1866	4a	*****	8.3%	306.3%			
27	1866	4a	*****	14.3%	300.0%	***	5.5%	93.3%
27a	1866	6a8p	*****	266.7%	1194.1%			
28	1868	8a	*****	55.6%	748.5%	*****	57.1%	266.7%
29	1866	6a	****	80.0%	227.3%	****	25.0%	112.1%
29a	1866	6a				*****	78.6%	376.2%
30	1866	6a	*****	89.2%	508.7%	*****	28.6%	172.7%
34	1876	12a				*****	18.2%	712.5%
35	1874	1r	*****	30.8%	507.1%	*****	25.0%	581.8%
36a	1882	0.5a	*****	133.3%	900.0%			
40a	1882	2a	*****	638.1%	2483.3%	*****	114.3%	900.0%
50	1895	2r	****	0.0%	120.0%	*****	45.0%	132.0%
51	1895	3r	***	-16.7%	81.8%	***	9.1%	92.0%
52	1895	5r	*****	18.2%	136.4%	*****	41.7%	240.0%

A Selection of Investment Grade Stamps
by Country - India

India Scott #	Issue Year	Value	Rating Mint	5 Year Mint Appreciation %	25 Year Mint Appreciation %	Rating Used	5 Year Used Appreciation %	25 Year Used Appreciation %
53a	1898	0.25a/0.5a	*****	140.0%	757.1%			
53b	1898	0.25a/0.5a	*****	130.8%	328.6%			
62a	1902	1a	***	89.2%	89.2%			
71	1902	2r	*****	31.6%	525.0%			
72	1904	3r	*****	66.7%	212.5%	*****	37.5%	139.1%
73	1902	5r	*****	37.9%	166.7%	*	6.3%	30.8%
74	1902	10r	****	36.0%	223.8%	****	66.7%	122.2%
75	1902	15r	*****	42.9%	170.3%	***	16.7%	75.0%
76	1902	25r	*****	51.4%	166.7%	*****	67.6%	287.5%
77a	1905	1/4a/1/2a				*****	0.0%	270.0%
78a	1906	1/2a	*****	157.1%	157.1%			
79a	1906	1a	(*)	0.0%	0.0%			
80a	1911	3p	****	100.0%	100.0%			
81a	1911	0.5a	(*)	0.0%	0.0%			
81b	1911	1/2a	****	114.3%	114.3%			
82b	1911	1a	****	100.0%	100.0%			
83a	1911	1a	***	88.2%	88.2%			
84a	1911	2a	***	88.2%	88.2%			
94	1911	2r	*****	22.2%	161.9%			
95	1911	5r	*****	13.6%	197.6%			
96	1911	10r	*****	5.3%	140.0%			
97	1911	15r	*	4.3%	41.2%	*****	25.0%	348.3%
98	1911	25r	*	10.5%	27.3%	*****	20.0%	125.0%
101a	1919	1/1/2a	**	71.4%	71.4%			
104a	1921	9p/1a	*****	18.8%	216.7%	*****	6.7%	433.3%
104b	1921	9p/1a	*****	18.8%	216.7%	*****	6.7%	433.3%
104c	1921	9p/1a	*****	14.3%	300.0%	*****	7.1%	309.1%
104e	1921	9p/1a	**	72.7%	72.7%			
105b	1922	0.25a/0.5a	*	4.2%	42.9%			

A Selection of Investment Grade Stamps
by Country - India Convention States

State/ Scott #	Issue Year	Value	Rating Mint	5 Year Mint Appreciation %	25 Year Mint Appreciation %	Rating Used	5 Year Used Appreciation %	25 Year Used Appreciation %
Chamba								
1a	1886	0.5a	*****	0.0%	500.0%	*****	0.0%	850.0%
2a	1886	1a	*****	0.0%	250.0%			
4a	1886	2a	*****	0.0%	400.0%			
6c	1886	3a	*****	0.0%	368.8%			
7a	1886	4a	*****	0.0%	300.0%			
8a	1886	8a	*****	0.0%	400.0%			
9a	1886	12a	*****	0.0%	681.3%			
9b	1886	12a	*****	0.0%	420.8%			
10a	1886	1r	*****	0.0%	600.0%			
11	1895	1r				*****	0.0%	809.1%
12	1886	2r	*****	87.5%	233.3%	*****	0.0%	727.6%
13	1886	3r	*****	0.0%	218.2%	*****	0.0%	556.3%
14	1886	5r	*****	0.0%	192.3%	*****	0.0%	842.9%
15	1890	6a				*****	0.0%	3150.0%
16a	1902	3p	*****	0.0%	166.7%			
19	1903	2a				*****	0.0%	577.4%
25	1904	4a				*****	0.0%	4233.3%
26	1905	6a				*****	0.0%	7191.7%
27	1904	8a				*****	0.0%	5733.3%
28	1903	12a				*****	0.0%	5488.2%
29	1905	1r				*****	0.0%	1172.7%
38	1924	3a				*****	0.0%	1300.0%
43	1913	1r	*****	0.0%	3337.5%	*****	0.0%	4900.0%
44	1921	9p/1a				*****	0.0%	4483.3%
45	1922	1.5a	*****	0.0%	185.7%	*****	90.0%	484.6%
47	1922	1.5a				*****	0.0%	7677.8%

A Selection of Investment Grade Stamps
by Country - India Convention States

State/ Scott #	Issue Year	Value	Rating Mint	5 Year Mint Appreciation %	25 Year Mint Appreciation %	Rating Used	5 Year Used Appreciation %	25 Year Used Appreciation %
Chamba								
49	1922	2a6p				*****	0.0%	7677.8%
54	1927	3a				*****	0.0%	2500.0%
59	1927	1r				*****	-82.0%	1284.6%
61	1932	9p				*****	0.0%	12400.0%
65	1932	2a				*****	0.0%	6718.2%
65a	1932	2a	*****	0.0%	268.4%	*****	0.0%	147.1%
68	1936	4a				*****	0.0%	614.3%
69	1932	6a	(*)	0.0%	0.0%	*****	0.0%	376.2%
70	1938	3p				*****	0.0%	2500.0%
72	1938	9p				*****	0.0%	2926.3%
75	1938	2a6p				*****	0.0%	1800.0%
76	1938	3a				*****	0.0%	672.7%
77	1938	2a6p				*****	0.0%	1400.0%
78	1938	4a	*****	0.0%	2042.9%	*****	0.0%	1536.4%
79	1938	6a	*****	0.0%	420.0%	*****	0.0%	900.0%
80	1938	8a	*****	0.0%	2300.0%	*****	0.0%	3150.0%
81	1938	12a				*****	0.0%	1460.0%
83	1938	2r	*****	0.0%	400.0%	*****	0.0%	2000.0%
84	1938	5r	*****	0.0%	220.0%	*****	0.0%	1455.6%
85	1938	10r	****	-5.5%	100.0%	*****	0.0%	1057.9%
86	1938	15r	*	0.0%	42.9%	*****	0.0%	689.5%
87	1938	25r	**	0.0%	52.6%	*****	0.0%	481.8%
O1a	1886	0.5a	*****	0.0%	733.3%	*****	0.0%	733.3%
O2a	1886	1a	*****	0.0%	674.2%	*****	0.0%	548.6%
O2c	1887	1a	(*)	0.0%	0.0%			
O2d	1887	1a	*****	0.0%	2300.0%	*****	0.0%	1180.0%
O3a	1886	2a	*****	0.0%	328.6%	*****	0.0%	766.7%
O4b	1886	3a	*****	0.0%	620.0%	*****	0.0%	624.1%
O5a	1886	4a	*****	0.0%	326.7%	*****	0.0%	712.5%

A Selection of Investment Grade Stamps
by Country - India Convention States

State/ Scott #	Issue Year	Value	Rating Mint	5 Year Mint Appreciation %	25 Year Mint Appreciation %	Rating Used	5 Year Used Appreciation %	25 Year Used Appreciation %
Chamba								
O5c	1886	4a	*****	0.0%	548.6%			
O6a	1886	8a	*****	0.0%	990.9%	*****	0.0%	860.0%
O7a	1886	12a	*****	0.0%	685.7%			
O8	1890	1r				*****	0.0%	4900.0%
O8a	1886	1r	*****	0.0%	500.0%			
O9	1898	1r				*****	0.0%	1090.5%
O14	1903	2a				*****	0.0%	740.0%
O19	1905	4a				*****	0.0%	2627.3%
O20	1905	8a				*****	0.0%	2300.0%
O22a	1907	1/2a	*****	1828.6%	629.7%			
O26	1913	2a	(**)	0.0%	-20.0%			
O32	1913	4a				*****	0.0%	16566.7%
O33	1913	8a				*****	0.0%	11900.0%
O34	1913	1r				*****	0.0%	12400.0%
O44	1927	12a				*****	0.0%	6150.0%
O45	1927	1r				*****	0.0%	1971.4%
O45A	1939	2r	*****	0.0%	242.9%			
O45B	1939	5r	*****	0.0%	200.0%			
O45C	1939	10r	*****	0.0%	153.8%			
O48a	1935	2a				*****	0.0%	12400.0%
O50	1938	9p	*****	50.0%	3900.0%	*****	0.0%	13233.3%
O51	1938	1a	*****	0.0%	4900.0%			
Faridkot								
8	1887	4a	*****	0.0%	557.9%	*****	0.0%	1347.4%
10	1887	1r	*****	0.0%	145.5%	*****	0.0%	1194.1%
11	1893	1r	*****	12.5%	800.0%	*****	0.0%	1490.9%
12a	1887	6a	*****	0.0%	1000.0%			
O7	1886	1r	*****	0.0%	266.7%	*****	0.0%	1233.3%
O9	1896	1r	*****	0.0%	330.8%	*****	0.0%	2005.3%

A Selection of Investment Grade Stamps
by Country - India Convention States

State/ Scott #	Issue Year	Value	Rating Mint	5 Year Mint Appreciation %	25 Year Mint Appreciation %	Rating Used	5 Year Used Appreciation %	25 Year Used Appreciation %
Gwalior								
1	1885	.5a	*****	0.0%	620.0%			
2	1885	1a	*****	0.0%	680.0%			
3	1885	1a6p	*****	0.0%	900.0%			
4	1885	2a	*****	0.0%	700.0%			
5	1885	8a	*****	0.0%	340.0%			
6	1885	1r	*****	0.0%	238.5%			
7	1885	4a	*****	0.0%	522.2%			
8	1885	6a	*****	0.0%	522.2%			
10	1885	2a	*****	0.0%	366.7%	*****	0.0%	633.3%
11	1885	1r				*****	0.0%	500.0%
12	1885	4a	*****	0.0%	431.3%			
13a	1885	0.5a	**	0.0%	66.7%	***	0.0%	87.5%
14	1885	9p	***	0.0%	97.9%	*****	0.0%	135.7%
24	1896	2a6p				*****	0.0%	757.1%
24a	1896	2a6p	*****	0.0%	263.6%			
25a	1896	1r	*****	0.0%	315.4%			
29a	1899	3p	*****	0.0%	725.0%	*****	0.0%	400.0%
30	1904	3p				*****	0.0%	718.2%
39	1905	2a6p	*****	0.0%	4587.5%	*****	0.0%	19900.0%
47	1908	3r	*****	0.0%	165.6%	*****	0.0%	233.3%
48	1908	5r	***	0.0%	96.4%	*****	0.0%	135.3%
53a	1912	1a	(*)	0.0%	0.0%			
63	1912	5r	****	0.0%	118.8%	*****	0.0%	171.4%
81	1929	5r	*****	0.1%	212.8%			
82	1930	10r	*****	0.0%	243.8%	*****	0.0%	197.6%
83	1930	15r	*****	0.0%	173.7%	****	0.0%	110.5%
84	1930	25r	*****	0.0%	340.0%	*****	0.0%	222.6%
92	1940	9p	*****	0.0%	150.0%	(**)	0.0%	-40.0%
94	1939	3a	*****	0.0%	1650.0%	*****	0.0%	275.0%

A Selection of Investment Grade Stamps
by Country - India Convention States

State/Scott #	Issue Year	Value	Rating Mint	5 Year Mint Appreciation %	25 Year Mint Appreciation %	Rating Used	5 Year Used Appreciation %	25 Year Used Appreciation %
Gwalior								
95	1938	4a	*****	0.0%	266.7%			
109	1948	6a	*****	0.0%	133.3%	*****	0.0%	433.3%
111	1942	12a	*	0.0%	27.3%	*****	0.0%	438.5%
113	1949	2r	*****	0.0%	900.0%	*****	0.0%	124.0%
114	1949	5r	*	0.0%	33.3%	*****	0.0%	185.7%
115	1949	10r	(*)	0.0%	6.7%	**	0.0%	66.7%
116	1933	15r	*	0.0%	25.7%	*****	0.0%	222.6%
117	1933	25r	****	0.0%	18.9%	****	0.0%	117.1%
O1a	1895	0.5a	*****			*****	0.0%	460.0%
O23a	1913	1a	**	0.0%	69.6%			
O27	1913	1r	*****	0.0%	1042.9%	*****	0.0%	900.0%
O37	1935	2r	*****	0.0%	2220.0%	*****	0.0%	1400.0%
O38	1932	5r	*****	0.0%	191.7%	*****	0.0%	941.7%
O39	1932	10r	*****	0.0%	900.0%	*****	0.0%	2066.7%
O48	1945	1r				*****	0.0%	2500.0%
O49	1945	2r				*****	0.0%	723.5%
O50	1945	5r	(*)	0.0%	0.0%	*****	0.0%	1220.0%
O51	1945	10r	**	0.0%	66.7%	*****	0.0%	1400.0%
O57	1942	1a3p	*****	0.0%	2100.0%			
O62	1942	1a/1a3p	*****	0.0%	380.0%			
Jind								
33a	1885	0.5a	*****	0.0%	166.7%	*****	0.0%	204.8%
34	1885	1a	*****	0.0%	8828.6%	*****	0.0%	9900.0%
34a	1885	1a	*****	0.0%	409.1%			
35	1885	2a	*****	0.0%	1557.1%	*****	0.0%	1610.5%
35a	1885	2a	*****	0.0%	566.7%			
36	1885	8a	*****	0.0%	380.8%			
36a	1885	8a	*****	0.0%	928.6%			
37	1885	1r	*****	0.0%	438.5%			

A Selection of Investment Grade Stamps
by Country - India Convention States

State/ Scott #	Issue Year	Value	Rating Mint	5 Year Mint Appreciation %	25 Year Mint Appreciation %	Rating Used	5 Year Used Appreciation %	25 Year Used Appreciation %
Jind								
37a	1885	1r	*****	0.0%	1100.0%			
38	1885	4a	*****	0.0%	413.2%	*****	0.0%	438.5%
39	1885	0.5a	*****	0.0%	460.0%			
40	1885	1a	*****	0.0%	460.0%			
41	1885	2a	*****	0.0%	394.1%			
42	1885	8a	*****	0.0%	480.0%			
43	1885	1r	*****	0.0%	404.3%			
44	1885	4a	*****	0.0%	544.4%			
45	1886	.5a	*****	0.0%	400.0%			
45a	1886	0.5a	*****	0.0%	700.0%			
46	1886	2a	*****	0.0%	360.0%			
46a	1886	2a	*****	0.0%	554.5%			
47	1886	1r	*****	0.0%	227.3%			
47a	1886	1r	*****	0.0%	161.9%			
48	1886	4a	*****	0.0%	542.9%			
49a	1886	0.5a	****	0.0%	100.0%			
50a	1886	1a	*****	0.0%	328.6%			
55	1886	8a				*****	0.0%	3900.0%
55a	1886	8a	*****	0.0%	220.0%			
56	1897	12a	*****	0.0%	1566.7%	*****	0.0%	4900.0%
57	1891	1r				*****	0.0%	842.9%
58	1898	1r				*****	0.0%	1100.0%
59	1886	2r	*****	0.0%	377.3%	*****	0.0%	1011.1%
60	1886	3r	*****	0.0%	581.8%	*****	0.0%	900.0%
61	1886	5r	*****	0.0%	316.7%	*****	0.0%	455.6%
71a	1903	3a	****	0.0%	100.0%			
73	1905	6a				*****	0.0%	6670.8%
74	1903	8a				*****	0.0%	6670.8%
76	1905	1r				*****	0.0%	3511.1%

A Selection of Investment Grade Stamps
by Country - India Convention States

State/ Scott #	Issue Year	Value	Rating Mint	5 Year Mint Appreciation %	25 Year Mint Appreciation %	Rating Used	5 Year Used Appreciation %	25 Year Used Appreciation %
Jind								
85	1913	6a				*****	0.0%	1788.9%
96	1913	12a				*****	0.0%	8471.4%
97	1913	1r				*****	0.0%	7191.7%
106	1927	2r				*****	0.0%	3500.0%
107	1927	5r	*****	0.0%	181.3%	*****	0.0%	1536.4%
116	1927	3a				*****	0.0%	7136.8%
119	1927	12a				*****	0.0%	2066.7%
121	1927	2r	*****	0.0%	478.9%	*****	0.0%	1945.5%
122	1927	5r				*****	0.0%	346.4%
O1a	1885	0.5a	*****	0.0%	185.7%	*****	0.0%	176.9%
O3	1885	2a	*****	0.0%	242.9%	*****	0.0%	314.3%
O3a	1885	2a	*****	0.0%	445.5%			
O4	1885	0.5a	*****	0.0%	328.6%			
O5	1885	1a	*****	0.0%	257.1%			
O6	1885	2a	*****	0.0%	229.4%			
O7	1886	.5a	*****	0.0%	203.6%			
O7a	1886	1/2a	*****	0.0%	452.6%			
O8	1886	2a	*****	0.0%	239.3%			
O8a	1886	2a	*****	0.0%	400.0%			
O10a	1886	1a	*****	0.0%	294.7%			
O14	1896	1r				*****	0.0%	614.3%
O17a	1903	0.5a				*****	0.0%	157.1%
O18a	1903	1a				*****	0.0%	128.6%
O46	1927	2r	*****	0.0%	1204.3%	*****	0.0%	861.5%
O47	1927	5r				*****	0.0%	2976.9%
O48	1927	10r	*****	0.0%	202.6%	*****	0.0%	765.4%
O52	1937	2a6p				*****	0.0%	2627.3%
O54	1937	6a				*****	0.0%	1900.0%
O55	1942	.5a	*****	0.0%	350.0%			

A Selection of Investment Grade Stamps by Country - India Convention States

State/ Scott #	Issue Year	Value	Rating Mint	5 Year Mint Appreciation %	25 Year Mint Appreciation %	Rating Used	5 Year Used Appreciation %	25 Year Used Appreciation %
Jind								
O58	1940	1r	*****	0.0%	350.0%	*****	0.0%	513.6%
O59	1937	2r	****	0.0%	111.1%	*****	0.0%	900.0%
O60	1937	5r	****	0.0%	122.2%	*****	0.0%	788.9%
O61	1937	10r	*****	0.0%	566.7%	*****	0.0%	1263.6%
Nabha								
2	1885	1a	*****	0.0%	334.2%	*****	52.6%	866.7%
3	1885	2a	*****	0.0%	294.7%	*****	0.0%	786.4%
4	1885	8a	*****	0.0%	216.7%			
5	1885	1r	*****	0.0%	266.7%			
6	1885	4a	*****	0.0%	233.3%	*****	0.0%	733.3%
9	1885	1r	*****	0.0%	216.7%	*****	0.0%	462.5%
10	1885	4a	*****	0.0%	285.7%	*****	0.0%	900.0%
14a	1885	1a6p	*****	0.0%	200.0%			
16	1885	3a				*****	0.0%	2066.7%
20	1885	1r				*****	0.0%	350.0%
22	1885	2r	*****	0.0%	223.1%	*****	0.0%	328.6%
23	1897	3r	*****	0.0%	223.1%	*****	0.0%	423.8%
24	1897	5r	*****	0.0%	190.3%	*****	0.0%	650.0%
28a	1903	.5a	*****	0.0%	900.0%			
30A	1903	2a6p				*****	0.0%	205.9%
33	1903	6a				*****	0.0%	3233.3%
34	1903	8a				*****	0.0%	4344.4%
35	1903	12a				*****	0.0%	2005.3%
36	1903	1r				*****	0.0%	1347.4%
58	1932	2r	*****	-0.8%	719.1%	*****	0.0%	2609.7%
59	1927	5r	*****	0.0%	358.3%	*****	0.0%	2081.8%
67	1937	3a				*****	0.0%	4445.5%
76	1938	3a6p				*****	0.0%	7712.5%
78	1938	6a				*****	0.0%	1500.0%

A Selection of Investment Grade Stamps
by Country - India Convention States

State/ Scott #	Issue Year	Value	Rating Mint	5 Year Mint Appreciation %	25 Year Mint Appreciation %	Rating Used	5 Year Used Appreciation %	25 Year Used Appreciation %
Nabha								
79	1938	8a				*****	0.0%	1150.0%
80	1938	12a				*****	0.0%	782.4%
81	1938	1r				*****	0.0%	624.1%
82	1938	2r	*****	0.0%	225.0%	*****	0.0%	872.2%
83	1938	5r	(*)	0.0%	6.3%	*****	0.0%	421.7%
84	1938	10r	(*)	0.0%	-13.3%	*****	0.0%	500.0%
85	1938	15r	***	0.0%	81.8%	*****	0.0%	525.0%
86	1938	25r	*	0.0%	20.0%	*****	0.0%	455.6%
O3	1885	2a	*****	0.0%	233.3%	*****	0.0%	334.8%
O6a	1885	0.5a	*****	0.0%	375.0%	****	0.0%	116.7%
O9	1885	3a	*****	0.0%	650.0%	*****	0.0%	1547.1%
O12	1889	12a				*****	0.0%	664.7%
O13	1889	1r	*****	0.0%	380.8%	*****	0.0%	2087.5%
O14	1897	1r	****	0.0%	100.0%	*****	0.0%	133.3%
O15	1889	6a	*****	0.0%	1200.0%	*****	0.0%	1809.1%
O26	1913	1r	(*)	0.0%	0.0%			
O36	1945	4a	*****	0.0%	400.0%			
Patiala								
1a	1884	0.5a	*****	0.0%	1800.0%	*****	0.0%	585.7%
2	1884	1a	*****	0.0%	435.7%	*****	0.0%	685.7%
2b	1884	1a	*****	0.0%	200.0%			
4	1884	8a	*****	0.0%	420.0%	*****	0.0%	788.9%
4a	1884	8a	*****	0.0%	406.7%			
5	1884	1r	*****	0.0%	150.0%	*****	0.0%	850.0%
6	1884	4a	*****	0.0%	900.0%	*****	0.0%	837.5%
8a	1885	2a	*****	0.0%	316.7%			
9	1885	1r				*****	0.0%	1090.5%
9a	1885	1r	*****	0.0%	282.4%			
10a	1885	4a	*****	0.0%	200.0%			

A Selection of Investment Grade Stamps
by Country - India Convention States

State/ Scott #	Issue Year	Value	Rating Mint	5 Year Mint Appreciation %	25 Year Mint Appreciation %	Rating Used	5 Year Used Appreciation %	25 Year Used Appreciation %
Patiala								
11a	1885	1a	*****	0.0%	400.0%			
12	1885	8a	*****	0.0%	677.8%	*****	0.0%	1733.3%
12a	1885	8a	*****	0.0%	175.0%			
15a	1891	1a	*****	0.0%	200.0%	*****	0.0%	525.0%
19a	1891	4a	*****	0.0%	368.8%	*****	0.0%	200.0%
22	1896	1r				*****	0.0%	1078.6%
23	1891	2r	*****	0.0%	200.0%			
24	1891	3r	*****	0.0%	222.2%			
25	1891	5r	*****	0.0%	195.5%			
39	1906	12a				*****	0.0%	3100.0%
56	1926	2r				*****	0.0%	3003.4%
57	1926	5r	*****	0.0%	221.4%	*****	0.0%	1900.0%
71	1928	2r				*****	0.0%	4025.0%
85	1938	2a6p				*****	0.0%	11900.0%
87	1938	3a6p				*****	0.0%	9768.4%
88	1938	4a				*****	0.0%	7712.5%
89	1938	6a	*****	0.0%	6150.0%	*****	0.0%	19900.0%
90	1938	8a	*****	0.0%	2650.0%	*****	0.0%	5581.8%
91	1938	12a	*****	0.0%	2400.0%	*****	0.0%	9445.5%
92	1938	1r	*****	0.0%	252.9%	*****	0.0%	635.3%
93	1938	2r	****	0.0%	114.3%	*****	0.0%	900.0%
94	1938	5r	**	0.0%	60.0%	*****	0.0%	1053.8%
O2a	1884	1a	*****	0.0%	900.0%	*****	0.0%	442.9%
O2d	1884	1a	*****	0.0%	2900.0%	*****	0.0%	515.4%
O3	1884	2a	*****	0.0%	233.3%	(*)	0.0%	-12.5%
O4a	1885	1/2 a				(*)	0.0%	0.0%
O6a	1885	1a	*****	0.0%	600.0%	***	0.0%	93.3%
O6d	1885	1a	*****	0.0%	1478.9%			
O9a	1900	1a	*	0.0%	24.1%			

A Selection of Investment Grade Stamps
by Country - Iran

Iran Scott #	Issue Year	Value	Rating Mint	5 Year Mint Appreciation %	25 Year Mint Appreciation %	Rating Used	5 Year Used Appreciation %	25 Year Used Appreciation %
1	1868	ls	*****	0.0%	400.0%			
1a	1868	ls	*****	0.0%	2976.9%			
2	1868	2s	*****	0.0%	450.0%			
2a	1868	2s	*****	0.0%	5614.3%			
3	1868	4s	*****	0.0%	350.0%			
4	1868	8s	*****	0.0%	511.1%			
4a	1868	8s	*****	0.0%	1900.0%			
11	1875	ls	*****	0.0%	150.0%	**	0.0%	50.0%
11a	1875	ls	*****	0.0%	775.0%	*****	0.0%	1150.0%
12	1875	2s	*****	0.0%	172.7%	**	0.0%	57.9%
12a	1875	2s	*****	0.0%	200.0%			
13	1875	4s	*****	0.0%	172.7%	*****	0.0%	135.3%
13b	1875	4s	*	0.0%	42.9%			
14	1875	8s	*****	0.0%	185.7%	*****	0.0%	337.5%
14b	1875	8s	*****	0.0%	50.0%	*****	0.0%	233.3%
15	1876	1s	*****	0.0%	233.3%	*****	0.0%	1066.7%
15a	1876	1s	*****	0.0%	200.0%			
15b	1876	1s	****	0.0%	100.0%			
16	1876	2s	*****	9.1%	300.0%	*****	0.0%	200.0%
16a	1876	2s	*****	0.0%	1066.7%			
17	1876	2s	****	0.0%	100.0%			
17a	1876	2s	****	0.0%	100.0%			
18	1876	4s	*****	0.0%	300.0%	*****	0.0%	233.3%
18a	1876	4s	*****	0.0%	1011.1%	*****	0.0%	1438.5%
19	1876	1k	*****	0.0%	809.1%	****	0.0%	100.0%
19a	1876	1k				*****	0.0%	742.1%
19b	1876	1k	*****	0.0%	1233.3%	*****	0.0%	700.0%
19c	1876	1k	*****	0.0%	600.0%			
19d	1876	1k				*****	0.0%	900.0%

A Selection of Investment Grade Stamps
by Country - Iran

Iran Scott #	Issue Year	Value	Rating Mint	5 Year Mint Appreciation %	25 Year Mint Appreciation %	Rating Used	5 Year Used Appreciation %	25 Year Used Appreciation %
20	1876	4k	*****	0.0%	500.0%	*****	0.0%	328.6%
20a	1876	4k				*****	0.0%	900.0%
20b	1876	4k	*****	0.0%	733.3%	*****	0.0%	172.7%
20c	1876	4k				****	0.0%	100.0%
27	1876	1s						
28	1876	2s	*****	0.0%	150.0%			
29	1876	5s	*	0.0%	20.0%			
30	1876	10s	*	0.0%	28.6%			
33	1878	lk	****	0.0%	533.3%	****	0.0%	100.0%
34	1878	lk	*****	0.0%	400.0%	*****	0.0%	150.0%
34a	1878	lk				*****	0.0%	150.0%
35	1878	4k	*****	0.0%	221.4%	*****	0.0%	250.0%
36	1878	5k	****	0.0%	50.0%	****	0.0%	100.0%
37	1878	5k	*****	0.0%	3300.0%	*****	0.0%	400.0%
38	1878	5k	*****	0.0%	1650.0%	*****	0.0%	614.3%
39	1878	5k	*****	0.0%	3150.0%	*****	6.7%	742.1%
40	1878	lt	*****	0.0%	400.0%	*****	0.0%	166.7%
41	1879	1k	*****	0.0%	1025.0%			
42	1879	5k	*****	0.0%	700.0%			
42a	1879	5k	*****	0.0%	650.0%	*****	0.0%	650.0%
43	1880	1s	*	0.0%	25.0%			
44	1880	2s	**	0.0%	70.0%			
44a	1880	2s				*****	0.0%	733.3%
45	1880	5s	*****	0.0%	600.0%			
46	1880	l0s	*****	0.0%	366.7%	****	0.0%	100.0%
47	1881	5c	*****	0.0%	233.3%	*****	0.0%	400.0%
48	1881	10c	*****	0.0%	150.0%	*****	0.0%	400.0%
49	1881	25c	*****	0.0%	1587.5%	****	0.0%	100.0%
50	1882	5c	*****	0.0%	233.3%	*****	0.0%	1900.0%

A Selection of Investment Grade Stamps
by Country - Iran

Iran Scott #	Issue Year	Value	Rating Mint	5 Year Mint Appreciation %	25 Year Mint Appreciation %	Rating Used	5 Year Used Appreciation %	25 Year Used Appreciation %
51	1882	10c	*****	0.0%	233.3%	*****	0.0%	1900.0%
52	1882	25c	*****	0.0%	1172.7%	*****	0.0%	300.0%
53	1882	5s	*****	0.0%	400.0%			
53a	1882	5s	*****	0.0%	400.0%			
54	1882	10s	*****	0.0%	325.0%			
55	1882	50c	*****	0.0%	1900.0%	*****	0.0%	300.0%
56	1884	50c	*****	0.0%	328.6%	*****	0.0%	600.0%
57	1882	1fr	*****	0.0%	328.6%	*****	0.0%	233.3%
58	1882	5fr	*****	0.0%	250.0%	*****	0.0%	300.0%
59	1882	l0f r	*****	0.0%	328.6%	*****	0.0%	300.0%
60	1885	1c	*****	0.0%	150.0%			
61	1885	2c	*****	0.0%	150.0%			
62	1885	5c	*****	0.0%	1233.3%			
62a	1885	5c						
63	1885	10c		0.0%	433.3%			
64	1885	1k		0.0%	1233.3%			
65	1886	5k	*****	0.0%	1233.3%	*****	0.0%	471.4%
66	1885	6c/5s	*****	0.0%	400.0%	*****	0.0%	650.0%
66a	1885	6c/5s	*****	0.0%	400.0%	*****	0.0%	400.0%
67	1885	12c/50c	****	0.0%	114.3%	*****	0.0%	100.0%
68	1885	18c/l0s	****	0.0%	114.3%	*****	0.0%	100.0%
69	1885	lt/5fr	*****	0.0%	150.0%	*****	0.0%	233.3%
70	1887	3c/5s	*****	83.3%	1000.0%	*****	0.0%	1328.6%
70a	1887	3c/5s	*****	0.0%	400.0%	*****	0.0%	400.0%
71	1887	6c/10s	*****	0.0%	500.0%	*****	0.0%	300.0%
72	1887	8c/50c	****	0.0%	100.0%	**	0.0%	50.0%
79	1889	2k	*****	0.0%	471.4%			
80	1889	5k	*****	0.0%	150.0%			
84	1889	7c	*****	0.0%	677.8%			

A Selection of Investment Grade Stamps
by Country - Iran

Iran Scott #	Issue Year	Value	Rating Mint	5 Year Mint Appreciation %	25 Year Mint Appreciation %	Rating Used	5 Year Used Appreciation %	25 Year Used Appreciation %
87	1889	1k	**	0.0%	71.4%			
88	1891	2k	*****	0.0%	833.3%	*****	0.0%	257.1%
89	1889	5k				*****	0.0%	566.7%
95	1894	16c	*****	0.0%	316.7%	*****	0.0%	650.0%
100	1894	50k	*****	0.0%	400.0%			
101	1897	5c/8c	*****	0.0%	1900.0%			
102	1897	1k/5k	*****	0.0%	1500.0%			
103	1897	2k/5k	*****	0.0%	1614.3%	*****	0.0%	1300.0%
118	1898	10k	*****	0.0%	471.4%			
119	1898	50k	*****	0.0%	300.0%	**	0.0%	66.7%
123	1899	4c				*****	0.0%	650.0%
125	1899	8c				*****	0.0%	2566.7%
128	1899	16c	*****	0.0%	525.0%	*****	0.0%	1100.0%
129	1899	1k	*****	0.0%	455.6%			
130	1899	2k	*****	0.0%	275.0%	*****	0.0%	316.7%
131	1899	3k	*****	0.0%	540.0%	*****	0.0%	2400.0%
132	1899	4k	*****	0.0%	700.0%	*****	0.0%	2400.0%
133	1899	5k	*****	0.0%	140.0%	*****	0.0%	220.0%
134	1899	10k	****	0.0%	100.0%	****	0.0%	100.0%
135	1899	50k	*****	0.0%	300.0%	*****	0.0%	400.0%
144	1899	16c	*****	0.0%	233.3%			
145	1899	lk	*****	0.0%	300.0%			
146	1899	2k	*****	0.0%	180.0%			
147	1899	3k	*****	0.0%	150.0%			
148	1899	4k	*****	0.0%	150.0%			
149	1899	5k	***	0.0%	77.8%			
150	1899	10k	*****	0.0%	566.7%	*****	0.0%	900.0%
151	1899	50k	**	0.0%	66.7%	*****	0.0%	328.6%

A Selection of Investment Grade Stamps
by Country - Italy

Italy Scott #	Issue Year	Value	Rating Mint	5 Year Mint Appreciation %	25 Year Mint Appreciation %	Rating Used	5 Year Used Appreciation %	25 Year Used Appreciation %
17	1862	10c	*****	-15.8%	233.3%	*****	-9.7%	306.3%
17a	1862	10c	*****	-48.4%	243.8%	*****	-23.9%	337.5%
17b	1862	10c	*****	-28.3%	127.6%	*****	-13.6%	295.8%
19	1862	10c				*****	-18.8%	261.1%
20	1862	40c	*****	-23.1%	127.3%	*****	-12.5%	191.7%
21	1862	80c	****	-23.1%	163.2%	****	-20.8%	111.1%
22	1863	80c	***	-28.1%	91.7%	*****	-18.2%	157.1%
22a	1863	15c				*****	-23.9%	366.7%
22b	1863	15c	****	-28.1%	155.6%	*****	-20.0%	191.7%
24a	1863	1c						
25	1865	2c	*****	-26.2%	433.3%			
25a	1865	2c	*****	40.0%	300.0%	*****	50.0%	122.2%
26	1863	5c	*****	-24.0%	769.0%			
27	1863	10c	*****	-22.5%	588.9%			
28	1877	10c	*****	-22.0%	588.2%			
29	1863	15c	*****	-21.7%	683.3%			
29a	1863	15c						
31	1863	40c	*****	-25.7%	796.6%			
31a	1863	40c		0.0%	1106.9%			
33	1863	2L	***	-26.2%	92.0%	*****	-28.0%	200.0%
34	1865	20c/15c	*****	-14.0%	377.8%			
34a	1865	20c/15c	*****	-16.7%	483.3%			
34b	1865	20c/15c	*****	-16.7%	311.8%			
34c	1865	20c/15c						
35	1867	20c	*****	100.0%	1085.2%			
36	1877	20c	*****	-20.0%	877.8%			
37	1877	2c/2c	*****	-10.0%	554.5%	*****	-23.1%	733.3%
37a	1877	2c/2c				*****	-18.8%	261.1%

A Selection of Investment Grade Stamps
by Country - Italy

Italy Scott #	Issue Year	Value	Rating Mint	5 Year Mint Appreciation %	25 Year Mint Appreciation %	Rating Used	5 Year Used Appreciation %	25 Year Used Appreciation %
38	1877	2c/5c	*****	0.0%	718.2%	*****	0.0%	650.0%
38a	1877	2c/5c				*****	-18.8%	271.4%
39	1877	2c/20c	*****	-8.6%	384.8%			
39a	1877	2c/20c	*****	-20.0%	590.9%	*****	-12.5%	150.0%
40	1877	2c/30c	*****	-12.5%	1233.3%			
40a	1877	2c/30c				*****	-18.8%	372.7%
41	1877	2c/IL	*****	-15.4%	358.3%			
41a	1877	2c/IL	*****	-20.0%	700.0%	*****	-14.3%	242.9%
42	1877	2c/2L	*****	-15.4%	340.0%			
42a	1877	2c/2L	*****	-20.0%	700.0%	*****	712.5%	271.4%
43	1877	2c/5I	*****	-8.6%	384.8%			
43a	1877	2c/5L				*****	-18.8%	271.4%
44	1877	2c/IOL	*****	-15.4%	478.9%			
44a	1877	2c/IOL				*****	-18.8%	271.4%
46	1879	10c	*****	-5.3%	592.3%			
47	1879	20c	*****	-5.6%	608.3%			
48	1879	25c	*****	0.0%	841.2%			
49	1879	30c	*****	-14.3%	185.7%	*****	-5.4%	194.4%
50	1879	50c	*****	-16.7%	175.9%			
51	1879	2L	*****	-19.2%	133.3%	*****	-12.5%	366.7%
52	1889	5c	*****	-11.4%	675.0%			
54	1889	45c	*****	-9.6%	487.5%			
55	1889	60c				(*)	-10.5%	0.0%
56a	1889	1L				*****	-10.0%	2060.0%
57	1889	5L	*****	16.7%	418.5%	*****	-10.4%	411.9%
58a	1890	2c/10c	*****	-9.1%	1011.1%	*****	-9.7%	2066.7%
60	1890	2c/50c	*****	-11.5%	538.9%	*****	-10.5%	844.4%
60a	1890	2c/50c				*****	-14.3%	847.4%
62	1890	2c/1.25I	*****	-9.1%	426.3%	*****	-6.3%	782.4%

A Selection of Investment Grade Stamps
by Country - Italy

Italy Scott #	Issue Year	Value	Rating Mint	5 Year Mint Appreciation %	25 Year Mint Appreciation %	Rating Used	5 Year Used Appreciation %	25 Year Used Appreciation %
62a	1890	2c/1.25l	*****	-10.5%	1316.7%	*****	-10.5%	794.7%
63	1890	2c/1.75l	*****	-8.3%	340.0%	*****	-8.3%	633.3%
64	1891	2c/5c	*****	-11.1%	166.7%	*****	-9.1%	300.0%
64a	1891	2c/5c	*****	-10.7%	127.3%	*****	-10.8%	222.2%
65	1890	20c/30c	*****	-10.5%	325.0%			
66	1890	20c/50c	*****	-9.1%	376.2%	*****	-10.5%	608.3%
67	1891	5c	*****	-9.1%	400.0%			
72	1891	5L	*****	-10.5%	209.1%	*****	-4.2%	513.3%
75	1897	5c	*****	-10.0%	620.0%			
76a	1901	1C	***	-11.1%	77.8%	**	-10.3%	62.5%
77a	1901	2c	*****	-12.0%	511.1%			
77b	1901	2c	*****	-8.0%	206.7%	*****	-8.6%	137.0%
78	1901	5c	*****	-8.6%	433.3%			
79	1901	10c	*****	-8.3%	511.1%			
79a	1901	10c				****	-4.8%	122.2%
81	1901	25c	*****	-9.1%	1150.0%			
81a	1901	25c	*****	-9.1%	1150.0%			
83	1901	40c	*****	-10.0%	500.0%			
84a	1901	45c	**	-9.4%	61.1%	(*)	-15.6%	15.2%
85	1901	50c	*****	-10.5%	608.3%			
87a	1901	1L	*****	-9.4%	222.2%	*****	-8.3%	193.3%
87b	1924	1L	*****	-9.4%	705.6%			

A Selection of Investment Grade Stamps
by Country - Japan

Japan Scott #	Issue Year	Value	Rating Mint	5 Year Mint Appreciation %	25 Year Mint Appreciation %	Rating Used	5 Year Used Appreciation %	25 Year Used Appreciation %
1	1871	48m	(*)	-13.5%	0.0%	(*)	-13.5%	7.1%
1a	1871	48m	**	0.0%	66.7%	***	0.0%	78.6%
1b	1871	48m	*	0.0%	30.4%	*	0.0%	25.0%
1c	1871	48m	*	-7.1%	30.0%	*	-7.1%	25.0%
1d	1871	48m	**	0.0%	53.8%	**	0.0%	53.8%
2	1871	100m	(*)	-13.5%	12.5%	(*)	-13.5%	15.4%
2a	1871	100m	**	0.0%	59.1%	**	0.0%	59.1%
2b	1871	100m	(*)	0.0%	10.0%	*	0.0%	29.4%
2c	1871	100m	*	0.0%	33.3%	*	0.0%	33.3%
3	1871	200m	(**)	-22.2%	16.7%	**	-23.5%	54.8%
3a	1871	200m	**	-4.8%	58.7%	**	-5.6%	54.5%
3b	1871	200m	*	0.0%	25.0%	**	0.0%	66.7%
4	1871	500m	**	-11.5%	53.3%	**	-15.4%	57.1%
4a	1871	500m	***	-7.1%	80.6%	***	-7.4%	83.8%
4b	1871	500m	*****	0.0%	150.0%	***	0.0%	75.0%
4c	1871	500m	*****	55.6%	311.8%	***	0.0%	81.8%
4d	1871	500m	****	-3.3%	101.4%	**	-3.8%	73.6%
4e	1871	500m	***	-3.2%	87.5%	***	0.0%	90.5%
4f	1871	500m	***	-3.2%	87.5%	***	0.0%	90.5%
4g	1871	500m	**	0.0%	66.7%	**	0.0%	66.7%
5	1872	1/2s	*	-15.4%	41.9%	(*)	-23.1%	17.6%
5a	1872	1/2s	**	-3.8%	61.3%	*	-15.4%	29.4%
5b	1872	1/2s	**	-3.8%	61.3%	*	-15.4%	29.4%
5c	1872	1/2s	(*)	0.0%	7.4%	(*)	0.0%	12.5%
5d	1872	1/2s	****	0.0%	110.5%	**	0.0%	53.8%
5e	1872	1/2s	****	0.0%	110.5%	**	0.0%	53.8%
5f	1872	1/2s	****	0.0%	110.5%	**	0.0%	53.8%
5g	1872	1/2s	****	0.0%	111.5%	*	0.0%	37.5%
6	1872	1s	***	-11.8%	92.3%	**	-23.5%	66.7%

A Selection of Investment Grade Stamps
by Country - Japan

Japan Scott #	Issue Year	Value	Rating Mint	5 Year Mint Appreciation %	25 Year Mint Appreciation %	Rating Used	5 Year Used Appreciation %	25 Year Used Appreciation %
6a	1872	1s	***	0.0%	77.6%	**	0.0%	68.8%
6b	1872	1s	**	0.0%	64.7%	**	0.0%	57.9%
6d	1872	1s	*****	50.0%	130.8%	***	0.0%	92.3%
7	1872	2s	**	-13.0%	66.7%	**	-17.4%	58.3%
7a	1872	2s	***	0.0%	98.4%	***	-8.0%	82.5%
8	1872	5s	****	-5.9%	100.0%	***	-14.7%	81.3%
8a	1872	5s	****	-2.9%	112.5%	****	-8.6%	100.0%
8b	1872	5s	*	0.0%	16.1%	*	0.0%	16.1%
9a	1872	1/2s	*	0.0%	16.7%	(*)	0.0%	-10.7%
10	1872	1s	(*)	0.0%	11.1%	(*)	0.0%	-5.5%
10a	1872	1s	*	0.0%	16.7%	(*)	0.0%	5.5%
11	1872	2s	(*)	0.0%	-9.1%	(*)	0.0%	11.1%
12	1872	2s	(**)	0.0%	-25.0%	(*)	0.0%	-6.7%
12a	1872	2s	*	0.0%	37.9%	***	0.0%	81.8%
13	1873	2s	(*)	0.0%	3.4%			
13a	1873	2s	(**)	-57.1%	-60.5%			
14	1873	4s	(*)	0.0%	12.5%	*	0.0%	30.0%
14a	1873	4s	(*)	0.0%	10.5%	*	0.0%	16.4%
15	1872	10s	(*)	-3.8%	11.1%	(*)	-6.3%	0.0%
16	1872	10s	(*)	-15.8%	-14.0%	(*)	-15.4%	-8.3%
16a	1872	10s	***	0.0%	91.7%	(*)	0.0%	-9.1%
17	1872	20s	**	-14.3%	66.7%	*	-17.6%	40.0%
17a	1872	20s	****	0.0%	108.3%	*	-17.6%	40.0%
18	1872	30s	*	0.0%	25.0%	(*)	0.0%	-6.3%
24	1874	4s	*	0.0%	23.8%	**	0.0%	66.7%
29 Syll.1	1874	6s	**	0.0%	70.0%	*	0.0%	39.7%
31 Syll.1	1874	30s	*	0.0%	33.3%	(*)	0.0%	0.0%
31a	1874	30s syll.1	*	0.0%	20.0%	(*)	0.0%	0.0%
34	1874	2s syll.1	(**)	-12.5%	-30.0%	*	0.0%	20.0%

A Selection of Investment Grade Stamps
by Country - Japan

Japan Scott #	Issue Year	Value	Rating Mint	5 Year Mint Appreciation %	25 Year Mint Appreciation %	Rating Used	5 Year Used Appreciation %	25 Year Used Appreciation %
35	1874	4s syll.1	***	0.0%	75.0%	**	0.0%	50.8%
36	1874	6s syll.10	*	-12.5%	40.0%	**	-7.1%	52.9%
37	1874	10s syll.1	*	-52.9%	42.9%	*****	-35.0%	136.4%
38	1874	20s syll.4	****	-15.0%	102.4%	**	-5.3%	50.0%
39	1874	30s syll.1	*****	-17.4%	171.4%	**	-5.0%	65.2%
41	1875	6-15y/2-5y	*	0.0%	16.7%			
42	1875	4s syll.1	*	0.0%	48.6%	**	0.0%	61.1%
43	1875	6s syll.10	(**)	0.0%	-40.0%	(**)	10.0%	-31.3%
44	1875	6s syll.19	*	22.2%	37.5%	***	10.0%	96.4%
45	1875	10s syll.4	**	2.9%	71.4%	***	9.1%	87.5%
46	1875	12s syll.1	**	-16.7%	63.0%	**	6.7%	52.4%
47	1875	15s syll.1	**	0.0%	66.7%	*	0.0%	18.5%
49	1875	30s syll.2	**	-2.8%	59.1%	**	0.0%	55.6%
50	1875	45s syll.1	****	-16.7%	100.0%	***	-12.7%	84.6%
51	1875	1s	*	15.4%	36.4%	(*)	-3.6%	12.5%
52	1875	4s	**	-28.6%	59.6%	**	0.0%	66.7%
53	1875	1s	***	-6.3%	87.5%			
54	1875	2s	**	15.8%	69.2%			
54A	1876	5s	*	10.0%	37.5%	*	10.0%	37.5%
55	1876	5r	**	0.0%	66.7%			
56	1876	1s	**	33.3%	53.8%			
57	1876	2s	***	71.4%	89.5%			
58	1876	4s	*	17.6%	25.0%			
58a	1876	4s	*	17.6%	25.0%			
59	1876	5s	(*)	0.0%	8.3%			
60	1877	6s	**	25.0%	60.0%	***	30.8%	88.9%
61	1877	8s	*	11.1%	25.0%			
62	1877	10s	*	0.0%	15.8%			

A Selection of Investment Grade Stamps
by Country - Japan

Japan Scott #	Issue Year	Value	Rating Mint	5 Year Mint Appreciation %	25 Year Mint Appreciation %	Rating Used	5 Year Used Appreciation %	25 Year Used Appreciation %
Offices in China								
18	1900	1y	(*)	-8.3%	0.0%			
20	1908	5y	(*)	0.0%	6.7%	*	0.0%	18.8%
21	1908	10y	(*)	0.0%	0.0%	(*)	0.0%	10.0%
24	1913	1.5s	(*)	-5.9%	0.0%			
25	1913	2s	(*)	-10.0%	0.0%			
27	1913	4s	(*)	-10.7%	4.2%	(*)	-10.7%	4.2%
28	1913	5s	(*)	-10.7%	4.2%	(*)	-9.1%	11.1%
29	1913	10s	(*)	-10.7%	4.2%			
30	1913	20s	(*)	-9.1%	4.2%	(*)	-6.7%	7.7%
32	1913	1y	(**)	-9.1%	-46.3%	(**)	-9.1%	-41.0%
44	1914	25s	*	-9.1%	25.0%	(*)	0.0%	-6.7%
45	1914	30s	(*)	-6.3%	7.1%	(*)	-5.2%	-8.3%
46	1914	50s	*	-5.3%	20.0%	(*)	-7.7%	-14.3%
47	1914	1y	*	-7.1%	18.2%			
48	1914	5y	**	-2.6%	54.2%	(*)	-4.5%	5.0%
49	1914	10y	*	-1.9%	18.2%	*	-5.9%	45.5%
Offices in Korea								
3	1900	1.5s	(*)	0.0%	11.1%	(**)	0.0%	-18.8%
6	1900	4s	(*)	0.0%	13.0%	(*)	0.0%	-8.3%
7	1900	5s	(*)	0.0%	12.5%	(*)	0.0%	-8.3%
8	1900	8s	(*)	0.0%	11.1%	(**)	0.0%	-25.0%
9	1900	10s	*	0.0%	16.7%	(*)	0.0%	-10.0%
10	1897	5p	(*)	0.0%	-16.7%	(*)	0.0%	-7.7%
11	1897	10p	(*)	0.0%	-16.7%	(*)	0.0%	-9.1%
12	1897	25p	(*)	0.0%	10.0%	(*)	0.0%	-8.3%
13	1900	50s	*	0.0%	16.7%	(*)	0.0%	-10.0%
14	1900	1y	(*)	0.0%	11.8%	(*)	0.0%	-6.7%
15	1900	3s	*	0.0%	47.1%	**	0.0%	57.1%

A Selection of Investment Grade Stamps
by Country - Korea

Korea Scott #	Issue Year	Value	Rating Mint	5 Year Mint Appreciation %	25 Year Mint Appreciation %	Rating Used	5 Year Used Appreciation %	25 Year Used Appreciation %
6	1895	5p	**	9.1%	66.7%	*	0.0%	33.3%
6a	1895	5p	*****	0.0%	200.0%	***	0.0%	83.3%
6b	1895	5p	*****	0.0%	750.0%			
6c	1895	5p	*****	0.0%	750.0%			
6d	1895	5p	*****	0.0%	672.7%			
6e	1895	5p	*****	0.0%	672.7%			
7	1895	10p	*****	-26.7%	478.9%	****	-6.3%	212.5%
7a	1895	10p	*****	0.0%	750.0%			
7b	1895	10p	*****	0.0%	962.5%			
8	1895	25p	*****	3.7%	133.3%	**	0.0%	57.9%
8a	1895	25p	*****	0.0%	476.9%	*****	0.0%	476.9%
8b	1895	25p	*****	0.0%	525.0%	*****	0.0%	525.0%
9a	1895	50p	*****	0.0%	471.4%	*****	0.0%	471.4%
9b	1895	50p	*****	0.0%	900.0%	*****	0.0%	900.0%
9c	1895	50p	*****	0.0%	900.0%	*****	0.0%	900.0%
9d	1895	50p	*****	0.0%	275.0%	*****	0.0%	185.7%
10	1900	15s	*	-12.5%	34.6%	*****	250.0%	250.0%
10a	1897	5p	*	0.0%	33.3%	*	0.0%	20.0%
10b	1897	5p	*	6.7%	28.0%	*	6.7%	28.0%
10c	1897	5p	*	0.0%	36.4%	*	0.0%	18.2%
10d	1897	5p	*	0.0%	36.4%	*	0.0%	18.2%
10f	1897	5p	(*)	0.0%	12.0%	(*)	0.0%	12.0%
10g	1897	5p	(*)	0.0%	6.7%	(*)	0.0%	6.7%
10h	1897	5p	(*)	0.0%	5.9%	(*)	0.0%	5.9%
10i	1897	5p	(*)	0.0%	10.0%			
11	1900	20s	*	4.5%	15.0%	*****	333.3%	333.3%
11a	1897	10p	**	0.0%	50.0%	**	0.0%	50.0%
11b	1897	10p	**	0.0%	50.0%	**	0.0%	50.0%
11c	1897	10p	*	0.0%	36.4%	*	0.0%	36.4%

A Selection of Investment Grade Stamps
by Country - Korea

Korea Scott #	Issue Year	Value	Rating Mint	5 Year Mint Appreciation %	25 Year Mint Appreciation %	Rating Used	5 Year Used Appreciation %	25 Year Used Appreciation %
11d	1897	10p	*	0.0%	40.0%	*	0.0%	40.0%
11e	1897	10p	*	0.0%	27.3%	*	0.0%	27.3%
11f	1897	10p	*	0.0%	28.6%			
12	1900	25s	*	8.3%	44.4%	*****	282.4%	282.4%
12a	1897	25p	*	0.0%	20.0%	*	0.0%	20.0%
12b	1897	25p	*	0.0%	20.0%	*	0.0%	20.0%
12c	1897	25p	*	0.0%	36.4%	*	0.0%	36.4%
12e	1897	25p	(*)	0.0%	12.5%	(*)	0.0%	12.5%
12f	1897	25p	(*)	0.0%	11.1%	(*)	0.0%	11.1%
12g	1897	25p	(*)	0.0%	13.3%	(*)	0.0%	13.3%
13	1897	50p	*	-17.5%	26.9%	*****	316.7%	316.7%
13F	1900	5p	****	25.0%	100.0%			
13G	1900	10p	*****	62.5%	160.0%			
13Gh	1900	10p	**	0.0%	50.0%			
13a	1897	50p	*	0.0%	20.0%	(*)	0.0%	10.0%
13b	1897	50p	*	0.0%	20.0%	(*)	0.0%	10.0%
13c	1897	50p	*	0.0%	33.3%	*	0.0%	22.2%
13e	1897	50p	(*)	0.0%	0.0%	(*)	0.0%	0.0%
14	1900	25p	****	106.3%	230.0%	****	100.0%	100.0%
14a	1900	25p	**	0.0%	63.6%			
14b	1900	25p	**	0.0%	63.6%			
14c	1900	25p	**	0.0%	63.6%			
15	1900	50p	*****	62.5%	160.0%			
15B	1900	1ch/5p	*****	71.4%	200.0%	*****	233.3%	400.0%
15a	1900	50p	**	0.0%	63.6%			
16	1900	1ch/25p	*****	160.0%	225.0%	*	8.3%	18.2%
16A	1900	1ch/5p	(*)	-2.5%	8.3%			
16Ab	1900	1ch/5p	*	5.0%	16.7%			
17C	1900	1ch/25p	****	-3.2%	114.3%	*****	271.4%	306.3%

A Selection of Investment Grade Stamps
by Country - Korea

Korea Scott #	Issue Year	Value	Rating Mint	5 Year Mint Appreciation %	25 Year Mint Appreciation %	Rating Used	5 Year Used Appreciation %	25 Year Used Appreciation %
17a	1900	1ch/25p	**	0.0%	53.8%			
17b	1900	1ch/25p	**	0.0%	63.6%	*	0.0%	27.3%
20	1900	2ch	*****	0.0%	150.0%	*****	0.0%	221.4%
20a	1900	2ch	*****	0.0%	383.3%			
21a	1900	3ch	*****	0.0%	135.3%	*****	0.0%	135.3%
22	1900	4ch	(*)	-15.0%	4.6%			
22a	1900	4ch	(*)	0.0%	12.5%			
23	1900	5ch	***	-15.4%	83.3%			
23a	1900	5ch	*****	0.0%	128.6%			
24	1900	6ch	****	-15.0%	112.5%			
24a	1900	6ch	*****	0.0%	150.0%			
25	1901	10ch	**	-15.8%	77.8%			
26	1900	15ch	*****	-13.8%	212.5%	*****	-11.1%	433.3%
26a	1900	15ch	*	0.0%	18.5%	*	0.0%	40.0%
27	1900	20ch	*****	-21.4%	358.3%	*****	10.5%	483.3%
27a	1900	20ch	*	0.0%	21.6%	**	0.0%	50.0%
31	1901	50ch	*****	-16.7%	150.0%	*****	-20.8%	245.5%
32	1901	1wn	***	-12.5%	75.0%	*****	8.3%	160.0%
33	1901	2wn	*	-13.3%	44.4%	*****	-7.7%	328.6%
35b	1902	1ch/25p	*****	0.0%	243.8%			
35c	1902	1ch/25p	***	0.0%	80.0%			
35d	1902	1ch/25p	*****	0.0%	450.0%			
36	1902	2ch/25p	**	12.1%	62.5%			
36E	1902	2ch/25p	(*)	0.0%	6.1%	*	0.0%	40.0%
36b	1902	2ch/25p	**	0.0%	66.7%			
36d	1902	2ch/25p	(*)	0.0%	0.0%	*	0.0%	28.6%
36f	1902	2ch/25p	(*)	0.0%	0.0%	*	0.0%	16.7%
37b	1902	3ch/50p	****	0.0%	100.0%	*	0.0%	18.8%
37g	1902	3ch/50p				*****	0.0%	380.0%

A Selection of Investment Grade Stamps
by Country - Mexico

Mexico Scott #	Issue Year	Value	Rating Mint	5 Year Mint Appreciation %	25 Year Mint Appreciation %	Rating Used	5 Year Used Appreciation %	25 Year Used Appreciation %
1	1856	.5r	*	0.0%	42.9%	*****	0.0%	157.1%
1b	1856	.5r	*****	0.0%	125.0%	*****	11.1%	127.3%
1c	1856	1/2r				*	0.0%	20.0%
2	1856	1r	**	0.0%	71.4%			
2b	1856	1r				****	0.0%	100.0%
2c	1856	1r	*****	0.0%	150.0%	*****	0.0%	150.0%
3a	1856	2r	***	0.0%	96.4%	***	12.5%	80.0%
3b	1856	2r	*	0.0%	42.9%	*	10.0%	37.5%
3c	1856	2r				**	0.0%	50.0%
3d	1856	2r	*****	0.0%	900.0%	*****	0.0%	221.4%
4	1856	4r	*	0.0%	59.1%	***	0.0%	83.3%
4a	1856	4r				***	0.0%	78.6%
4b	1856	4r				*****	0.0%	180.0%
4c	1856	4r	**	0.0%	55.6%	*	0.0%	33.3%
4d	1856	4r				**	0.0%	71.4%
5	1856	8r	***	0.0%	75.0%	**	0.0%	53.8%
5a	1856	8r	**	0.0%	50.0%	**	0.0%	53.8%
5b	1856	8r	***	0.0%	87.5%	**	0.0%	50.0%
5c	1856	8r				*****	0.0%	600.0%
5d	1856	8r				*	0.0%	40.6%
5e	1856	8r				*****	0.0%	260.0%
6	1861	1/2r	*	0.0%	42.9%	*****	0.0%	125.0%
6a	1861	1/2r	**	0.0%	70.0%	*****	0.0%	127.3%
7a	1861	1r				****	66.7%	114.3%
7f	1861	1r				*	0.0%	20.0%
8a	1861	2r	*****	0.0%	400.0%			
8b	1861	2r				*****	0.0%	150.0%
8d	1861	2r				(*)	0.0%	12.5%

A Selection of Investment Grade Stamps
by Country - Mexico

Mexico Scott #	Issue Year	Value	Rating Mint	5 Year Mint Appreciation %	25 Year Mint Appreciation %	Rating Used	5 Year Used Appreciation %	25 Year Used Appreciation %
8e	1861	2r				(*)	0.0%	0.0%
9	1861	4r	****	0.0%	100.0%	*****	0.0%	150.0%
9a	1861	4r				(*)	0.0%	8.6%
9b	1861	4r	*	0.0%	42.9%	***	0.0%	81.8%
9c	1861	4r				*****	0.0%	154.5%
9d	1861	4r				*****	0.0%	1300.0%
10	1861	4r	*	0.0%	42.9%	**	14.3%	60.0%
10a	1861	4r				****	0.0%	111.1%
10b	1861	4r	*	0.0%	37.5%	*	0.0%	40.0%
10c	1861	4r				*****	0.0%	500.0%
10d	1861	4r				*****	0.0%	1900.0%
11	1861	8r	**	0.0%	50.0%	**	0.0%	66.7%
11b	1861	8r				**	0.0%	66.7%
11c	1861	8r				*****	-90.1%	172.7%
11d	1861	8r	*	0.0%	46.7%	**	0.0%	50.0%
11e	1861	8r				*****	0.0%	1400.0%
12	1861	8r	*	0.0%	42.9%	**	0.0%	71.4%
12b	1861	8r	**	0.0%	50.0%	**	0.0%	60.0%
12d	1861	8r	*****	0.0%	900.0%	*****	0.0%	900.0%
14	1864	1r	**	0.0%	50.0%	*****	0.0%	200.0%
15	1864	2r	****	0.0%	144.4%	****	0.0%	118.8%
16	1864	4r	*	0.0%	25.0%	*	0.0%	37.1%
17	1864	1p	*	0.0%	30.0%	(*)	0.0%	0.0%
18	1864	3c	*	0.0%	30.0%	**	30.0%	71.1%
18a	1864	3c	*	0.0%	27.3%			
18b	1864	3c	*	0.0%	28.6%	(*)	0.0%	9.1%
19	1864	1/2r	*	0.0%	33.3%	*	0.0%	19.0%
19a	1864	1/2r	*	0.0%	46.7%	*****	0.0%	125.0%

A Selection of Investment Grade Stamps
by Country - Mexico

Mexico Scott #	Issue Year	Value	Rating Mint	5 Year Mint Appreciation %	25 Year Mint Appreciation %	Rating Used	5 Year Used Appreciation %	25 Year Used Appreciation %
19b	1864	1/2r	*	0.0%	42.9%	***	0.0%	85.7%
20	1864	1/2r	(*)	0.0%	9.1%	*	0.0%	22.2%
20a	1864	1/2r	*****	0.0%	133.3%	*	0.0%	36.4%
20c	1864	1/2r				(*)	0.0%	0.0%
20d	1866	1/2r	(*)	0.0%	7.7%	*	0.0%	23.1%
21a	1864	1r	*****	0.0%	300.0%	*****	0.0%	233.3%
21c	1864	1r				*****	233.3%	233.3%
22	1864	1r	*	0.0%	20.0%	(*)	0.0%	9.1%
22a	1864	1r	*	0.0%	20.0%	(*)	0.0%	14.3%
22b	1864	1r	*	0.0%	23.1%	*	0.0%	25.0%
22c	1864	1r				*****	0.0%	141.7%
23b	1864	2r	*	0.0%	25.0%			
23c	1864	2r	*	0.0%	16.7%	*	0.0%	30.0%
23e	1864	2r				*****	0.0%	500.0%
24	1864	4r	*	0.0%	17.6%	(*)	0.0%	0.0%
24a	1864	4r	*	0.0%	33.3%	*	0.0%	29.2%
24b	1864	4r	*	0.0%	35.7%	*****	0.0%	1260.0%
24d	1864	4r				(*)	0.0%	3.7%
25	1864	8r	*	0.0%	20.0%	*	0.0%	20.0%
25a	1864	8r	*	0.0%	16.7%	***	0.0%	78.6%
25b	1864	8r	*	0.0%	33.3%	**	0.0%	52.2%
25c	1864	8r	*	0.0%	33.3%	*****	0.0%	130.0%
25f	1864	8r				*****	0.0%	400.0%
26	1866	7c	*	0.0%	30.0%	*	0.0%	31.6%
26a	1866	7c	*	0.0%	21.4%	*	0.0%	47.4%
27	1866	13c	***	0.0%	94.4%	***	0.0%	94.4%
27b	1866	13c	(*)	0.0%	11.1%	(*)	0.0%	11.1%

A Selection of Investment Grade Stamps
by Country - Mexico

Mexico Scott #	Issue Year	Value	Rating Mint	5 Year Mint Appreciation %	25 Year Mint Appreciation %	Rating Used	5 Year Used Appreciation %	25 Year Used Appreciation %
29a	1866	25c	*	0.0%	33.3%	*****	0.0%	150.0%
29b	1866	25c	*****	0.0%	142.9%	***	0.0%	90.0%
29c	1866	25c	****	0.0%	120.0%	*****	0.0%	183.3%
30	1866	50c	*	0.0%	38.9%	**	0.0%	66.7%
34	1866	50c	*	0.0%	27.3%	*	0.0%	27.3%
35	1867	1/2r	****	0.0%	108.3%	*****	25.0%	233.3%
36	1867	1r	**	0.0%	50.0%	**	0.0%	66.7%
37a	1867	2r				*	0.0%	40.0%
38	1867	4r	*****	0.0%	150.0%	*****	0.0%	257.1%
38a	1867	4r				*	0.0%	16.7%
39	1867	4r	**	0.0%	50.0%	*****	0.0%	170.8%
40	1867	8r	*****	0.0%	218.2%	*	0.0%	37.5%
41	1867	8r				****	0.0%	100.0%
42	1867	1/2r	*	0.0%	37.5%	*	0.0%	26.7%
42a	1867	1/2r	(*)	0.0%	9.4%	(*)	0.0%	9.4%
43	1867	1r	(*)	0.0%	14.3%	(*)	0.0%	8.3%
43b ?	1867	1r	(*)	0.0%	0.0%	***	0.0%	78.6%
44	1867	2r	*****	0.0%	185.7%	*****	0.0%	328.6%
44a	1867	2r	*****			*****	0.0%	288.9%
44b	1867	2r	*****	0.0%	300.0%	*****	0.0%	150.0%
45	1867	4r	*****	0.0%	150.0%	*	0.0%	36.4%
46	1868	6c	*	0.0%	45.5%	*	0.0%	42.9%
47	1868	12c	***	0.0%	80.0%	**	0.0%	66.7%
47a	1868	12c				*	0.0%	37.5%
48	1868	25c	**	0.0%	66.7%	****	0.0%	100.0%
48a	1868	25c	*	0.0%	25.0%			
49	1868	50c	****	0.0%	118.2%	**	0.0%	50.0%
50	1868	100c	*****	0.0%	158.3%	**	0.0%	55.6%
51	1868	100c	****	0.0%	118.8%	***	0.0%	88.7%

A Selection of Investment Grade Stamps
by Country - New Zealand

New Zealand Scott #	Issue Year	Value	Rating Mint	5 Year Mint Appreciation %	25 Year Mint Appreciation %	Rating Used	5 Year Used Appreciation %	25 Year Used Appreciation %
1	1855	1p	*****	13.3%	277.8%	*****	-7.0%	233.3%
2	1855	2p	*****	0.0%	433.3%	***	0.0%	87.5%
3	1855	1sh	*****	4.8%	266.7%	**	0.0%	50.0%
3a	1855	1sh				*****	0.0%	150.0%
4	1855	1p	*****	7.7%	300.0%	*****	2.3%	300.0%
5	1856	2p	****	23.1%	100.0%	***	0.0%	85.7%
6	1858	1sh	*****	11.1%	455.6%	*****	-10.5%	325.0%
6a	1858	1sh				*****	0.0%	132.0%
7	1858	1p	*****	14.3%	788.9%	*****	0.0%	400.0%
7a	1859	1p				*****	0.0%	200.0%
7b	1859	1p				**	0.0%	57.1%
7c	1859	1p	***	0.0%	77.3%	****	0.0%	120.0%
8	1858	2p	*****	0.0%	188.9%	****	0.0%	100.0%
8a	1859	2p				*****	0.0%	153.3%
8b	1859	2p				****	0.0%	105.0%
8c	1859	2p	*	0.0%	26.9%	*****	0.0%	133.3%
8d	1862	2p	*****	0.0%	135.7%	***	0.0%	90.0%
9	1859	6p	*****	0.0%	566.7%	***	0.0%	97.0%
9a	1859	6p				***	0.0%	84.0%
9b	1859	6p				***	0.0%	90.0%
9c	1859	6p	***	0.0%	82.4%	****	0.0%	100.0%
9d	1862	6p				*	0.0%	16.7%
9e	1859	6p	*****	0.0%	355.6%	*****	0.0%	144.4%
9f	1859	6p	*****	0.0%	300.0%	****	0.0%	109.7%
10	1861	1sh	*****	0.0%	236.4%	*****	0.0%	185.7%
10a	1859	1sh				*	0.0%	37.5%
10b	1859	1sh				*****	0.0%	211.1%
10c	1859	1sh				*	0.0%	31.3%
10e	1861	1sh	*****	0.0%	300.0%	****	0.0%	116.2%

A Selection of Investment Grade Stamps
by Country - New Zealand

New Zealand Scott #	Issue Year	Value	Rating Mint	5 Year Mint Appreciation %	25 Year Mint Appreciation %	Rating Used	5 Year Used Appreciation %	25 Year Used Appreciation %
11	1862	1p	*****	-4.5%	320.0%	*****	-8.3%	197.3%
11b	1862	1p				****	-4.0%	108.7%
11c	1862	1p	*****	-5.0%	137.5%	*****	-2.9%	161.5%
11d	1863	1p	***	-5.0%	90.0%	*****	-7.7%	224.3%
11e	1862	1p	*****	3.2%	220.0%	*****	-8.3%	197.3%
12	1862	2p	*****	-5.0%	280.0%	****	-4.8%	100.0%
12b	1862	2p				(*)	0.0%	13.0%
12c	1862	2p	*****	-1.3%	167.9%	**	-4.8%	66.7%
12d	1862	2p	**	-4.8%	60.0%	(*)	-7.0%	-7.0%
13	1863	3p	*****	0.0%	192.3%	*****	0.0%	150.0%
13b	1862	3p				*	0.0%	21.9%
13c	1862	3p	*****	0.0%	204.0%	*****	0.0%	250.0%
14	1863	6p	*****	-2.9%	518.2%	***	-8.0%	91.7%
14a	1862	6p				*****	0.0%	125.0%
14b	1862	6p				(*)	0.0%	0.0%
14c	1862	6p	*****	0.0%	180.0%	****	0.0%	120.0%
14d	1862	6p	*****	0.0%	281.8%	**	-7.1%	52.9%
14e	1862	6p	*****	-4.5%	265.2%	*	-3.8%	38.9%
15	1862	1sh	*****	-9.1%	400.0%	*****	-3.8%	240.9%
15b	1862	1sh				***	-5.3%	80.0%
15c	1862	1sh	****	0.0%	100.0%	*****	0.0%	166.7%
15d	1862	1sh	*****	-5.2%	400.0%	*****	58.5%	333.3%
16	1863	1p	*****	-16.7%	400.0%	*****	-3.4%	335.9%
17	1863	2p	*****	-16.7%	1011.1%	*****	-10.0%	1284.6%
18	1863	3p	*****	18.2%	550.0%	*****	-4.5%	483.3%
19	1863	6p	*****	0.0%	361.5%	*****	-7.7%	220.0%
20	1863	1sh	*****	-5.0%	776.9%	*****	-6.3%	316.7%
21	1862	1p	*****	25.0%	252.9%	*****	0.0%	150.0%
21a	1863	1p	****	-6.3%	100.0%	(*)	-6.7%	-6.7%

A Selection of Investment Grade Stamps
by Country - New Zealand

New Zealand Scott #	Issue Year	Value	Rating Mint	5 Year Mint Appreciation %	25 Year Mint Appreciation %	Rating Used	5 Year Used Appreciation %	25 Year Used Appreciation %
21b	1862	1p				****	0.0%	136.4%
22	1862	2p	****	-4.5%	110.0%	*****	-9.1%	150.0%
22a	1863	2p	*****	-2.7%	157.1%	*****	-6.4%	175.0%
22ab	1863	2p	*****	-3.0%	128.6%	*****	-6.4%	175.0%
22c	1862	2p	*****	16.7%	180.0%	*****	-9.1%	150.0%
24	1862	6p	*****	-5.7%	230.0%	*****	-11.1%	175.9%
24a	1863	6p	*****	-3.0%	166.7%	***	-11.1%	77.8%
24b	1862	6p	****	6.3%	112.5%	****	-4.5%	110.0%
24c	1862	6p				***	0.0%	92.3%
25	1862	1sh	*****	0.0%	215.8%	*****	0.0%	212.5%
25a	1863	1sh	*****	-6.7%	211.1%	****	-6.7%	110.0%
25b	1862	1sh	*****	-3.3%	205.3%	*****	0.0%	212.5%
25c	1862	1sh	*****	-6.3%	252.9%	*****	25.0%	150.0%
26	1863	2p	*****	0.0%	150.0%	*****	-18.2%	227.3%
26a	1863	2p	**	-7.0%	60.0%	*****	4.5%	318.2%

A Selection of Investment Grade Stamps
by Country - Nigeria

Nigeria Scott #	Issue Year	Value	Rating Mint	5 Year Mint Appreciation %	25 Year Mint Appreciation %	Rating Used	5 Year Used Appreciation %	25 Year Used Appreciation %
8b	1914	1sh	*****	100.0%	605.9%	*****	50.0%	566.7%
8c	1920	1sh				*****	10.5%	556.3%
10	1914	5sh				*****	0.0%	575.7%
11	1914	10sh	*****	20.8%	141.7%	****	5.3%	100.0%
11a	1914	10sh	*	0.0%	33.3%	*****	13.6%	177.8%
11b	1914	10sh	**	20.0%	60.0%	***	8.8%	76.2%
11c	1914	10sh	*****	6.7%	255.6%	*****	25.0%	257.1%
12	1914	1L	*	0.0%	35.7%	*	15.6%	48.6%
12a	1927	1L	**	22.2%	57.1%	***	7.7%	75.0%
16	1914	5sh	***	16.7%	75.0%	*****	0.0%	243.8%
17	1914	10sh	*	0.0%	25.0%	*****	5.9%	200.0%
28a	1921	6p	*****	0.0%	522.2%	*****	23.1%	2062.2%
30	1921	2sh6p	**	0.0%	61.1%			
30a	1932	2sh6p	*****	11.1%	177.8%	*****	0.0%	372.2%
31	1926	5sh	(*)	0.0%	6.7%	*****	6.7%	255.6%
31a	1932	5sh	****	3.4%	100.0%	*****	0.0%	455.6%
32	1921	10sh	**	0.0%	68.8%	*****	0.0%	350.0%
32a	1932	10sh	***	8.3%	92.6%	*****	0.0%	300.0%
37	1935	1sh	*****	3.8%	350.0%	*****	26.7%	850.0%
40a	1936	1.5p	*****	6.3%	507.1%			
42a	1936	3p	*****	7.1%	361.5%	**	0.0%	66.7%
46	1936	2sh6p	*	45.5%	23.1%	*****	45.5%	515.4%
47	1936	5sh	**	37.5%	83.3%	***	26.3%	300.0%
48	1936	10sh	*****	20.0%	200.0%	*****	27.3%	300.0%
49	1936	1L	***	30.0%	85.7%	*****	17.6%	142.4%
59	1938	4p	***	-18.8%	85.7%			
63c	1938	2sh6p	*****	-11.8%	240.9%			
64c	1842	5sh	*****	-10.0%	200.0%			

A Selection of Investment Grade Stamps
by Country - Norway

Norway Scott #	Issue Year	Value	Rating Mint	5 Year Mint Appreciation %	25 Year Mint Appreciation %	Rating Used	5 Year Used Appreciation %	25 Year Used Appreciation %
1	1855	4s	(*)	0.0%	-5.6%	***	0.0%	75.0%
1a	1855	4s				*	0.0%	20.0%
2	1857	2s	***	0.0%	77.8%	*	0.0%	28.0%
3	1857	3s	****	0.0%	100.0%	***	0.0%	84.6%
4	1856	4s	*****	0.0%	200.0%			
4a	1856	4s				(*)	0.0%	11.1%
5	1856	8s	***	0.0%	81.3%	*****	15.4%	172.7%
6	1865	2s	****	0.0%	177.8%	****	0.0%	100.0%
7	1866	3s	**	0.0%	70.0%	***	0.0%	84.6%
8	1863	4s	*****	0.0%	323.1%	*****	0.0%	200.0%
9	1863	8s	****	0.0%	108.7%	*****	0.0%	146.2%
10	1863	24s	*	0.0%	37.5%	*	0.0%	23.8%
11	1868	1s	*	0.0%	33.3%	****	0.0%	100.0%
12	1867	2s	***	0.0%	75.0%	*****	0.0%	266.7%
13	1868	3s	*****	0.0%	140.0%	*****	0.0%	146.2%
14	1867	4s	*****	0.0%	288.9%			
15	1867	8s	***	0.0%	87.5%	*****	0.0%	133.3%
15a	1867	8s	*****	0.0%	153.3%	***	0.0%	83.3%
16	1875	1s				*****	0.0%	156.4%
16a	1873	1s	*****	0.0%	177.8%	****	0.0%	122.2%
16b	1872	1s	(*)	0.0%	11.1%	*****	-50.0%	172.7%
17	1874	2s				*****	0.0%	185.7%
17a	1874	2s	*****	0.0%	353.3%	**	0.0%	66.7%
17b	1872	2s				***	0.0%	87.5%
18	1872	3s	****	0.0%	112.5%	*****	0.0%	600.0%
18a	1872	3s	*****	0.0%	137.5%	*****	0.0%	220.0%
18b	1872	3s	*****	0.0%	260.0%	*****	0.0%	212.5%
19	1873	4s				****	0.0%	114.3%
19a	1873	4s	***	0.0%	86.7%	**	0.0%	60.0%

A Selection of Investment Grade Stamps
by Country - Norway

Norway Scott #	Issue Year	Value	Rating Mint	5 Year Mint Appreciation %	25 Year Mint Appreciation %	Rating Used	5 Year Used Appreciation %	25 Year Used Appreciation %
19b	1872	4s	***	0.0%	86.7%	****	0.0%	100.0%
20	1875	6s	***	0.0%	80.0%	*****	0.0%	200.0%
21	1873	7s	*****	0.0%	150.0%	****	0.0%	116.7%
23	1877	3o	***	0.0%	78.6%	*****	0.0%	157.1%
24	1877	5o	*	0.0%	33.3%	*****	0.0%	300.0%
24a	1877	5o	*****	0.0%	1233.3%	*****	0.0%	1685.7%
24b	1877	5o	*****	0.0%	233.3%	*****	0.0%	400.0%
24c	1877	5o	*	0.0%	15.0%	*****	0.0%	150.0%
24d	1877	5o	*****	0.0%	263.6%	*****	0.0%	212.5%
24e	1877	5o	*****	0.0%	164.7%	*****	0.0%	129.2%
25	1877	10o	*****	0.0%	140.0%			
25b	1877	10o	*****	0.0%	140.0%			
26	1877	12o	***	0.0%	76.5%	*****	0.0%	130.8%
27	1877	20o	***	0.0%	95.7%			
28	1877	25o	*****	0.0%	140.0%	**	0.0%	57.9%
29	1877	35o	***	0.0%	87.5%			
29a	1878	35o	*****	0.0%	150.0%	**	0.0%	57.1%
30	1877	50o	***	0.0%	85.7%			
31	1878	60o	****	0.0%	115.4%			
32	1878	1k	****	0.0%	100.0%			
33	1878	1.50k	**	0.0%	66.7%	**	0.0%	66.7%
34	1878	2k	**	0.0%	57.1%	*	0.0%	25.0%
35	1886	1o	**	0.0%	56.3%	****	0.0%	114.3%
35a	1882	1o	(*)	0.0%	9.1%	(*)	0.0%	9.1%
35b	1882	1o	(*)	0.0%	9.1%	(*)	0.0%	9.1%
38	1883	3o	****	0.0%	110.5%	****		
38a	1883	3o	*****	0.0%	531.6%	*****	0.0%	809.1%
38b	1889	3o				*****	0.0%	166.7%
39	1889	5o	*****	0.0%	137.5%			
39a	1889	5o	****	0.0%	118.2%			

StampFinder

A Selection of Investment Grade Stamps
by Country - Norway

Norway Scott #	Issue Year	Value	Rating Mint	5 Year Mint Appreciation %	25 Year Mint Appreciation %	Rating Used	5 Year Used Appreciation %	25 Year Used Appreciation %
39b	1888	5o	****	0.0%	100.0%			
39c	1891	5o	*****	0.0%	185.7%			
39d	1892	5o				**	0.0%	50.0%
40	1882	10o	****	0.0%	100.0%			
40a	1886	10o	*****	0.0%	128.6%			
40b	1886	10o	**	0.0%	68.4%			
40c	1882	10o	*****	0.0%	200.0%	*****	0.0%	175.0%
41	1884	12o	*	0.0%	20.0%	**	0.0%	66.7%
42	1884	12o	****	0.0%	100.0%	*****	0.0%	169.2%
42a	1883	12o	*****	0.0%	185.7%	*****	0.0%	133.3%
43	1882	20o	*****	0.0%	166.7%	*****	0.0%	177.8%
44	1886	20o	*****	0.0%	163.2%			
44a	1883	20o	*****	0.0%	376.2%	*****	0.0%	284.6%
44b	1885	20o	*****	0.0%	133.3%	*****	0.0%	150.0%
44c	1882	20o	*****	0.0%	127.3%	*****	0.0%	172.7%
45	1884	25o	****	0.0%	100.0%	*****	0.0%	233.3%
47a	1899	1o	*****	0.0%	138.1%	******	0.0%	328.6%
52	1908	15o	**	0.0%	52.9%			
53a	1895	20o	*	0.0%	46.7%			
54	1901	25o	**	0.0%	61.9%			
54a	1898	25o	***	0.0%	86.7%	*****	0.0%	175.0%
55	1907	30o	*	0.0%	44.4%			
56a	1895	35o	*	0.0%	33.3%	**	0.0%	50.0%
57	1801	50o	**	0.0%	50.0%			
57a	1897	50o	*****	0.0%	204.3%	***	0.0%	92.3%
58	1900	60o	*	0.0%	41.7%			
59	1905	1k/2s	**	0.0%	64.3%	***	0.0%	92.3%
60	1905	1.50k/2s	**	0.0%	60.0%	*	0.0%	36.0%
61	1905	2k/2s	**	0.0%	69.2%	****	0.0%	110.5%

A Selection of Investment Grade Stamps
by Country - Philippines

Philippines Scott #	Issue Year	Value	Rating Mint	5 Year Mint Appreciation %	25 Year Mint Appreciation %	Rating Used	5 Year Used Appreciation %	25 Year Used Appreciation %
1	1854	5c	*****	-11.1%	300.0%	*****	0.0%	133.3%
2	1854	10c	*****	-17.6%	133.3%	*****	0.0%	127.3%
4	1854	1r	*****	11.1%	233.3%	****	0.0%	114.3%
4a	1854	1r	****	0.0%	113.3%	**	0.0%	57.9%
4c	1854	1r	***	0.0%	80.0%	*****	0.0%	400.0%
5	1854	2r	*****	29.0%	150.0%	****	0.0%	100.0%
6	1855	5c	*	6.7%	33.3%	***	0.0%	81.8%
7	1855	5c	(*)	-17.6%	-12.5%	*	0.0%	29.4%
10b	1859	5c	*	0.0%	30.0%			
11	1859	10c				*****	27.3%	483.3%
12	1861	5c	*****	6.7%	166.7%	*****	-5.9%	416.1%
13	1862	5c	*****	0.0%	850.0%	*****	0.0%	985.7%
15	1863	10c	*****	0.0%	150.0%	*****	0.0%	1685.7%
16	1863	1r	*****	0.0%	183.3%	*****	0.0%	1614.3%
17	1863	2r	*****	0.0%	225.0%	*****	100.0%	1233.3%
18	1863	1r	*****	25.0%	488.2%	****	0.0%	115.4%
20	1863	1r	*****	0.0%	321.1%	*****	0.0%	140.0%
25	1874	1r	*	16.7%	47.4%	*	0.0%	31.3%
25A	1874	2r	****	79.5%	100.0%	*****	-12.5%	803.2%
26	1873	1r	**	0.0%	50.0%	*	0.0%	45.5%
27	1873	2r	*****	0.0%	132.1%	*****	0.0%	350.0%
28	1874	10c	**	0.0%	60.0%	*	0.0%	28.6%
29	1873	5c	*****	0.0%	316.7%	*****	0.0%	483.3%
30	1872	5c	*****	0.0%	155.6%	*	0.0%	40.0%
31	1872	1r	**	0.0%	55.6%	*****	0.0%	140.0%
32	1872	2r	*	-4.8%	25.0%	***	0.0%	88.9%
33	1871	1r	*****	0.0%	311.8%	*****	0.0%	466.7%
34	1871	1r	*****	0.0%	525.0%	*****	0.0%	900.0%
37	1868	12 4/8c	(*)	-11.3%	10.0%			

A Selection of Investment Grade Stamps
by Country - Philippines

Philippines Scott #	Issue Year	Value	Rating Mint	5 Year Mint Appreciation %	25 Year Mint Appreciation %	Rating Used	5 Year Used Appreciation %	25 Year Used Appreciation %
38	1868	25c	****	0.0%	114.8%			
39	1871	5c	*****	0.0%	375.0%			
41	1871	20c	*****	0.0%	340.0%	*****	0.0%	400.0%
42	1871	40c	*****	0.0%	385.7%	*****	0.0%	823.1%
44	1872	16c	*****	-5.0%	322.2%	*****	0.0%	212.5%
46	1872	62c	*****	0.0%	166.7%			
47	1872	1p25c	*****	0.0%	183.3%	*****	0.0%	431.3%
50	1874	62c	*****	0.0%	188.9%			
51	1874	1p25c	*****	0.0%	252.9%	*****	0.0%	450.0%
53	1877	2c	*****	0.0%	225.0%	*****	0.0%	135.3%
58	1876	25c	*****	0.0%	316.7%			
59	1877	12c	*****	0.0%	209.1%			
60	1879	12c/25m	*****	0.0%	200.0%	*****	0.0%	331.8%
61	1879	12c/25m	*****	0.0%	218.2%	*****	0.0%	190.3%
63	1879	25m	****	0.0%	107.7%	*****	0.0%	525.0%
64	1878	25m	*****	0.0%	183.3%			
66	1878	100m	*****	0.0%	144.4%	*****	0.0%	150.0%
69	1879	200m	*****	0.0%	212.5%			
70	1879	200m	*****	0.0%	191.7%	*****	0.0%	1400.0%
72	1879	2c/25m	****	0.0%	100.0%			
73	1879	8c/100m	***	0.0%	90.9%			
73a	1879	8c/100m	*****	0.0%	130.8%	*****	0.0%	146.2%
74	1879	2c/25m	*****	0.0%	361.5%	*****	0.0%	202.6%
75	1879	8c/100m	*****	33.3%	515.4%	*****	0.0%	202.6%
83	1880	8c	*****	0.0%	414.3%			
84	1880	10c	*****	-23.8%	128.6%	*****	-4.8%	400.0%
93	1883	1r/2c	*****	0.0%	484.6%	*****	0.0%	1705.6%
97	1883	1r/2c	*****	0.0%	192.3%	*****	50.0%	900.0%
112	1881	2c/10c	*****	0.0%	257.1%			

A Selection of Investment Grade Stamps
by Country - Philippines

Philippines Scott #	Issue Year	Value	Rating Mint	5 Year Mint Appreciation %	25 Year Mint Appreciation %	Rating Used	5 Year Used Appreciation %	25 Year Used Appreciation %
114	1881	24/8c /2r	*	0.0%	42.9%	*****	0.0%	133.3%
115	1881	8c/10c	*****	0.0%	221.4%	*****	0.0%	9130.8%
123	1881	2r/8c	****	0.0%	120.0%	*****	0.0%	250.0%
126	1883	1r/10p	*****	0.0%	216.7%			
127	1881	1r	*****	0.0%	438.5%	*****	0.0%	1300.0%
127A	1881	2r	*****	0.0%	542.9%	*****	0.0%	1337.5%
128	1883	1r/1p	*****	0.0%	757.1%	*****	0.0%	441.7%
129	1883	1r/200m	*****	380.0%	990.9%	*****	433.3%	2566.7%
139	1888	6c				*****	0.0%	3066.7%
172	1890	20c	(*)	0.0%	0.0%	*****	12.5%	275.0%
180	1897	80c	***	0.0%	81.8%	*****	0.0%	627.3%
187	1897	5c/5c	*****	0.0%	525.0%			
189	1897	20c/20c	*****	0.0%	169.2%			
190	1897	20c/25c	*****	0.0%	257.1%			
191	1897	15c/15c				*****	0.0%	1400.0%
195	1898	4m				*****	0.0%	6053.8%
200	1898	4c						
211	1898	2p	*****	-20.0%	400.0%			
212	1899	50c	(**)	0.0%	-20.0%	(*)	0.0%	0.0%
214b	1900	2c	(**)	-20.0%	-20.0%	*****	0.0%	233.3%
216a	1899	5c				**	0.0%	73.3%
217	1899	10c	****	0.0%	100.0%			
217A	1899	10c	(**)	0.0%	-37.5%	(*)	0.0%	10.0%
218	1899	15c	*	0.0%	33.3%			
219	1899	50c	(*)	0.0%	13.6%	*	0.0%	25.0%
219a	1899	50c	*	0.0%	25.0%			
220	1901	4c	****	0.0%	100.0%			
221	1901	6c	***	0.0%	77.8%			

A Selection of Investment Grade Stamps
by Country - Poland

Poland Scott #	Issue Year	Value	Rating Mint	5 Year Mint Appreciation %	25 Year Mint Appreciation %	Rating Used	5 Year Used Appreciation %	25 Year Used Appreciation %
1	1860	10k	*****	0.0%	405.3%	**	20.0%	71.4%
1a	1860	10k	*****	4.0%	300.0%	**	15.4%	50.0%
1b	1860	10k	*****	0.0%	361.5%	**	21.4%	70.0%
1c	1860	10k	*****	66.7%	925.6%	****	0.0%	100.0%
11a	1918	5f/2gr	*****	0.0%	433.3%	*****	0.0%	515.4%
13a	1918	25f/10gr	*****	0.0%	205.6%	*****	0.0%	243.8%
14a	1918	50f/20gr	*****	0.0%	169.2%	*****	0.0%	250.0%
15	1919	3pf	*****	0.0%	133.3%	*****	0.0%	161.9%
21a	1918	20pf	*****	0.0%	121.4%	*****	0.0%	542.9%
27a	1918	10h	*****	0.0%	357.1%	*****	0.0%	321.1%
28a	1918	20h	*****	0.0%	185.7%	*****	0.0%	163.2%
29a	1918	45h	*****	0.0%	185.7%	*****	0.0%	163.2%
30	1918	3hal/3h	*	-1.8%	35.0%	(*)	0.0%	5.3%
30a	1918	3hal/3h	*****	11.4%	1633.3%	*****	11.4%	1633.3%
30b	1918	3hal/3h	*	0.0%	66.7%	*	0.0%	31.0%
31a	1918	3hal/15h	(*)	0.0%	12.5%	**	0.0%	50.0%
32a	1918	10hal/30h	*	11.1%	25.0%	**	0.0%	50.0%
32b	1918	10hal/30h	*	0.0%	25.0%	*	0.0%	30.0%
34a	1918	25hal/40h	*	0.0%	25.0%	*	0.0%	41.7%
34b	1918	25hal/40h	*****	5.0%	250.0%	****	0.0%	205.6%
35a	1918	45hal/60h	**	20.0%	50.0%	*	0.0%	37.5%
36a	1918	45hal/80/h	*	0.0%	16.7%	*	0.0%	16.7%
37a	1918	50hal/60h	*****	5.0%	162.5%	***	0.0%	75.0%
39a	1918	50h	*****	0.0%	400.0%	*****	0.0%	400.0%
40a	1918	90h	*****	40.0%	600.0%	*****	0.0%	400.0%
41	1919	3h	*****	0.0%	185.7%	*****	11.1%	233.3%
42	1919	5h	*****	-12.0%	214.3%	*****	15.8%	266.7%
43	1919	6h	*****	0.0%	300.0%	*****	0.0%	333.3%

A Selection of Investment Grade Stamps
by Country - Poland

Poland Scott #	Issue Year	Value	Rating Mint	5 Year Mint Appreciation %	25 Year Mint Appreciation %	Rating Used	5 Year Used Appreciation %	25 Year Used Appreciation %
44	1919	10h	*****	0.0%	185.7%	*****	11.1%	212.5%
45	1919	12h	*****	7.1%	328.6%	*****	7.1%	435.7%
46	1919	40h	*****	0.0%	150.0%	*****	0.0%	127.3%
46a	1919	40h	*****	57.1%	450.0%			
46b	1919	40h	*****	25.0%	525.0%			
48a	1919	60h	*****	0.0%	250.0%	****		
49a	1919	80h	*****	8.3%	225.0%	*****	0.0%	233.3%
49b	1919	80h	*****	0.0%	1300.0%			
50	1919	90h	*****	25.0%	172.7%	*****	40.0%	194.7%
51	1919	1k	*****	-16.7%	257.1%	*****	-9.1%	400.0%
53	1919	3k	*****	0.0%	322.2%	*****	0.0%	337.5%
54	1919	4k	*****	0.0%	207.7%	*****	0.0%	191.7%
55	1919	10k	*****	16.7%	344.4%	*****	0.0%	261.1%
56	1919	15h	*****	3.7%	1066.7%	*****	85.7%	1200.0%
57	1919	20h	*****	0.0%	400.0%	*****	14.3%	190.9%
58	1919	25h	*****	5.3%	207.7%	*****	-15.8%	146.2%
59	1919	30h	*****	9.1%	380.0%	*****	14.3%	300.0%
60a	1919	25h/80h	*****	-6.3%	275.0%	*****	-6.7%	133.3%
78	1919	10pf/7.5pf	*****	-12.5%	180.0%	***	12.0%	75.0%
92	1919	5m	*	0.0%	16.7%	*****	0.0%	416.1%
134a	1919	15f	(*)	0.0%	0.0%			
153a	1921	3m/40f	*	0.0%	25.0%	*	0.0%	25.0%
158a	1921	4m	*****	0.0%	200.0%			
187	1923	80m						
188	1923	100m						
189	1923	200m				*****	-25.0%	1233.3%
190	1923	300m				*****	-25.0%	1100.0%
195a	1923	10000m/25m	**	66.7%	1900.0%			
195b	1923	10000m/25m	****	114.3%	900.0%			
196	1923	25000m/20m	*****	0.0%	13233.3%			
196b	1923	25000m/20m	*****	114.3%	650.0%			

A Selection of Investment Grade Stamps
by Country - Poland

Poland Scott #	Issue Year	Value	Rating Mint	5 Year Mint Appreciation %	25 Year Mint Appreciation %	Rating Used	5 Year Used Appreciation %	25 Year Used Appreciation %
197a	1923	50000m/10m	*****	66.7%	1900.0%			
197b	1923	50000m/10m	*****	114.3%	900.0%			
213	1924	1000000m				*****	-25.7%	845.5%
214	1924	2000000m						
222a	1924	25g	*****	0.0%	300.0%	*	0.0%	41.2%
223a	1924	30g	(*)	0.0%	0.0%			
251	1928	Sheet of 2	(*)	0.0%	11.1%	(*)	0.0%	8.3%
251a	1928	50g	(**)	0.0%	-75.0%	(**)	0.0%	-32.0%
251b	1928	1z	(**)	0.0%	-75.0%	(**)	0.0%	-32.0%
255a	1928	1z	(**)	60.0%	-38.5%			
275	1933	60g	(*)	27.3%	0.0%			
280	1934	20g	(*)	12.5%	-13.5%	***	0.0%	90.5%
281	1934	30g	*	8.3%	25.0%	****	0.0%	114.3%
B14	1921	20m+30m	**	44.4%	85.7%	*****	-14.3%	269.2%
B15	1925	1g	(**)	0.0%	-55.0%	*****	0.0%	169.2%
B16	1925	2g	(**)	0.0%	-55.0%	*****	0.0%	169.2%
B17	1925	3g	(**)	0.0%	-55.0%	*****	0.0%	169.2%
B18	1925	5g	(**)	0.0%	-55.0%	*****	0.0%	169.2%
B19	1925	10g	(**)	0.0%	-55.0%	*****	0.0%	169.2%
B20	1925	15g	(**)	0.0%	-55.0%	*****	0.0%	169.2%
B21	1925	20g	(**)	0.0%	-55.0%	*****	0.0%	169.2%
B22	1925	25g	(**)	0.0%	-55.0%	*****	0.0%	169.2%
B23	1925	30g	(**)	0.0%	-55.0%	*****	0.0%	169.2%
B24	1925	40g	****	0.0%	266.7%	*****	0.0%	169.2%
B25	1925	50g	(**)	0.0%	-55.0%	*****	0.0%	169.2%
B29	1938	Sheet of 4	(**)	0.0%	-27.6%	**	0.0%	60.0%
B31	1938	75g	(**)	0.0%	-27.3%	*	0.0%	30.0%
B35	1939	SS of 3	(**)	0.0%	-25.0%	*	30.0%	30.0%
J2	1919	10h	*****	0.0%	200.0%	*****	0.0%	385.7%
J3a	1919	15h	*****	0.0%	2233.3%			
J4	1919	20h	*****	0.0%	200.0%	*****	-81.4%	136.4%

A Selection of Investment Grade Stamps
by Country - Romania

Romania Scott #	Issue Year	Value	Rating Mint	5 Year Mint Appreciation %	25 Year Mint Appreciation %	Rating Used	5 Year Used Appreciation %	25 Year Used Appreciation %
1	1858	27pa	*****	0.0%	215.8%	*****	0.0%	400.0%
2	1858	54pa	*****	0.0%	269.0%	*****	0.0%	400.0%
3	1858	108pa	*****	0.0%	150.0%	*****	0.0%	255.6%
4	1858	81pa	*****	0.0%	138.1%	*****	0.0%	161.9%
5	1858	5pa	*	0.0%	30.4%	*****	0.0%	252.9%
6	1858	40pa	****	0.0%	120.0%	*****	0.0%	164.7%
6a	1858	40pa	*****	0.0%	100.0%	**	0.0%	51.4%
7	1858	80pa	(*)	0.0%	14.8%	*****	0.0%	191.7%
8	1859	5pa	***	0.0%	87.5%	*****	0.0%	135.3%
8b	1859	5pa	*****	0.0%	133.3%			
8c	1859	5pa	****	0.0%	100.0%			
9	1859	40pa	*****	0.0%	133.3%	*****	0.0%	245.5%
9b	1859	40pa	****	0.0%	116.7%	**	0.0%	50.0%
10	1859	80pa	*****	0.0%	156.8%	*****	0.0%	200.0%
10b	1859	80pa	***	0.0%	79.5%	(*)	0.0%	8.3%
11	1862	3pa	**	0.0%	50.0%	(*)	0.0%	0.0%
11a	1862	3pa	**	0.0%	50.0%	(*)	0.0%	0.0%
12	1862	6pa	***	0.0%	81.8%	*****	0.0%	163.9%
13	1862	6pa	***	0.0%	81.8%	*****	0.0%	163.9%
14	1862	30pa	***	0.0%	94.4%	***	0.0%	91.7%
14a	1862	30pa	*	0.0%	40.7%			
15	1862	3pa	*****	0.0%	183.3%	*****	0.0%	205.6%
15a	1862	3pa	*	0.0%	41.7%	*****	0.0%	205.6%
15b	1862	3pa	***	0.0%	75.0%	**	0.0%	60.0%
16	1862	6pa	*****	0.0%	295.8%	*****	0.0%	205.6%
16a	1862	6pa	*****	0.0%	189.5%			
17	1862	6pa	*****	0.0%	330.6%	*****	0.0%	309.1%
17a	1862	6pa	*****	0.0%	162.1%			
18	1862	30pa	****	0.0%	118.2%	*****	0.0%	364.3%

A Selection of Investment Grade Stamps
by Country - Romania

Romania Scott #	Issue Year	Value	Rating Mint	5 Year Mint Appreciation %	25 Year Mint Appreciation %	Rating Used	5 Year Used Appreciation %	25 Year Used Appreciation %
18a	1862	30pa	**	0.0%	66.7%			
19	1864	3pa	*****	0.0%	166.7%	*	0.0%	20.0%
19a	1864	3pa	*****	0.0%	268.4%			
19b	1864	3pa	*****	0.0%	150.0%			
20a	1864	6pa	*****	0.0%	275.0%			
20b	1864	6pa	*****	0.0%	677.8%			
21	1864	30pa				*****	0.0%	376.2%
21a	1864	30pa	*****	0.0%	283.3%			
21b	1864	30pa	*****	0.0%	666.7%			
21c	1864	30pa	****	0.0%	100.0%			
22	1865	2pa	*****	0.0%	180.0%	*****	0.0%	233.3%
22a	1865	2pa	*****	0.0%	269.0%	*****	0.0%	261.1%
22b	1865	2pa	*****	0.0%	333.3%	***	0.0%	97.0%
23	1865	5pa	*****	0.0%	520.7%	*****	0.0%	205.6%
24	1865	20pa	*****	0.0%	1066.7%	*****	0.0%	900.0%
24a	1865	20pa	*****	0.0%	191.7%			
25	1865	20pa	*****	0.0%	1066.7%	*****	0.0%	742.1%
25a	1865	20pa	*****	0.0%	191.7%			
26	1865	2pa	*****	0.0%	233.3%	*****	0.0%	358.3%
26a	1865	2pa	*****	0.0%	177.8%			
27	1865	5pa	*****	0.0%	192.3%	*****	0.0%	100.0%
29	1866	2pa	*****	0.0%	976.9%	*****	0.0%	352.4%
29a	1866	2pa	*****	0.0%	136.4%	*****	0.0%	142.4%
30	1866	5pa	*****	0.0%	252.9%	*****	0.0%	248.5%
30a	1866	5pa	**	0.0%	66.7%			
30b	1866	5pa	*****	0.0%	133.3%	*****	0.0%	150.0%
31	1866	20pa	*****	0.0%	650.0%	*****	0.0%	430.0%
31a	1866	20pa	(*)	0.0%	14.3%	*	0.0%	42.9%
31b	1866	20pa	*****	0.0%	133.3%	*****	0.0%	169.2%

A Selection of Investment Grade Stamps
by Country - Romania

Romania Scott #	Issue Year	Value	Rating Mint	5 Year Mint Appreciation %	25 Year Mint Appreciation %	Rating Used	5 Year Used Appreciation %	25 Year Used Appreciation %
31c	1866	20pa	*	0.0%	25.0%	*	0.0%	20.8%
32	1866	20pa	*****	0.0%	500.0%	*****	0.0%	360.9%
32a	1866	20pa	*****	0.0%	133.3%	*****	0.0%	150.0%
33	1868	2b	*****	0.0%	254.2%	*****	0.0%	471.4%
33a	1868	2b	***	0.0%	87.5%	*	0.0%	33.3%
34	1870	3b	*****	0.0%	203.6%	*****	0.0%	233.3%
35	1868	4b	**	0.0%	69.2%	*****	0.0%	179.4%
36	1868	18b	**	0.0%	60.7%	*****	0.0%	445.5%
36a	1868	18b	**	0.0%	60.7%	*****	0.0%	445.5%
37	1869	5b	****	0.0%	107.1%	*****	0.0%	226.9%
37a	1869	5b	***	0.0%	87.5%	*****	0.0%	226.9%
38	1869	10b	*****	0.0%	135.3%	*****	0.0%	400.0%
38a	1869	10b	***	0.0%	93.8%	*****	0.0%	320.0%
38b	1869	10b	**	0.0%	70.0%	*****	0.0%	128.6%
40	1869	15b	(*)	0.0%	0.0%	*****	0.0%	250.0%
41	1869	25b	***	0.0%	77.8%	*****	0.0%	221.2%
42	1869	50b	(*)	0.0%	7.1%	*****	0.0%	337.5%
42a	1869	50b	(*)	0.0%	-5.4%	*****	0.0%	358.3%
43	1871	5b	**	0.0%	54.5%	(**)	0.0%	-46.2%
43a	1871	5b	**	0.0%	50.0%	*****	0.0%	480.6%
44	1871	10b	*	0.0%	37.5%	*****	0.0%	191.7%
44a	1871	10b	**	0.0%	63.6%	***	0.0%	80.0%
45	1871	10b	*	0.0%	25.0%	*****	0.0%	268.4%
46	1871	15b	****	0.0%	110.0%	*****	0.0%	300.0%
47	1871	25b	*****	0.0%	137.5%	*****	0.0%	239.3%
48	1872	10b	*****	0.0%	203.6%	*****	0.0%	275.0%
48a	1872	10b	*****	0.0%	159.3%	*****	0.0%	275.0%
48b	1872	10b	**	0.0%	57.9%	***	0.0%	94.4%
49	1872	50b	**	0.0%	73.1%	**	0.0%	60.0%

A Selection of Investment Grade Stamps
by Country - Romania

Romania Scott #	Issue Year	Value	Rating Mint	5 Year Mint Appreciation %	25 Year Mint Appreciation %	Rating Used	5 Year Used Appreciation %	25 Year Used Appreciation %
50	1872	5b	*****	0.0%	136.4%	*****	0.0%	425.0%
50a	1872	5b	*	0.0%	48.6%	****	0.0%	115.4%
51	1872	10b	*	0.0%	43.8%	*****	0.0%	303.8%
51a	1872	5b	*	0.0%	41.2%	***	0.0%	78.6%
52	1872	25b	*****	0.0%	239.3%	*****	0.0%	375.0%
53	1872	1/2b	*****	0.0%	809.1%			
54	1872	3b	*****	0.0%	282.4%			
57	1872	15b	*****	0.0%	154.5%	*****	0.0%	445.5%
58	1872	25b	*****	0.0%	141.7%	*****	0.0%	393.3%
59	1872	50b	****	0.0%	122.2%	*****	0.0%	639.1%
61b	1876	5b				(*)	0.0%	0.0%
62	1877	10b	***	0.0%	96.4%			
62a	1876	10b	****	0.0%	108.3%			
62b	1876	10b	*****	0.0%	150.0%			
62d	1879	5b/10b	*****	0.0%	129.7%	*****	0.0%	431.3%
63	1877	10b	*****	0.0%	137.5%			
64	1876	15b	***	0.0%	81.3%			
65	1878	30b	**	0.0%	72.7%	*****	0.0%	952.6%
65a	1876	30b				(*)	0.0%	0.0%
69b	1879	10b	*****	0.0%	275.0%	(*)	0.0%	-20.8%
70	1879	15b	**	0.0%	66.7%	*****	0.0%	400.0%
71	1879	25b	*****	0.0%	483.3%	*****	0.0%	1011.1%
72	1879	50b	*****	0.0%	220.0%	*****	0.0%	1455.6%
77	1885	5b	****	0.0%	114.3%			
87	1885	50b	***	0.0%	87.5%			
88	1889	1 1/2b	*	0.0%	33.3%			
92	1889	15b	**	0.0%	61.1%			
93	1889	25b	***	0.0%	90.0%			
95	1890	3b	*****	0.0%	900.0%			

A Selection of Investment Grade Stamps
by Country - Russia

Russia Scott #	Issue Year	Value	Rating Mint	5 Year Mint Appreciation %	25 Year Mint Appreciation %	Rating Used	5 Year Used Appreciation %	25 Year Used Appreciation %
1	1857	10k	*****	150.0%	1685.7%	****	-8.8%	121.4%
2	1858	10k	*****	-22.2%	1300.0%	*	-6.7%	40.0%
3	1858	20k	*****	30.0%	420.0%	*****	-8.6%	220.0%
4	1858	30k	*****	48.0%	428.6%	*****	-8.3%	175.0%
5	1864	1k	*****	13.3%	423.1%	*****	-10.0%	321.9%
5a	1864	1k	*****	70.0%	946.2%	*****	-26.7%	243.8%
6	1864	3k	*****	131.6%	1900.0%	*****	25.0%	263.6%
7	1864	5k	*****	233.3%	1566.7%	*****	-10.0%	157.1%
8	1858	10k	*****	-65.6%	1122.2%			
9	1858	20k	*****	0.0%	700.0%	*****	-11.1%	255.6%
10	1858	30k	*****	17.5%	1075.0%	*****	25.0%	177.8%
11	1863	5k	*****	20.0%	328.6%	(**)	-8.6%	-20.0%
12	1865	1k	*****	87.5%	1150.0%	*****	87.5%	368.8%
12a	1865	1k	*****	100.0%	1233.3%	*****	41.7%	608.3%
13	1865	3k	*****	0.0%	614.3%	*****	16.7%	311.8%
14	1865	5k	*****	36.4%	650.0%	*****	100.0%	595.7%
15	1865	10k	*****	362.5%	1441.7%			
15a	1865	10k	*****	290.0%	747.8%			
17	1865	20k	*****	129.2%	2100.0%	*****	0.0%	220.0%
18	1865	30k	*****	62.5%	1014.3%	***	-20.0%	77.8%
19b	1866	1k				*****	-96.0%	160.9%
19c	1866	1k	*****	40.0%	152.0%	*****	-10.0%	125.0%
19d	1866	1k	*	-12.0%	46.7%	*****	-8.3%	340.0%
20b	1866	3k				*****	36.0%	2166.7%
20c	1866	3k	*****	6.7%	166.7%	**	-9.1%	66.7%
20d	1870	3k	*****	0.0%	150.0%	(*)	-73.3%	14.3%
22a	1866	5k	*****	92.0%	300.0%	*****	62.5%	225.0%
22b	1866	5k	*****	0.0%	133.3%	*****	112.5%	448.4%
22c	1866	5k	*****	0.0%	1438.5%	**	-8.6%	60.0%

A Selection of Investment Grade Stamps
by Country - Russia

Russia Scott #	Issue Year	Value	Rating Mint	5 Year Mint Appreciation %	25 Year Mint Appreciation %	Rating Used	5 Year Used Appreciation %	25 Year Used Appreciation %
23a	1866	10k	*****	110.0%	707.7%			
23b	1866	10k				*****	-16.7%	733.3%
23c	1866	10k				*****	-10.0%	1025.0%
24	1866	20k	*****	5.0%	133.3%			
24a	1866	20k	*****	5.0%	677.8%	*****	6.7%	220.0%
25	1866	30k	***	-9.1%	81.8%	***	-14.3%	76.5%
25a	1866	30k	**	33.3%	53.8%	*****	128.6%	380.0%
26	1875	2k	*****	25.0%	900.0%			
26a	1875	2k	*****	-10.0%	1400.0%	*****	28.0%	166.7%
26b	1875	2k				*****	-11.5%	666.7%
27	1879	7k	*****	-36.0%	700.0%			
27b	1875	7k	**	-70.0%	50.0%	*	0.0%	30.0%
27c	1879	7k				*****	54.5%	1900.0%
27e	1875	7k	*****	0.0%	3233.3%	*****	0.0%	900.0%
28a	1875	8k	*****	11.1%	525.0%	*	17.9%	37.5%
28b	1875	8k				*****	-10.0%	1400.0%
28c	1875	8k	*****	225.0%	2500.0%	*****	-9.1%	900.0%
29a	1875	10k				*****	-7.7%	650.0%
30	1875	20k	*****	-32.5%	125.0%	*****	-9.1%	135.3%
30a	1875	20k	**	36.0%	70.0%	(*)	-8.3%	10.0%
30b	1875	20k				*****	-11.8%	837.5%
31a	1883	1k				*****	-10.7%	16566.7%
31b	1883	1k				*****	-10.0%	200.0%
32b	1883	2k	*****	57.1%	193.3%	****	0.0%	100.0%

A Selection of Investment Grade Stamps
by Country - Russia

Russia Scott #	Issue Year	Value	Rating Mint	5 Year Mint Appreciation %	25 Year Mint Appreciation %	Rating Used	5 Year Used Appreciation %	25 Year Used Appreciation %
32c	1883	2k	**	0.0%	55.6%	*	0.0%	33.3%
32d	1883	2k				*****	-10.0%	950.0%
33a	1883	3k	*****	0.0%	650.0%	*****	0.0%	650.0%
33b	1883	3k				*****	-14.3%	900.0%
33c	1883	3k	(*)	0.0%	0.0%	(*)	0.0%	3.7%
34a	1883	5k				*****	21.4%	112.5%
35a	1883	7k	****	6.7%	100.0%	*	-5.0%	35.7%
35b	1883	7k	*****	6.3%	151.9%	*****	0.0%	166.7%
36	1883	14k	*****	183.3%	3300.0%			
36a	1883	14k	*****	400.0%	661.9%	*****	275.0%	566.7%
36b	1883	14k	(*)	0.0%	0.0%	(*)	0.0%	4.2%
37	1883	35k	*****	0.0%	300.0%			
38	1883	70k	*****	-10.0%	275.0%			
39	1884	3.50r	*****	20.0%	200.0%	*****	-10.7%	127.3%
39a	1884	3.50r	*****	75.0%	2400.0%	****	0.0%	114.3%
40	1884	7r	****	-27.3%	100.0%	*****	-10.0%	145.5%
41a	1889	4k				*****	-20.0%	966.7%
45	1889	1r	*****	-5.0%	216.7%			
45a	1889	1r	*****	20.0%	157.1%	**	-40.0%	50.0%
45b	1889	1r	*****	70.0%	240.0%	**	-15.0%	70.0%
47a	1889	2k	*****	23.1%	300.0%	*****	0.0%	163.2%
48a	1889	3k	****	21.4%	112.5%	***	0.0%	75.0%
49b	1889	5k						
50a	1889	7k				*****	-10.0%	2900.0%
50b	1889	7k				*****	-10.0%	309.1%
51a	1889	14k	**	-10.0%	68.8%	(*)	-10.0%	12.5%
54	1889	7r	*****	-5.0%	484.6%	*	-8.3%	29.4%
54a	1889	7r				*****	-10.0%	16263.6%
55a	1902	1k				****	0.0%	300.0%

A Selection of Investment Grade Stamps
by Country - Spain

Spain Scott #	Issue Year	Value	Rating Mint	5 Year Mint Appreciation %	25 Year Mint Appreciation %	Rating Used	5 Year Used Appreciation %	25 Year Used Appreciation %
1	1850	6c	*****	0.0%	293.9%	*****	0.0%	126.7%
1a	1850	6c	*****	0.0%	225.0%			
1b	1850	6c	*****	0.0%	347.4%			
1c	1850	6c	*****	0.0%	314.6%			
2	1850	12c	*	-16.7%	25.0%	*	-20.0%	48.1%
2a	1850	12c	**	0.0%	63.6%	***	0.0%	116.7%
3	1850	5r	*	-10.0%	35.0%	**	-20.0%	60.0%
4	1850	6r	*	-6.7%	27.3%	*****	-12.5%	154.5%
5	1850	10r	**	-14.5%	66.7%	(*)	-11.8%	0.0%
6	1851	6c	*****	0.0%	200.0%			
6a	1851	6c	*****	0.0%	266.7%			
7	1851	12c	*****	7.1%	172.7%	***	-12.5%	75.0%
8	1851	2r	***	0.0%	92.0%	(*)	-14.3%	9.1%
9	1851	5r	**	0.0%	50.0%	*****	-22.2%	150.0%
9a	1851	5r	*	0.0%	46.7%			
10	1851	6r	***	0.0%	75.0%	****	-13.3%	116.7%
10a	1851	2r				(*)	0.0%	13.6%
11	1851	10r	***	0.0%	87.5%	*****	-18.2%	172.7%
12	1852	6c	*****	0.0%	196.3%			
12a	1852	6c	*****	0.0%	177.8%			
13	1852	12c	***	0.0%	92.6%	****	0.0%	114.3%
14	1852	2r	*	-11.1%	45.5%	(*)	-22.2%	0.0%
15	1852	5r	****	1.7%	122.2%	*	-20.0%	42.9%
16	1852	6r	***	0.0%	84.0%	***	-4.8%	81.8%
17	1853	1c	*	-16.7%	25.0%	**	-12.5%	55.6%
18	1853	3c	**	0.0%	63.6%	*	-14.3%	33.3%
19	1853	6c	*****	0.0%	316.7%			
19a	1853	6c	*****	0.0%	254.5%			

A Selection of Investment Grade Stamps
by Country - Spain

Spain Scott #	Issue Year	Value	Rating Mint	5 Year Mint Appreciation %	25 Year Mint Appreciation %	Rating Used	5 Year Used Appreciation %	25 Year Used Appreciation %
19b	1853	6c	*****	0.0%	225.0%			
20	1853	12c	****	0.0%	103.7%	*****	0.0%	125.0%
21	1853	2r	*	-20.0%	33.3%	*	-20.0%	33.3%
21a	1853	2r	****	0.0%	142.9%	*****	0.0%	150.0%
22	1853	5r	***	0.0%	85.2%	***	0.0%	85.7%
23	1853	6r	***	-5.1%	85.0%	***	0.0%	87.5%
24	1854	2c	***	0.0%	76.7%	*****	0.0%	162.5%
25	1854	4c	*****	0.0%	172.7%			
26	1854	6c	*****	-12.5%	133.3%			
27	1854	1r	***	-12.5%	75.0%	*****	0.0%	133.3%
28	1854	2r	****	0.0%	110.0%	****	0.0%	118.2%
29	1854	5r	****	0.0%	100.0%	**	0.0%	57.1%
30	1854	6r	*****	-11.1%	128.6%	*****	0.0%	140.7%
31	1854	2c	*	-5.7%	32.0%	**	-28.6%	50.0%
32	1854	4c	*****	-4.8%	163.2%			
33	1854	1r				(*)	-13.3%	-7.1%
34	1854	2r	**	-6.7%	55.6%	*	-14.3%	44.6%
36	1855	2c	**	0.0%	51.1%	*****	0.0%	133.3%
36a	1855	2c	*	0.0%	45.5%	***	0.0%	75.0%
37	1855	4c	*****	0.0%	140.0%			
37a	1855	4c	*****	0.0%	225.9%			
37b	1855	4c	*****	0.0%	159.3%			
38	1855	1r	*****	0.0%	160.0%			
38a	1855	1r	***	0.0%	77.8%			
38b	1855	2r	**	0.0%	66.7%	****	0.0%	103.1%
39	1855	2r	*****	0.0%	176.9%	****	0.0%	114.3%
39a	1855	2r	*****	0.0%	222.2%	*****	0.0%	158.1%
40	1856	2c	**	0.0%	60.0%	*****	0.0%	150.0%
42	1856	1r	****	0.0%	120.0%	****	0.0%	122.2%

A Selection of Investment Grade Stamps
by Country - Spain

Spain Scott #	Issue Year	Value	Rating Mint	5 Year Mint Appreciation %	25 Year Mint Appreciation %	Rating Used	5 Year Used Appreciation %	25 Year Used Appreciation %
42a	1856	1r	***	0.0%	76.9%	*****	0.0%	205.6%
43	1856	2r	****	0.0%	100.0%	***	0.0%	92.3%
43a	1856	2r	*****	0.0%	181.8%	***	0.0%	80.0%
44	1856	2c	*****	0.0%	250.0%	*****	0.0%	165.6%
44a	1856	2c	*****	0.0%	230.0%	****	0.0%	100.0%
46	1856	1r	*****	-1.8%	145.5%	*****	0.0%	316.7%
46a	1856	1r	*****	0.0%	150.0%	*****	0.0%	209.5%
47	1856	2r	*****	-22.2%	115.4%			
47a	1856	2r	****	0.0%	122.2%	***	0.0%	191.7%
48	1859	12c	****	0.0%	100.0%			
49	1860	2c	*****	-12.5%	133.3%			
50	1860	4c	*****	9.1%	166.7%			
51	1860	12c	*****	0.0%	133.3%			
52	1861	19c	*	0.0%	25.0%	**	0.0%	50.0%
53	1860	1r	*****	0.0%	225.0%			
54	1860	2r	*****	0.0%	196.3%			
55	1862	2c	***	0.0%	97.4%			
57	1862	12c	**	0.0%	70.0%			
58	1862	19c	*****	0.0%	135.3%	*****	0.0%	164.7%
58a	1862	19c	****	0.0%	100.0%	*****	0.0%	150.0%
59	1862	1r	*****	0.0%	130.0%			
60	1862	2r	*****	0.0%	134.4%			
61	1864	2c	*****	0.0%	163.2%			

A Selection of Investment Grade Stamps
by Country - Switzerland

Switzerland Scott #	Issue Year	Value	Rating Mint	5 Year Mint Appreciation %	25 Year Mint Appreciation %	Rating Used	5 Year Used Appreciation %	25 Year Used Appreciation %
2	1850	2.5r	*****	24.0%	148.0%	**	14.3%	68.4%
3	1850	2.5r	****	16.7%	112.1%	**	7.3%	73.5%
4	1850	2.5r	**	0.0%	61.5%	**	8.0%	58.8%
5	1850	5r	***	18.1%	77.1%	**	10.0%	52.8%
5a	1850	5r	***	7.8%	90.8%	*	10.0%	37.5%
6	1850	10r				*****	13.0%	136.4%
7	1850	5r	**	10.0%	67.4%	*	27.8%	43.8%
7a	1850	5r	*	28.3%	42.6%	*	27.8%	15.0%
7b	1850	5r				*****	-15.5%	165.7%
7c	1850	5r	*****	15.0%	130.0%	***	44.4%	85.7%
8	1850	10r	*	0.0%	17.6%	****	28.0%	100.0%
8a	1850	10r	****	0.0%	112.5%	*****	0.0%	181.3%
8b	1850	10r	*	0.0%	47.1%	**	0.0%	66.7%
8c	1850	10r				**	-35.9%	56.3%
9	1851	5r				*****	0.0%	211.1%
10	1851	5r	**	-3.8%	66.7%	****	28.0%	100.0%
11	1852	15r	*****	33.3%	263.6%	**	10.7%	72.2%
12	1852	15r	***	8.0%	92.9%	***	28.0%	88.2%
13	1852	15c	*****	32.1%	131.3%	**	15.0%	70.4%
14	1854	5r	*****	86.7%	273.3%	**	2.9%	59.1%
15	1854	5r	*****	0.0%	127.3%	*****	0.0%	128.6%
16	1854	10r	*****	3.0%	126.7%	*****	6.3%	466.7%
17	1854	10r	*****	16.7%	133.3%	****	8.6%	111.1%
17a	1854	15r	*****	0.0%	125.0%	****	0.0%	111.1%
18	1854	40r	*****	22.1%	21995.2%	**	0.0%	62.5%
19	1854	40r	*****	48.0%	270.0%	*****	15.4%	150.0%
20	1854	5r	****	19.2%	106.7%	*****	6.3%	142.9%
21	1854	10r	*****	43.8%	178.8%	****	0.0%	108.3%

A Selection of Investment Grade Stamps
by Country - Switzerland

Switzerland Scott #	Issue Year	Value	Rating Mint	5 Year Mint Appreciation %	25 Year Mint Appreciation %	Rating Used	5 Year Used Appreciation %	25 Year Used Appreciation %
22	1854	15r	****	24.3%	109.1%	*****	0.0%	175.0%
23	1854	20r	****	21.4%	100.0%	*****	5.3%	150.0%
24	1855	5r	*****	13.6%	127.3%	*****	0.0%	130.0%
25	1856	5r	***	7.7%	89.2%	*****	0.0%	207.7%
26	1855	10r	*****	55.0%	342.9%	*****	15.0%	283.3%
27	1855	10r	***	8.3%	85.7%	*****	-5.0%	265.4%
27a	1856	10r	****	8.0%	116.0%	***	0.0%	90.0%
28	1855	15r	***	4.5%	91.7%	*****	-6.7%	133.3%
29	1855	40r	*****	10.0%	158.8%	*****	0.0%	214.3%
30	1855	1fr	*****	26.8%	208.7%	*****	0.0%	185.7%
31	1856	1fr	****	14.8%	113.8%	*****	0.0%	185.7%
31a	1857	1fr				**	3.0%	71.7%
32	1856	5r	*****	20.0%	134.8%	*	10.0%	46.7%
33	1857	15r	***	6.9%	98.6%	****	0.0%	100.0%
34	1857	20r	*****	25.0%	142.9%	*****	5.5%	190.0%
35	1862	2r	****	0.0%	120.0%	*****	0.0%	130.0%
36	1858	5r	*****	11.1%	212.5%	*****	25.0%	500.0%
36a	1858	5r	****	0.0%	120.0%	*****	0.0%	137.5%
37	1858	10r	*****	8.3%	188.9%	*****	18.2%	712.5%
38	1858	15r	****	6.7%	100.0%	*****	7.7%	250.0%
39	1858	20r	*****	10.5%	176.3%	*****	3.3%	181.8%
40	1858	40r	*****	5.6%	150.0%	*****	-7.5%	270.0%
41	1862	2c	*****	40.0%	337.5%			
42	1862	3c				*****	39.1%	236.8%
43a	1862	5c	***	0.0%	84.0%			
43b	1862	5c	*****	4.5%	187.5%	*****	0.0%	550.0%
43c	1862	5c	*	0.0%	41.7%	*	-6.0%	34.3%
43d	1862	5c				**	3.3%	55.0%
44	1862	10c	*****	12.0%	366.7%			

A Selection of Investment Grade Stamps
by Country - Switzerland

Switzerland Scott #	Issue Year	Value	Rating Mint	5 Year Mint Appreciation %	25 Year Mint Appreciation %	Rating Used	5 Year Used Appreciation %	25 Year Used Appreciation %
44a	1862	10c				(*)	-5.6%	13.3%
45a	1862	20c	*****	-2.5%	875.0%			
46	1862	30c	*****	23.3%	164.3%	*****	0.0%	375.0%
47	1862	40c	*****	21.4%	325.0%	*****	19.2%	244.4%
48	1862	60c	*****	10.7%	264.7%	*****	19.4%	207.1%
50	1862	1fr	****	-10.0%	104.5%	*****	8.3%	333.3%
50a	1864	1fr	*****	10.9%	153.6%	*****	12.7%	313.3%
52a	1867	2c	***	10.7%	72.2%	****	5.5%	123.1%
54	1867	15c				*****	5.6%	239.3%
55a	1867	25c	*****	0.0%	700.0%	*****	0.0%	1042.9%
55b	1867	25c				(*)	-45.5%	9.1%
56	1867	30c	*****	30.5%	313.3%			
56a	1867	30c	****	4.5%	109.1%	**	-1.8%	68.8%
58	1867	40c				*****	6.3%	423.1%
59	1867	50c	**	13.6%	56.3%	*****	40.9%	287.5%
60a	1881	2c	*	30.0%	30.0%			
61a	1881	5c				**	5.6%	72.7%
61b	1881	5c				**	0.0%	78.6%
63	1881	15c				****	20.0%	116.0%
64	1881	20c				*****	25.9%	183.3%
65	1881	25c				*****	10.0%	144.4%
66	1881	40c				****	14.0%	115.3%
67	1881	50c				*****	31.6%	127.3%
67b	1881	50c	(*)	-38.5%	0.0%	****	11.1%	100.0%
68	1881	1fr				*****	27.3%	133.3%
70a	1882	3c	*****	0.0%	364.3%	*****	0.0%	417.9%
71	1882	5c	***	-4.0%	92.0%			

A Selection of Investment Grade Stamps
by Country - Turkey

Turkey Scott #	Issue Year	Value	Rating Mint	5 Year Mint Appreciation %	25 Year Mint Appreciation %	Rating Used	5 Year Used Appreciation %	25 Year Used Appreciation %
1	1863	20pa	*****	0.0%	172.7%	(*)	0.0%	14.3%
1a	1863	20pa	****	0.0%	100.0%	**	0.0%	60.0%
1b	1863	20pa	****	0.0%	122.2%			
2	1863	1pi	*****	0.0%	316.7%	(*)	0.0%	0.0%
2a	1863	1pi	*****	0.0%	316.7%	(*)	0.0%	7.5%
2b	1863	1pi	****	0.0%	166.7%	****	0.0%	100.0%
2c	1863	1pi	*****	0.0%	229.4%			
2d	1863	1pi				(*)	0.0%	0.0%
2e	1863	1pi	**	0.0%	66.7%	*	0.0%	20.0%
4	1863	2pi	*****	0.0%	228.6%			
4a	1863	2pi	*****	0.0%	228.6%			
4b	1863	2pi	****	0.0%	166.7%	****	0.0%	100.0%
4c	1863	2pi	*****	0.0%	180.0%			
5	1863	5pi	*****	0.0%	309.1%	**	0.0%	63.6%
5a	1863	5pi	****	0.0%	100.0%	**	0.0%	60.0%
5b	1863	5pi	*****	0.0%	233.3%			
5c	1863	5pi	*****	0.0%	189.5%			
5d	1863	5pi	*****	0.0%	189.5%			
6	1863	20pa	*****	0.0%	455.6%	*	0.0%	25.0%
6b	1863	20pa	*	0.0%	18.2%	*	0.0%	18.2%
6c	1863	20pa	*****	0.0%	542.9%	*****	0.0%	542.9%
6d	1863	20pa	*****	0.0%	200.0%	*****	0.0%	200.0%
7	1863	1pi	*****	0.0%	500.0%	(*)	0.0%	-17.6%
7a	1863	1pi	*****	0.0%	157.1%	*****	0.0%	157.1%
7d	1863	1pi	*****	0.0%	180.0%	***	0.0%	80.0%
8	1865	10pa				*****	0.0%	536.4%
8c	1865	10pa	(*)	0.0%	0.0%	(*)	0.0%	0.0%
9b	1865	20pa	(*)	0.0%	0.0%	(*)	0.0%	0.0%
10b	1865	1pi	(*)	0.0%	11.1%	(*)	0.0%	0.0%
11a	1865	2pi	(*)	0.0%	11.1%	(*)	0.0%	0.0%

A Selection of Investment Grade Stamps
by Country - Turkey

Turkey Scott #	Issue Year	Value	Rating Mint	5 Year Mint Appreciation %	25 Year Mint Appreciation %	Rating Used	5 Year Used Appreciation %	25 Year Used Appreciation %
12b	1865	5pi	*	0.0%	36.4%	(*)	0.0%	0.0%
12d	1865	5pi				(**)	0.0%	-70.7%
13	1865	25pi	*****	0.0%	182.6%	*****	0.0%	127.3%
13a	1865	25pi	*	0.0%	28.6%	*	0.0%	28.6%
14a	1867	10pa	(*)	0.0%	10.0%			
15a	1867	20pa	(*)	0.0%	7.1%			
16a	1867	1pi	*	0.0%	15.8%			
16b	1867	2pi	*****	0.0%	1233.3%			
17a	1867	2pi						
18a	1867	5pi						
19	1867	25pi	*****	0.0%	860.0%			
20b	1869	10pa	(*)	0.0%	12.5%	(*)	0.0%	0.0%
20c	1869	10pa				(*)	0.0%	0.0%
20e	1869	10pa				*	0.0%	20.0%
21	1869	20pa	*****	0.0%	1354.5%	*****	0.0%	1766.7%
21a	1869	20pa	*****	0.0%	400.0%	*****	0.0%	205.6%
22c	1869	1pi	*	0.0%	25.0%			
23b	1869	2pi	(*)	0.0%	-3.8%	(*)	0.0%	-3.8%
23c	1869	2pi				(*)	0.0%	-3.8%
23d	1869	2pi	(*)	0.0%	0.0%	(*)	0.0%	0.0%
23e	1869	2pi				(*)	0.0%	0.0%
26	1869	25pi	*****	0.0%	167.9%	*****	0.0%	900.0%
27	1870	10pa	*****	0.0%	266.7%			
28	1870	10pa	*****	0.0%	1566.7%			
29	1870	20pa	*****	0.0%	733.3%			
30	1870	1pi	*****	0.0%	2344.4%			
30a	1870	1pi	*****	0.0%	400.0%	(*)	0.0%	0.0%
31b	1870	2pi				*	0.0%	23.1%

A Selection of Investment Grade Stamps
by Country - Turkey

Turkey Scott #	Issue Year	Value	Rating Mint	5 Year Mint Appreciation %	25 Year Mint Appreciation %	Rating Used	5 Year Used Appreciation %	25 Year Used Appreciation %
33	1870	5pi	*****	0.0%	433.3%	*****	0.0%	733.3%
33b	1870	5pi				*****	0.0%	146.2%
34	1870	25pi	*****	0.0%	220.0%	*****	0.0%	500.0%
35	1870	10pa	*****	0.0%	1627.3%	*****	0.0%	1011.1%
35a	1870	10pa				(*)	0.0%	0.0%
36	1870	10pa	*****	0.0%	214.3%			
36a	1870	10pa	*****	0.0%	175.0%			
40a	1874	1pi	(*)	0.0%	0.0%	(*)	0.0%	0.0%
41a	1874	10pa	(*)	0.0%	0.0%	(*)	0.0%	0.0%
42a	1876	10pa	(*)	0.0%	0.0%			
44a	1876	1pi	(*)	0.0%	0.0%	(*)	0.0%	0.0%
46	1876	5pi	*****	0.0%	580.0%			
47	1876	210Pa	*****	0.0%	580.0%			
50a	1876	1 1/4pi	(*)	0.0%	0.0%			
51	1876	2pi/2pi	*****	0.0%	515.4%			
52	1876	5pi/5pi	*****	0.0%	900.0%	*****	0.0%	4150.0%
54	1876	20pa	*****	0.0%	316.7%			
57b	1876	25pi	(*)	0.0%	0.0%	(*)	0.0%	0.0%
58	1876	25pi				*****	0.0%	1033.3%
58a	1876	25pi	(*)	0.0%	0.0%			
59a	1881	5pa	(*)	0.0%	0.0%			
61	1881	20pa	*****	0.0%	34275.0%	*****	0.0%	1233.3%
62	1880	1pi	*****	0.0%	49900.0%	*****	0.0%	1900.0%
62a	1880	1pi	*****	0.0%	53025.0%			
62b	1881	1pi	**	0.0%	50.0%			
63	1881	1pi	*****	0.0%	1592.3%			
64b	1881	20pa	(*)	0.0%	0.0%			
66	1886	5pa	*****	0.0%	627.3%	*****	0.0%	566.7%
66a	1886	5pa	(*)	0.0%	0.0%			

A Selection of Investment Grade Stamps
by Country - Turkey

Turkey Scott #	Issue Year	Value	Rating Mint	5 Year Mint Appreciation %	25 Year Mint Appreciation %	Rating Used	5 Year Used Appreciation %	25 Year Used Appreciation %
67a	1884	10pa	****	0.0%	100.0%			
68b	1884	20pa	****	0.0%	100.0%			
69b	1884	1pi	****	0.0%	100.0%			
71	1884	5pi	*****	0.0%	9900.0%	*****	0.0%	6150.0%
73	1886	25pi	*****	0.0%	300.0%	*****	0.0%	466.7%
73a	1886	25pi	(*)	0.0%	0.0%			
74a	1886	5pa	**	0.0%	50.0%			
75b	1886	2pi	****	0.0%	100.0%			
76b	1886	5pi	****	0.0%	100.0%			
83a	1888	5pa	****	0.0%	100.0%			
84a	1888	2pi	****	0.0%	100.0%			
85a	1888	5pi	****	0.0%	100.0%			
86	1888	25pi	*****	0.0%	300.0%	*****	0.0%	2400.0%
86a	1888	25pi	**	0.0%	60.0%			
89a	1890	1pi	*****	0.0%	400.0%			
90b	1890	2pi	*****	0.0%	300.0%			
91a	1890	5pi	(*)	0.0%	0.0%			
96b	1892	20pa	*****	0.0%	775.0%			
97	1892	1pi	*****	0.0%	2100.0%			
98a	1892	2pi	*****	0.0%	500.0%	*****	0.0%	500.0%
99a	1892	5pi	*****	0.0%	300.0%	*****	0.0%	260.0%
108	1901	25pi	*****	0.0%	733.3%	*****	0.0%	300.0%
109	1901	50pi	*****	0.0%	733.3%	*****	0.0%	400.0%
116a	1901	25pi	*	0.0%	25.0%			
117	1901	50pi	*****	0.0%	400.0%			
117a	1901	50pi	*****	0.0%	175.0%			
127	1905	50pi	*****	0.0%	566.7%	*****	0.0%	990.9%

A Selection of Investment Grade Stamps
by Country - Uruguay

Uruguay Scott #	Issue Year	Value	Rating Mint	5 Year Mint Appreciation %	25 Year Mint Appreciation %	Rating Used	5 Year Used Appreciation %	25 Year Used Appreciation %
1	1856	60c	***	0.0%	80.0%			
1a	1856	60c	**	0.0%	62.5%			
1b	1856	60c	*	0.0%	42.9%			
2	1856	80c	****	0.0%	122.2%			
3	1856	1r	****	0.0%	100.0%			
3B	1856	1r	***	0.0%	83.3%			
3Bc	1856	1r	**	0.0%	71.9%			
3Bd	1856	1r	***	0.0%	87.5%			
3a	1856	1r	***	0.0%	80.0%			
4	1858	120c	*****	0.0%	228.6%	*****	0.0%	333.3%
4a	1858	120c	*****	0.0%	242.9%			
4b	1858	120c	*****	0.0%	271.4%			
5	1858	180c	*****	0.0%	200.0%	*****	0.0%	166.7%
5a	1858	180c	*****	0.0%	150.0%			
5b	1858	180c	*	0.0%	40.0%			
6	1858	240c	*****	0.0%	200.0%	*****	0.0%	300.0%
6a	1858	240c	*****	0.0%	180.0%			
6b	1858	240c	****	0.0%	100.0%			
7	1859	60c	*****	0.0%	150.0%	****	-12.5%	100.0%
7a	1859	60c	****	-10.0%	114.3%	****	0.0%	100.0%
8	1859	80c	*****	38.5%	157.1%	*****	15.4%	130.8%
8a	1859	80c	*	-33.3%	20.0%	*	-20.0%	41.2%
9	1859	100c	****	-9.1%	100.0%	***	-6.7%	86.7%
9a	1859	100c	*****	0.0%	140.0%	*****	0.0%	166.7%
10	1859	120c	**	-15.4%	69.2%	*****	0.0%	140.0%
10a	1859	120c	***	0.0%	76.5%	****	20.0%	100.0%
11	1859	180c	***	-12.0%	76.0%	**	-13.3%	73.3%
12	1859	240c	****	0.0%	100.0%	****	0.0%	100.0%

A Selection of Investment Grade Stamps
by Country - Uruguay

Uruguay Scott #	Issue Year	Value	Rating Mint	5 Year Mint Appreciation %	25 Year Mint Appreciation %	Rating Used	5 Year Used Appreciation %	25 Year Used Appreciation %
13	1860	60c	****	-16.7%	100.0%			
13a	1860	60c	*****	33.3%	166.7%			
13b	1860	60c	****	0.0%	100.0%			
13c	1860	60c	*****	0.0%	700.0%	*****	0.0%	900.0%
13d	1859	60c	****	0.0%	100.0%	*	0.0%	20.0%
14	1860	80c	*****	0.0%	185.7%	*****	0.0%	150.0%
14a	1860	80c	*****	0.0%	150.0%	****	-5.5%	108.0%
15	1860	100c	*****	0.0%	135.3%	*****	0.0%	175.0%
15a	1860	100c	*****	0.0%	158.8%	*****	0.0%	175.0%
16	1860	120c	*****	0.0%	125.0%	*****	0.0%	212.5%
17	1859	180c	*****	0.0%	286.4%	*****	0.0%	400.0%
17a	1859	180c	*****	0.0%	240.0%	*****	0.0%	414.3%
18a	1864	6c	*****	0.0%	220.0%	*****	0.0%	200.0%
18b	1864	6c	*****	0.0%	185.7%	*****	0.0%	200.0%
18c	1864	6c	*****	0.0%	157.1%	**	0.0%	71.4%
20	1864	12c	*****	0.0%	566.7%			
21a	1864	8c	*****	0.0%	138.5%			
22	1864	10c	***	0.0%	85.7%	****	0.0%	108.3%
22a	1864	10c	****	0.0%	100.0%	****	0.0%	108.3%
23a	1864	12c	*****	0.0%	150.0%			
23b	1864	12c	*****	0.0%	150.0%			
24	1866	5c/12c	*****	0.0%	140.0%	****	0.0%	120.0%
24a	1866	5c/12c	**	0.0%	50.0%	**	0.0%	71.4%
24b	1866	5c/12c	*****	0.0%	300.0%			
24c	1866	5c/12c	*****	0.0%	650.0%			
24e	1866	5c/12c	*	0.0%	29.4%			
25	1866	10c/8c	*****	0.0%	140.0%	****	0.0%	120.0%
25a	1866	10c/8c	*****	0.0%	140.0%	****	0.0%	120.0%
25b	1866	10c/8c	****	0.0%	100.0%			

A Selection of Investment Grade Stamps
by Country - Uruguay

Uruguay Scott #	Issue Year	Value	Rating Mint	5 Year Mint Appreciation %	25 Year Mint Appreciation %	Rating Used	5 Year Used Appreciation %	25 Year Used Appreciation %
25c	1866	10c/8c	*****	0.0%	500.0%			
26	1866	15c/10c	*****	0.0%	133.3%	*****	0.0%	140.0%
26a	1866	15c/10c	*****	0.0%	133.3%	*****	0.0%	140.0%
26b	1866	15c/10c	*****	0.0%	252.9%			
27	1866	20c/6c	*****	0.0%	128.6%	****	0.0%	113.3%
27a	1866	20c/6c	**	0.0%	50.0%	****	0.0%	100.0%
27b	1866	20c/6c	*****	0.0%	233.3%			
27c	1866	20c/6c	*****	0.0%	500.0%			
28	1866	20c/6c	*****	0.0%	300.0%			
28a	1866	20c/6c	*****	0.0%	400.0%			
30b	1866	5c	***	0.0%	85.7%			
30c	1866	5c	**	0.0%	66.7%			
30d	1866	5c	**	0.0%	66.7%			
30e	1866	5c	**	0.0%	66.7%			
30f	1866	5c	*****	0.0%	185.7%			
30g	1866	5c	*****	0.0%	700.0%	*****	0.0%	1328.6%
31b	1866	10c	*	0.0%	22.2%			
31c	1866	10c	*	0.0%	22.2%			
31d	1866	10c	*	0.0%	22.2%			
32	1866	15c	*****	0.0%	150.0%			
32a	1866	15c	*****	0.0%	150.0%			
33	1866	20c	*****	0.0%	150.0%			
33a	1866	20c	*****	0.0%	150.0%			
33b	1866	20c	**	0.0%	66.7%			
35b	1866	5c	*****	0.0%	177.8%			
35c	1866	5c	*****	0.0%	150.0%			
35d	1866	5c	*****	0.0%	150.0%			
35f	1866	5c	*****	0.0%	1100.0%			
36b	1866	10c	*****	0.0%	180.0%			

A Selection of Investment Grade Stamps
by Country - Uruguay

Uruguay Scott #	Issue Year	Value	Rating Mint	5 Year Mint Appreciation %	25 Year Mint Appreciation %	Rating Used	5 Year Used Appreciation %	25 Year Used Appreciation %
36c	1866	10c	*****	0.0%	180.0%			
36d	1866	10c	*****	0.0%	180.0%			
36e	1866	10c	*****	0.0%	620.0%			
37b	1866	15c	***	0.0%	78.6%			
38	1866	20c	*****	0.0%	316.7%			
38a	1866	20c	*****	0.0%	316.7%			
38b	1866	20c	**	0.0%	50.0%			
38c	1866	20c	*****	0.0%	172.7%			
43A	1879	1p	*****	0.0%	122.2%			
120a	1894	25c				*	0.0%	33.3%
126	1895	2p	****	0.0%	116.7%			
128	1895	3p	****	0.0%	116.7%			
174a	1908	1c	*	0.0%	33.3%	*	0.0%	33.3%
174b	1906	1c	**	0.0%	50.0%			
175a	1908	2c	*	0.0%	33.3%	*	0.0%	33.3%
175b	1906	2c	**	0.0%	50.0%			
176a	1908	5c	*	0.0%	33.3%	*	0.0%	33.3%
176b	1906	5c	**	0.0%	50.0%			
277	1923	1p	****	0.0%	103.1%	****	0.0%	100.0%
278	1923	2p	*****	0.0%	196.9%	****	0.0%	100.0%
378	1929	3p	*****	0.0%	177.8%			
380	1929	2c	****	0.0%	100.0%			
382	1929	5p	***	0.0%	85.7%			
383	1932	5p	****	0.0%	114.3%			
384	1933	10p	***	0.0%	85.0%	****	0.0%	100.0%
385	1933	10p	***	0.0%	85.0%	****	0.0%	100.0%
409	1930	5p	**	0.0%	55.6%			
C1a	1921	25c	***	0.0%	77.8%	***	0.0%	77.8%
C2a	1921	25c	**	0.0%	66.7%	**	0.0%	66.7%

A Selection of Investment Grade Stamps
by Country - Uruguay

Uruguay Scott #	Issue Year	Value	Rating Mint	5 Year Mint Appreciation %	25 Year Mint Appreciation %	Rating Used	5 Year Used Appreciation %	25 Year Used Appreciation %
C7	1925	14c	***	0.0%	75.0%	*****	0.0%	150.0%
C8	1925	14c	***	0.0%	75.0%			
C22	1928	1.14p	*****	0.0%	246.2%	*****	0.0%	204.3%
C23	1928	1.52p	*****	0.0%	275.0%	*****	0.0%	200.0%
C24	1928	1.90p	*****	0.0%	295.8%	*****	0.0%	240.9%
C25	1928	3.80p	*****	0.0%	181.3%	*****	0.0%	142.9%
C57	1929	3p	*****	0.0%	166.7%	*****	0.0%	150.0%
C58	1930	3p	*****	0.0%	200.0%	*****	0.0%	150.0%
C59	1929	4.50p	*****	0.0%	188.5%	*****	0.0%	129.2%
C60	1930	4.5p	*****	0.0%	150.0%	****	0.0%	118.8%
C61a	1934	17c	**	0.0%	60.0%			
C61b	1934	17c	**	0.0%	50.0%			
C61c	1934	17c	**	0.0%	50.0%			
C62a	1934	36c	**	0.0%	60.0%			
C82	1935	5p	*****	0.0%	200.0%	*****	0.0%	200.0%
C89	1938	1.38p	*****	0.0%	177.8%			
C105	1940	10p	*****	0.0%	233.3%	*****	0.0%	225.0%

A Selection of Investment Grade Stamps
by Country - Vatican City

Scott #	Issue Year	Value	Rating Mint	5 Year Mint Appreciation %	25 Year Mint Appreciation %	Rating Used	5 Year Used Appreciation %	25 Year Used Appreciation %
19a	1933	5c	*****	0.0%	166.7%	*****	0.0%	135.7%
22a	1933	vert.pair im	*****	0.0%	328.6%			
23a	1933	imperf.pair	*****	0.0%	240.0%	*****	0.0%	263.6%
30	1933	2l	****	0.0%	110.0%	****	0.0%	108.3%
31	1933	2.75l	*****	0.0%	145.5%	*****	0.0%	200.0%
35	1934	40c/80c	*****	0.0%	3990.9%	*****	0.0%	515.4%
36	1934	1.30L/1.25L	***	-5.3%	89.5%	****	0.0%	110.5%
36a	1934	"30"in"1.30"	*****	0.0%	1820.0%	*****	0.0%	966.7%
37	1934	2.05L/2L	***	0.0%	92.0%	*****	0.0%	209.5%
37a	1934	2.05L/2L	*****	0.0%	161.9%	*	0.0%	23.1%
38	1934	2.55 l/2.50	**	0.0%	57.9%	***	0.0%	83.3%
38a	1934	2.55l/2.50l	*	0.0%	33.3%	****	0.0%	100.0%
39	1934	3.05L/5L	**	0.0%	66.7%	**	0.0%	50.0%
40	1934	3.70L/10L	**	0.0%	50.0%	(*)	0.0%	4.3%
43	1935	25c	*****	0.0%	1415.2%	*****	0.0%	900.0%
44	1935	75c	*****	0.0%	188.9%	*****	0.0%	328.6%
45	1935	80c	*****	0.0%	189.5%	*****	0.0%	325.0%
46	1935	1.25l	*****	0.0%	195.5%	*****	0.0%	425.0%
49	1936	25c	*****	0.0%	221.4%	*****	0.0%	233.3%
51	1936	75c	***	0.0%	90.0%	*****	0.0%	166.7%
60	1938	1.25l	***	0.0%	81.3%	*****	0.0%	132.0%
61	1939	5c	(*)	0.0%	-5.5%			
65a	1939	pair,1 w/o ovpt	*****	0.0%	300.0%			
B3	1933	80c+20c	****	0.0%	114.3%			
J2a	1931	10c	*****	0.0%	1212.5%			
J5	1931	60c/2l	(*)	0.0%	14.3%	**	0.0%	66.7%

A Selection of Investment Grade Stamps
by Country - Venezuela

Venezuela Scott #	Issue Year	Value	Rating Mint	5 Year Mint Appreciation %	25 Year Mint Appreciation %	Rating Used	5 Year Used Appreciation %	25 Year Used Appreciation %
1	1859	1/2r	*****	0.0%	242.9%			
1b	1859	.50r	(*)	0.0%	12.5%			
2	1859	1r	***	0.0%	80.0%	(*)	0.0%	-6.3%
3	1859	2r	*	0.0%	30.8%			
3a	1859	2r	*	0.0%	37.5%			
3b	1859	2r				*****	0.0%	525.0%
3c	1859	2r	(*)	0.0%	12.5%	(*)	0.0%	12.0%
4a	1859	.50r	*	0.0%	17.6%	**	0.0%	50.0%
4b	1859	.50r	*	0.0%	15.4%	(*)	0.0%	16.7%
4c	1859	.50r	(*)	0.0%	9.5%			
5a	1859	1r	*	0.0%	40.0%			
5b	1859	1r	*	0.0%	40.0%			
5c	1859	1r				*****	0.0%	3650.0%
5d	1859	1r	(*)	0.0%	14.3%			
6	1862	2r	****	0.0%	100.0%	*****	0.0%	540.0%
6a	1859	2r	****	0.0%	100.0%	*****	0.0%	471.4%
6b	1859	2r	****	0.0%	122.2%			
6c	1859	2r				*****	0.0%	142.4%
6d	1859	2r	(*)	0.0%	12.5%			
7	1862	1/4c				*****	0.0%	150.0%
8	1862	.50c				**	0.0%	60.0%
8a	1862	.50c	*	0.0%	45.5%	*	0.0%	31.3%
9	1862	1c	*	0.0%	30.8%	*****	0.0%	135.3%
10	1864	.50c	*	0.0%	37.5%	*****	0.0%	515.4%
10a	1864	.50c	*	0.0%	33.3%	*****	0.0%	300.0%
11	1864	1c	*	0.0%	38.9%	****	0.0%	113.3%
13a	1863	1r	*	0.0%	33.3%	****	0.0%	30.0%
13b	1863	1r				*****	0.0%	650.0%
14a	1863	2r	*	0.0%	33.3%			

A Selection of Investment Grade Stamps
by Country - Venezuela

Venezuela Scott #	Issue Year	Value	Rating Mint	5 Year Mint Appreciation %	25 Year Mint Appreciation %	Rating Used	5 Year Used Appreciation %	25 Year Used Appreciation %
14b	1863	2r				*****	0.0%	3650.0%
14c	1863	2r				*****	0.0%	1233.3%
16	1867	.50c	**	0.0%	66.7%	*	0.0%	20.0%
17	1867	1c	**	0.0%	66.7%	*	0.0%	25.0%
19b	1866	.50r	****	0.0%	122.2%	*****	0.0%	380.0%
20	1865	1r	*	0.0%	38.5%			
20a	1866	1r				*****	0.0%	400.0%
21	1866	2r	*	0.0%	45.5%	*	0.0%	29.2%
21a	1866	2r				*****	0.0%	900.0%
23e	1874	2c	(*)	0.0%	0.0%	(*)	0.0%	0.0%
33	1871	15r	****	0.0%	100.0%			
33a	1876	10r	****	0.0%	100.0%			
33b	1871	15r	(*)	0.0%	0.0%	(*)	0.0%	0.0%
34	1871	20r	*	0.0%	19.2%			
34a	1875	20r	(*)	0.0%	10.0%	(*)	0.0%	7.7%
35	1871	30r	*	0.0%	25.0%	(*)	0.0%	10.0%
35a	1876	30r	(*)	0.0%	4.3%	(*)	0.0%	6.7%
36	1871	50r	*	0.0%	20.0%	(*)	0.0%	9.1%
37	1873	.50r	*	0.0%	27.3%			
37a	1873	.50r	*	0.0%	27.3%			
37b	1873	.50r	**	0.0%	52.2%	***	0.0%	76.5%
37c	1873	1/2r	*	0.0%	20.0%	(*)	0.0%	5.3%
38	1873	1r	*	0.0%	30.8%	*	0.0%	42.9%
39	1873	2r	****	0.0%	140.0%	****	0.0%	100.0%
40	1873	1c	*	0.0%	33.3%	*	0.0%	30.0%
41	1873	2c	*	0.0%	47.1%	*	0.0%	28.6%
41a	1873	2c	*	0.0%	23.1%	*	0.0%	17.6%
42	1873	.50r	*	0.0%	31.8%	*	0.0%	30.0%

A Selection of Investment Grade Stamps
by Country - Venezuela

Venezuela Scott #	Issue Year	Value	Rating Mint	5 Year Mint Appreciation %	25 Year Mint Appreciation %	Rating Used	5 Year Used Appreciation %	25 Year Used Appreciation %
42a	1873	1/2r		0.0%	33.3%			
42b	1873	.50r	*	0.0%	20.0%	*	0.0%	18.9%
43	1873	1r	*	0.0%	30.8%	*	0.0%	31.4%
43a	1873	1r	*	0.0%	27.3%			
44	1873	2r	*	0.0%	44.4%	**	0.0%	60.0%
44a	1873	2r	*	0.0%	15.8%	*	0.0%	25.0%
45	1875	.50r	*	0.0%	30.8%			
45a	1875	.50r	(*)	0.0%	13.6%	*	0.0%	25.0%
45b	1875	.50r	(*)	0.0%	10.3%	(*)	0.0%	12.5%
46	1875	1r	**	0.0%	68.4%			
46a	1875	1r	(*)	0.0%	14.3%	(*)	0.0%	14.3%
46b	1875	1r	(*)	0.0%	7.7%	(*)	0.0%	9.1%
47	1876	.50r	*	0.0%	19.2%			
47a	1876	.50r	(*)	0.0%	0.0%			
47b	1876	.50r	(*)	0.0%	0.0%			
47c	1876	.50r	(*)	0.0%	0.0%			
47d	1876	.50r	(*)	0.0%	0.0%			
47e	1876	.50r	(*)	0.0%	0.0%	(*)	0.0%	0.0%
48	1876	1r	*	0.0%	23.3%			
48a	1876	1r	(*)	0.0%	0.0%			
48b	1876	1r	(*)	0.0%	0.0%	(*)	0.0%	0.0%
54	1879	90c	*	0.0%	33.3%			
55	1879	1v	*	0.0%	19.2%	****	0.0%	105.7%
56	1879	3v	*	0.0%	18.2%	**	0.0%	57.1%
57	1879	5v	*	0.0%	18.4%	*	0.0%	19.2%
58b	1880	5c	(*)	0.0%	0.0%	(*)	0.0%	0.0%
60b	1880	25c	(*)	0.0%	0.0%	(*)	0.0%	0.0%
60c	1880	25c	(*)	0.0%	0.0%	(*)	0.0%	0.0%

A Selection of Investment Grade Stamps
by Country - Venezuela

Venezuela Scott #	Issue Year	Value	Rating Mint	5 Year Mint Appreciation %	25 Year Mint Appreciation %	Rating Used	5 Year Used Appreciation %	25 Year Used Appreciation %
61c	1880	50c	(*)	0.0%	0.0%	(*)	0.0%	0.0%
61d	1880	50c	(*)	0.0%	0.0%	(*)	0.0%	0.0%
64	1880	5b	*	0.0%	23.1%			
65	1880	10b	*	0.0%	21.2%	(*)	0.0%	7.7%
66	1880	20b	*	0.0%	20.0%	*	0.0%	21.2%
67	1880	25b	*	0.0%	17.6%	(*)	0.0%	0.0%
68a	1880	5c	(*)	0.0%	12.5%	(*)	0.0%	12.0%
69b	1880	10c	(*)	0.0%	12.5%	*	0.0%	15.4%
69c	1880	10c	*	0.0%	15.4%	*	0.0%	15.4%
70a	1880	10c	*	0.0%	15.4%	*	0.0%	15.4%
72	1880	50c	****	0.0%	131.3%	****	0.0%	100.0%
72a	1880	50c	****	0.0%	131.3%	****	0.0%	100.0%
72b	1880	50c	(*)	0.0%	12.5%	(*)	0.0%	12.0%
73	1880	1B	*****	0.0%	133.3%	**	0.0%	66.7%
73a	1880	1B	*	0.0%	20.0%	*	0.0%	20.0%
76a	1882	25c	(*)	0.0%	0.0%	(*)	0.0%	0.0%
88	1887	25c	*	0.0%	29.4%			
92	1887	5c	*	0.0%	33.3%	(*)	0.0%	13.3%
95	1887	1b	*	0.0%	25.0%	*	0.0%	33.3%
100	1892	25c/5c	*	0.0%	33.3%	*	0.0%	33.3%
110c	1893	25c	****	0.0%	100.0%	****	0.0%	100.0%
140	1896	50c	*	0.0%	37.5%	*	0.0%	25.0%
140a	1896	50c	*	0.0%	31.3%	*	0.0%	31.3%
140b	1896	50c	*****	0.0%	275.0%	*****	0.0%	275.0%
141	1896	1b	*	0.0%	33.3%	*	0.0%	37.5%
147	1899	1b	*	0.0%	30.0%	*	0.0%	20.0%
149	1899	2B	*	0.0%	33.3%	*	0.0%	18.4%
155a	1900	2b	*	0.0%	27.3%	*	0.0%	27.3%
155b	1900	2b	(*)	0.0%	0.0%	(*)	0.0%	0.0%

A Selection of Investment Grade Stamps
by Country - Venezuela

Venezuela Scott #	Issue Year	Value	Rating Mint	5 Year Mint Appreciation %	25 Year Mint Appreciation %	Rating Used	5 Year Used Appreciation %	25 Year Used Appreciation %
156	1900	5c	*****	0.0%	400.0%	*****	0.0%	400.0%
157	1900	10c	*****	0.0%	400.0%	*****	0.0%	400.0%
158	1900	25c	****	0.0%	100.0%	*****	0.0%	300.0%
160a	1900	1b	***	0.0%	75.0%			
253a	1911	25c	(*)	0.0%	0.0%	(*)	0.0%	0.0%
256	1914	5c	**	0.0%	56.3%			
257	1914	10c	**	0.0%	66.7%			
267	1915	75c	*	0.0%	27.8%			
267a	1915	75c	*	0.0%	27.8%			
268	1915	1b	***	0.0%	75.0%			
269b	1924	5c	(*)	0.0%	0.0%	(*)	0.0%	0.0%
277a	1924	25c	(*)	0.0%	0.0%	(*)	0.0%	0.0%
280a	1924	50c	**	0.0%	70.7%			
282a	1924	1b	*	0.0%	30.8%	*	0.0%	35.0%
289a	1928	10c	(*)	0.0%	0.0%			
303	1932	3b	***	0.0%	90.0%			
304	1932	5b	****	0.0%	100.0%			
306a	1933	25c	(*)	0.0%	0.0%	(*)	0.0%	0.0%
318c	1937	25c/40c	(*)	0.0%	0.0%	(*)	0.0%	0.0%
319	1937	25c/40c	*	0.0%	35.4%	*	0.0%	27.3%
324	1937	3b	***	0.0%	150.0%	*****	0.0%	200.0%
337	1938	50c	*	0.0%	37.5%			